D1071049

The Organization of African Unity After Ten Years

edited by
Yassin El-Ayouty

The Praeger Special Studies program—
utilizing the most modern and efficient book
production techniques and a selective
worldwide distribution network—makes
available to the academic, government, and
business communities significant, timely
research in U.S. and international economic, social, and political development.

The Organization of African Unity After Ten Years;
Comparative Perspectives.

Praeger Publishers   New York   Washington   London

PRAEGER SPECIAL STUDIES IN INTERNATIONAL POLITICS AND GOVERNMENT

Library of Congress Cataloging in Publication Data

El-Ayouty, Yassin, 1928-
  The Organization of African Unity after ten years.

  (Praeger special studies in international politics
and government)
  Includes papers presented at the 16th annual meeting
of the African Studies Association, held in 1973.
  Includes index.
  1. Organization of African Unity—Congresses.
I. African Studies Association.   II. Title.
DT1.0752E4   341.24'9   74-15421
ISBN 0-275-09910-5

PRAEGER PUBLISHERS
111 Fourth Avenue, New York, N.Y. 10003, U.S.A.
5, Cromwell Place, London SW7 2JL, England

Published in the United States of America in 1975
by Praeger Publishers, Inc.

In connection with the tenth anniversary (1973) of the Organization of African Unity, this book is dedicated to a regional intergovernmental organization whose success is bound with the success of Africa and the rest of the Third World in their struggle for universal equality and justice

LIST OF CONTRIBUTORS

Berhanykun Andemicael
(Ethiopia)
UNITAR Fellow, New York

Boutros Boutros-Ghali
(Egypt)
University of Cairo, Egypt

Zdenek Cervenka
(Sweden)
The Scandanavian Institute of African Studies,
Uppsala University, Sweden

Yassin El-Ayouty
(Egypt)
State University of New York
   at Stony Brook

Leonard T. Kapungu
(Zimbabwe)
University of Maryland

Mansour Khalid
(Sudan)
Minister for Foreign Affairs of The Sudan

B. David Meyers
(United States)
University of North Carolina, Greensboro

Peter Onu
(Nigeria)
Assistant Secretary General
Political Affairs and Decolonization
OAU, Addis Ababa, Ethiopia

Galobawi M. Salih
(Sudan)
Chief, Local Government Section
Public Administration Division
United Nations, New York

W. Scott Thompson
(United States)
Fletcher School of Law and Diplomacy
Tufts University
Medford, Massachusetts

Claude E. Welch, Jr.
(United States)
State University of New York at Buffalo

Jon Woronoff
(United States)
Author and consultant

Romain Yakemtchouk
(Belgium)
University of Louvain, Belgium

I. William Zartman
(United States)
New York University
New York

Peter Onu

Ten years in the life of an international organization is a very short time. However, during the short span of its existence the Organization of African Unity has, among other things, succeeded in promoting and accelerating the struggle for freedom of the 30 million Africans still under the yoke of colonialism, racial discrimination, and apartheid. OAU's efforts in this regard have been deployed mainly in the military, political, and diplomatic fields. Through its 17-nation Liberation Committee, OAU has effectively coordinated the financial, material, and military assistance of independent Africa to liberation movements.

The armed liberation struggle has thus developed to such an extent that Guinea-Bissau has successfully attained its freedom and independence through armed struggle and has now become the forty-second member state of the OAU. Similarly, the Angolan freedom fighters have successfully liberated over one-third of their motherland with a population of over one million. The Mozambique patriots have liberated over one-quarter of the territory, with a population of about one million. In the liberated areas of Angola and Mozambique, the liberation movements have launched programs of national reconstruction. Numerous schools and clinics have been built. Trade and commercial centers have mushroomed in the liberated regions. The armed struggle in Zimbabwe, Namibia, and apartheid South Africa also has been further intensified. Political struggles, some of them underground, have been intensified in territories still under French, British, and Spanish colonial domination.

As a result of the political and diplomatic action of the OAU, the international community, through the United Nations, has recognized the legitimacy of the armed struggle of the African people against the colonial and minority racist regimes in Southern Africa. By resolution 2704(XXV) and subsequent resolutions, the United Nations has decided to give material assistance to the liberation movements. Thus, UNESCO, FAO, and WHO have gone a long way in implementing the said U.N. resolutions. The other specialized agencies are also in the process of consultation with the OAU with the view of formulating their respective programs of assistance to the liberation movements. Such assistance by the U.N. and its various bodies to the liberation movements will no doubt help the liberation movements to consolidate their gains in the military field. It must also be pointed out that the assistance by the United Nations High Commission for Refugees and other benevolent nongovernmental organizations has helped to alleviate the suffering of African refugees, most of whom were forced to flee the territories under minority and racist domination as a result of political repression and indiscriminate bombing and the constant use of napalm by the fascist authorities in Southern Africa, especially against the liberated regions of Angola and Mozambique.

The OAU has also stood up successfully to the various other challenges and problems. Among these may be mentioned border disputes, interstate disputes, and internal conflicts within member states. All such problems were contained and resolved by the OAU without recourse to the United Nations or the World Court.

Finally, the OAU has contributed immensely to the consolidation of the unity and solidarity among the independent African states, members of the OAU. Through its happy relations with the United Nations, its specialized agencies, and such other international and regional organizations, the OAU has also successfully managed to project the genuine aspirations and the authentic image of Africa to the outside world.

THEORIES AND
INSTITUTIONS

1

THE DEVELOPMENT OF
NORMS IN THE
AFRICAN SYSTEM

W. Scott Thompson and
I. William Zartman

When new social entities—persons, groups, societies—come into existence and enter into new relations with each other, they naturally, if often unconsciously, seek to work out conventions, rules of interactions, and basic assumptions—norms, in other words—to regulate their expectations and to provide a working basis for their relationship. These norms can be formalized and given a semblance of permanence. But like any kind of social relations, the norms, although influencing the substance of relations, are at the mercy of that substance. They are perpetually being tested for relevance by the impact of reality, and they are open to reevaluation when important changes take place in the nature of the social entities or of their relations. Permanence is a far more striking feature of this evaluation than it is of the norms themselves.

In the African regional system, norms are being set up and reevaluated, much as in Europe during the period of dynastic relations and in the Western hemisphere through attention to "inter-American law." Although the Organization of African Unity is not the only place where norms are discussed in Africa, it is an apt forum for the conception, application, and testing of conventions. Indeed conference diplomacy since the late 1950s has been a far more important setting for doing intergovernmental business of any kind for Africa than for any other region, for which there are several reasons. By advertising their presence to the rest of the world, as they were doing through conferences, African states were consciously trying to appear more organized and powerful than they actually were, thus eliminating the cause of some national insecurities. In Africa, unlike Asia, there is neither so great a diversity of peoples, cultures, and historical background nor such great distances that a semblance of coherence is impossible. In Africa, unlike Latin America, no single power overshadows the continent to make meetings a monologue by the powerful to the weak and thus injure the chance for internally engendered unity.

3

A final reason for using OAU discussions as the illustrations for the norms discussed is intrinsic to the level of political development in Africa during this period. Foreign policy decisions in Africa tended to be made only at the highest level because the amount of power with which to give direction to states is small and leaders cannot afford, or are not willing, to surrender very much of it. Even foreign ministers, as we shall see, went to conferences with little negotiating power. Foreign policy decisions were thus facilitated by conferences where busy heads of state could conduct business with their peers. Bilateral diplomatic networks of course became somewhat rusty, but as a rule professional African diplomats have not preferred those postings in any event.

The first of the African norms we have chosen for consideration is the predominance of national independence over continental unity. We are using selections from a debate at the first annual OAU conference of heads of state (and of the foreign ministers' meeting that preceded it), which met in Cairo in July 1964, a year or so after the founding of the OAU in Addis Ababa. The argument took place on several levels. For the majority, the OAU was created to defend, rather than to abolish, member states. But since even the narrow notion of defense implied common action, the notion of unity was written into the OAU in practice, as it was written into African politics as a hope and a myth. Since sovereign independence predominated over but did not abolish the notion of unity, the argument divided on tactics and implementation. Was unity to be prepared for now, or only anticipated in the future? Was it to result from a political act, like independence, or from an economic growth process, the development of common and complementary interests, and the strengthening of mutual acquaintance through such instruments as the regional associations? Was subregionalism a midpoint on the way to continental unity, as President Nyerere argued, or an obstacle, as President Nkrumah argued? Behind these arguments of substance lay an additional difference of motivation: Some raised their arguments to oppose the principle—as well as the proposal—of unity, while others sought to further it.

Underlying the entire debate, finally was the basic and unresolved question: What is unity? Are we all Africans, by definition of condition and geography, or does unity imply a certain conduct and structure? The answer of 1963—the creation of the OAU—was a partial and temporary solution. The answer of 1964 on the Ghana resolution for a "continental union government" implicitly reaffirmed the norm of the previous year but went no further, and the proposal shuttled back and forth between presidents and ministers with neither group willing to give body to the dream they wished to keep alive. But procedures and form kept substance alive in this manner. As the fatigued

4

Emperor of Ethiopia put it at the end of a seemingly interminable session, "We will discuss [union government] again, because, in the long run we are all for its unity."

A second norm related to the first one prohibits intervention in internal affairs. The OAU discussions chosen occupied the entire special Council of Ministers meeting at Lagos on June 10-11, 1965, called to discuss the boycott of the 1965 Assembly by those threatened by Ghanaian subversion. The Assembly was, as a result of the procedures and compromises of Cairo the previous year, to be held in Accra—hence the problem.

It was clearly stated from the outset that neither the principle of the annual summit nor the norm of nonintervention itself was to be questioned. But behind the problems of interpreting and applying the norm lay the deeper question of African unity. Were all African governments to be considered equally legitimate (as the conservative states argued) or was there a higher standard of "Africanness" with which the sovereignty of brother African states could be questioned (as President Nkrumah implicitly argued)? Where did the rights of asylum to brother Africans and the duties of support to brother African states stop? Similarly, was boycott a means of intervention or a permissible means of influence in extremis? It is no exaggeration to say that the life of the OAU itself was in danger; old quarrels among members were threatening to take on more importance than common action.

The meeting also was a test of the problem-solving capabilities of the OAU and hence of another norm: that African problems shall have African solutions. In the end, after delicate maneuvering and wily arguments, the meeting, the organization, and the anti-interventionist norm were all preserved. The subversives were somewhat curbed, the Assembly was held in October 1965, in Accra, and scarcely three months later the Nkrumah government was overthrown (from within).

The third norm, the sanctity of boundaries, was inherited at independence. Carefully worded to avoid reference to colonial "artificiality," it was twice included in the OAU documents: in the Addis Ababa Charter and, in reinforced form, in the 1964 resolutions. Despite its clarity, it could not cover all cases. The Somali boundaries, discussed in the 1964 summit, brought out a strengthened consensus for the norm—as well as some hidden assumptions that were to remain in conflict. In the case of the Ethiopian boundary, the state could claim two millennia of more or less uninterrupted existence, but its shape was constantly changing, with many consequences for its relations with neighbors. Even more important conceptually was the debate between Somalia and Kenya, which also applied to Ethiopia. Somalia claimed that the legitimate referent was the nation, in whose

5

name the nationalist movement (in this unique case) had struggled for independence. Kenya, on the other hand, claimed that the legitimate referent was the state—the sovereign, independent, territorial unit. In almost no case in Africa are nation (ethnically construed) and state strictly coincident, but Somalia is the only one of a few largely homogeneous states whose ethnic group extends significantly beyond its borders; it is thus unique, but the consequences for its argument are not, as Kenya points out in the debate. The African states are stuck with their boundaries, something the Nigerian civil war settled—at least for the time being. Ethnically plural most of them are, but the most important elite group in the new African states is the governmental elite, which is defined by the existence of the state and invariably multiethnic in composition. The existence of the boundaries as they are, colonially derived though they be, is one of the most important bases of legitimacy of these elite groups; thus, the boundaries will not be changed without a struggle.

⁜ The last norm concerns neutralism and nonalignment. The debate at the Lagos Council of Ministers in February 1964 has moments of frank bewilderment that would be wryly amusing in a world of slogans if they did not again uncover serious problems in applying neat principles to untidy politics. As in the case of unity, who was so neutral as to be able to decide who else was neutral? Dr. John Karefa Smart of Sierra Leone complained that "certain countries set up themselves as judges as to what is nonaligned. . . . They look down on us with a kind of disdain and sometimes even venture to regard us as a stooge . . . when in fact we can point accusing fingers at them as stooges because they are stooges to certain ideas of nonalignment." And who was neutral at all, between what, in a world where characteristic interdependence inevitably contained elements of dependence, and where any chosen position already had its committed supporters outside the continent? In all cases, the norm did not meet the reality ready-made and cut to measure. It had to be adjusted, remodeled, sometimes discarded, but always dealt with. In many cases, it had to be reconciled with another norm, but the necessity showed that the norm or norms existed and were considered important.

The whole debate on nonalignment illustrates aspects of all of the norms and also illustrates the remarkable success of the OAU in developing a forum of African unity. Whereas the 1961 Belgrade nonaligned conference divided Africa, because only a few of the purportedly nonaligned African states were invited, the 1964 nonaligned conference in Cairo, and still more that in Lusaka in 1971, united them. In the OAU framework—and as a specific result of that framework—"Africa" decided it would hang together. The Sudanese representative said, not without irony, that there was an old English

6

proverb stating, "If you invite an Arab, you invite the whole tribe"—
and it is the same with Africa, he noted. There was even a reluctance
by some delegates to be involved in a nonaligned conference at all,
for reasons different from those impinging on foreign policy in the
first few years of independence. The Camerounian foreign minister
feared that, since nonalignment had become associated with one bloc,
and the Afro-Asian movement with another, paralleling the split
between the Soviet Union and China, the invitations to the 1964 conference were "merely a trap." He added, "I would like to know whether
we could not have our own stand. Can Africa not constitute a school
which might inspire other continents?"

To be sure, the declining content to nonalignment, as the great
blocs softened their conflicts (which nonalignment had been designed
to soften), it became easier for Africa to be united on this issue.
This was the success and dilemma of the organization in all areas:
greater unity in principle, but over less and less momentous issues;
success in maintaining a coherence, but a putting aside of such elegant
edifices as a "continental union government." Perhaps it was only
through such a strategy, if it can be called a strategy, that Africa,
in the long run, could develop substantive unity.

THE PREEMINENCE OF NATIONAL
INDEPENDENCE AS A NORM

Report of the Council of Ministers and of the Assembly
of Heads of State and Government, Cairo, 14-21
July 1964

Council of Ministers

Chairman (Ali Amer, United Arab Republic): This afternoon
we are going to start with Item 3—Promotion of the Unity and Solidarity of African States in pursuance of Resolution 28 (2) of the Council
of Ministers' Resolution. I give the floor to the Delegate of Ghana.

Ghana (Kojo Botsio): Mr. Chairman, distinguished foreign
ministers. We have before us now the proposals of the Government
of Ghana, for the consideration of this Council, for the establishment
of a Union government. These are not new proposals, but the continuation of what Dr. Kwame Nkrumah, President of the Republic of
Ghana, put before the Summit Conference last year at Addis Ababa.
But the charter nevertheless makes provision for political and pragmatic cooperation in accordance with Article 2, paragraph 2(a) of the

Charter. At the time, every African who was sincerely committed to the progress and prosperity of the continent received with joy the unanimous resolution adopted by the Addis Ababa conference. Nevertheless, experience has come to convince us that the instrument we formed at Addis Ababa had only led to creating more complicated problems in the way of achieving real African unity. We scarcely had settled down after Addis Ababa before the conflicts flared up in several member states. It would appear that all of us underestimate the neocolonialist structure of the former metropolitan and other imperialist powers.

Today what we have already achieved is nothing short of OAU, which allows for an association of individual African states with only paper coordination and void of any centralized political direction. Today, instead of the Africa we dreamed of at Addis Ababa, Africa strong and united to face the strong task before us, we have now developed an Africa which is balkanized and fighting itself and therefore profits no member state. The President of the Republic of Ghana cannot forever keep silent about this dangerous position, and I am sure there are other member states which strongly share our views. There are many and varied arguments that have been advanced in favor of a union government of Africa of which we are all aware. . . .

The argument is often put forward that it is economic cooperation and emancipation—and not political unification under a union government—which should come first. Such an argument ignores the realities of the colonial struggle. Which of our states represented here can deny the fact that, because we have got our independence, we can now endeavor to attain economic development and a higher standard of living for our people? What is good for our states is also good for the whole continent. The imperative need now is a union government which would crystallize our political institutions and plan continentally in the supreme interests of Mother Africa.

It has also been said that establishment of commissions under the Charter provides an alternative to a union government. Why should we waste our time and deceive ourselves? The commissions we have set up are so many forums which issue reports for our consideration. Who can seriously think that the Economic and Cultural Commission of the OAU can bring about the much-needed development of Africa without any centralized political direction?

Some people also maintain that a union government of Africa is not practicable. It is difficult to see what is meant by such a statement. Is it the elections to the national assembly of the union or the appointment of a council of ministers which is not practicable? The Ghana proposals in the draft constitution, for instance, are easier, cheaper, and more effective to implement than the numerous commissions, meeting often and only issuing reports.

8

Here I would like to point out that the outline constitution submitted by Ghana is only meant to provide a basis for discussing a constitution for union government. It is never meant to impose a final constitution for union government upon this conference.

The lead now is for the Assembly of Heads of State and Government to accept the recommendation on the need for the establishment of a union government now, so that the necessary machinery could be set up to implement it. Our draft constitution emphasizes that, under a union government, the sovereignty of individual states will be preserved, and in fact strengthened. There is therefore no purpose in any member state hesitating regarding the establishment of a union government. Rather, we must all endeavor to establish it now so that we might not perish separately or be recolonized.

Will the member states, joining a union of Africa, lose the foreign aid on which some states so heavily depend? Such a question has been asked before and continues to be asked. I would like to say here that this is no colonialist blackmail and an empty threat. On the contrary, real positive unification under a union government is the best guarantee for an African common market and an African development bank whose resources can be utilized by all member states for their economic development. Neither will such a union mean less trade with foreign countries, for with rapid industrialization there will be an ever-expanding trade among ourselves, and an expanding purposeful trade with foreign countries.

Mr. Chairman, distinguished foreign ministers, now is the time to act and we must act now, for every day that passes constitutes a dangerous delay which, for example, may lead to the regime of tariff wars, the tribulation of border conflicts, and the waging of trade wars. That is why we must declare ourselves for a union government of Africa now and take the necessary steps to realize it without delay.

In conclusion, I would like to emphasize that the establishment of OAU in Addis Ababa was an act of faith. In the same way, we must now regard the establishment of a union of Africa now as another act of faith for the salvation of Africa. This is the moment of decision and action, and we must not fail to take it. Let it not be said of us, when we are dead and gone, that at the psychological moments in the history of our continent, we did shirk our responsibility. Let the Council of Foreign Ministers, in response to the compelling mandate of the African peoples, pass on the Ghana proposals to our heads of state and government for their consideration. This is the firm recommendation of the Ghana delegation. I thank you.

Tunisia: ... The Charter which we drew up in Addis Ababa on 25 May 1962, mentions, in Article 2, paragraph (a), ways and means of reinforcing African unity and solidarity. Reinforcing unity does not mean creating units, and it is only a year since we began to experiment with these units by conferring, by trying to develop cooperation between the African states in every field; and it seems to me that, despite the very laudable efforts which have been made up to now, we are not yet ready to form an African government. I say this very frankly and in complete loyalty toward our colleagues, and I would like everyone to express himself clearly and frankly, because silence on such an important matter might well give the impression that it is agreement on the immediate creation of an African government which is implied by this silence in the Council. . . .

We have still all of us too much to do in our own countries if we are to consolidate stability in our own countries and try to create the framework necessary to the development of our own people. It is our duty and our right to promote and create every kind of cooperation and the ways and means for cooperation between our countries and our peoples, in order to facilitate the gradual advent of a closer unity between our countries. But to speak at the present time of a union government for Africa seems to me to be premature. Article 2, paragraph (a), which is itself the subject of this discussion since we are discussing a recommendation coming from the last Council of Ministers at Lagos, also speaks of African solidarity, Mr. Ali Amer.

Do we feel that this solidarity is in fact being practiced? When we speak of solidarity, we speak of a feeling of tolerance and support toward each one of us; if we find that we are in conflict or in difficulties with a country outside of Africa, do we not have precedents which would be painful for me to dwell upon here? Or perhaps one or more African countries are in conflict with one or more countries outside of Africa, and it is in this case and in the cases I have just mentioned that our solidarity is unfortunately not yet working adequately.

Mr. Chairman, before speaking of unity, we must first speak of solidarity. We are, one and all and all of us together, striving to make that solidarity more and more effective between us and to make cooperation between ourselves also increasingly effective. When this solidarity and this cooperation have developed sufficiently and reached the stage when we will have managed to consider ourselves as really one united whole, bound together by our aims, by our political aspirations, by the means of development to be found in each of our countries—that is to say the means of economic, cultural, and social production—then, I think, the time will have come to think of setting up a pan-African government . . .

Ghana (Kojo Botsio): Mr Chairman, the paper [proposal on union government] is for the heads of state and government, but as foreign ministers we should take cognizance of it. So I suggest that we take note of it, then the paper will go to the heads of state and

10

government for their consideration, as already notified in the agenda for this meeting of heads of state and government. So just take note of it and then go on to other business.

Madagascar: . . . The delegation of Madagascar does not agree in any way to creation of a union government of Africa, a pan-African government, or supranational government. After having lost our liberty for years, having been under the yoke of colonialism, when we have now, with the granting of independence, just recovered this liberty, must we today lose it again to a supranational government with all the attributes which are comprised therein? How can internal sovereignty, or perhaps just the internal or external sovereignty of a country, be reconciled with the attributes of a supranational government?

Besides, what would a pan-African government bring us? Every one of us here is animated by feelings of the purest patriotism, we have with unceasing care striven according to our lights to elaborate a constitution which we are, one and all, trying to put into practice, in order to promote our advancement in every field, whether economic, political, social, or cultural. Despite this patriotism which animates us all, we must in good faith admit that we did not succeed in all these domains while we were each only aiming at the welfare of our own country. So I do not see how a supranational government, which would have to take into account 24 countries, could do better than each of us did within our own countries . . .

Senegal: A union government on a continental scale is certainly the most ardent wish of all the member states of the OAU. This ideal, toward which all our efforts tend, must be the final step in the development of African unity. But Senegal believes that while reaching this ideal we must remain aware of the real facts; otherwise there is a risk of failing, of never reaching one's ideal. By this I mean that a union government of Africa on a continental scale must be prepared in successive stages, by degrees, by successive relays. We believe that we must not at present have ambitions beyond regional integration; let us begin to constitute, at the regional level, common cooperation bodies. We will thus learn to know ourselves, to work together toward the same goals, progressively to reduce our national idiosyncrasies.

For example, let us begin, on the level of a given region, to form a monetary union, a customs union, to form a common airline, as has been done in West Africa with the creation of Air Afrique, a company set up by 12 African states. Let us begin with the coordination of our educational systems and of our teaching methods, and we will gradually come to the first stage of African unity, to the first relay which tomorrow will lead us to a unified government on the continental level. It is only after this, when regional integration has

11

been realized on the level of the various large regions of Africa, that we will have to consider the next relays, the next steps, the next stages, the regrouping on the continental level.

Despite our wish to realize the ideal expressed by Ghana, we think that this is a realistic and wise method of work. As has already been said, African unity cannot be the work of one generation only; its work is on a many-generations scale. . . . Let us follow nature in that respect. The ancients said "natura non falcis soltus"—nature makes no jumps. For the creation of man, plants, and all living biological bodies, there are unforeseeable delays, and if these delays are not respected, nothing that is born can live.

Guinea: . . . In expressing the thanks of the Guinean delegation to the delegation of Ghana for having suggested something that each delegation here present feels deeply, I wish to say that this problem of a union government of Africa is an idea which is dear to us all; it is not even really an idea—it is the goal toward which we are all directing our efforts. The Addis Ababa Charter has already established certain principles which must lead us, slowly perhaps but surely, toward this goal. Consequently, we think it is an idea to which we must give thought, which we must not put aside a priori. But in view of its importance, since the Addis Ababa Charter was signed by our heads of state themselves, it was a fundamental act in the life of the OAU. Likewise, this plan, this worthy project of the delegation of Ghana, will be a fundamental act. During the second stage in the life of our organization, we think this act will have to be examined and possibly taken up by our Heads of State exactly because the problem is of such capital importance . . . .

No one here will positively oppose the union government of Africa. It was therefore to gain time that the delegation of Guinea suggested that the Council take cognizance of the delegation of Ghana's noble idea and put it forward for examination by our Heads of State, who are to assemble here. I would therefore like the matter to appear on the agenda of our Heads of State.

Cameroun: This question we are discussing is extremely delicate. It is actually the second time that we are discussing this problem. You will certainly remember discussions at Lagos in the course of which, in order to clarify discussion regarding this question, we set up a subcommittee composed of five countries, including my own. This subcommittee at Lagos, in which the delegation of Ghana was represented, had received a mandate to try to discover the possibilities of accelerating the process of unification of African countries. So, bearing in mind the short time at our disposal at Lagos, this subcommittee was unable to study the fundamental problem and, its mandate terminating at the end of the Conference, these studies also came to a stop. We are once again meeting, this time in Cairo, and once again the same question is on the agenda. . . .

12

Our states, gathered at Addis Ababa, set up a process of unification of African states. They elaborated a Charter and a philosophy
for this meeting. But unfortunately, have we actually attained anything
concrete? Can each of our states sincerely say here: "You eminent
ministers are responsible for the politics of your respective governments"? Can we really state here that the process of unification of
African countries elaborated at Addis Ababa last year has started to
be implemented? As far as any country is concerned, the answer is
no. We are, on the contrary, beating around the bush. Since last year,
new problems have arisen. Most of us acquired independence in 1960;
up to 1963 we lived extremely peacefully, but since last year there
have been many border disputes. What a number of refugee problems
among ourselves!

At a time such as this, how can we speak of a continental government, that is to say, of the perfection at the top, when the very basis
of the edifice is not yet well planted? As I have already said, Ghana's
initiative is certainly laudable; it is an ideal, but when one is responsible for the politics and respective governments of African states,
one must guard against acting on impulse. This impulse can precipi-
tate things, especially when it is a question of political decisions. . . .

Let us begin by foreseeing concrete measures for a sincere
cooperation among our peoples, on the level of the young people, on
the level of movements, on the level of all this, so that the African,
the man from Cameroun, who leaves his country finds himself at home
in Malawi, finds himself at home in Tanganyika, or in Algeria, or in
any other part of Africa. This is the first concrete achievement which
will allow Africa to win the challenge it has taken up since last year.

Besides, in the opinion of my delegation, the Ghanaian proposal
seems to be somewhat incomplete. For it to be effectively implemented, we must define the number of members of the continental
government, how it will function, what are to be its relations with the
governments whose independence must be preserved but in whose
respect it will first be necessary to pass through a continental government. It would be of interest to us to know the sources of finance and
the constitutional regulations at the same time as this proposition,
in order to allow our Heads of State to pronounce themselves on a
concrete and explicit project. A while ago the honorable Foreign
Minister of Ghana said that the file should be immediately transferred
to the Heads of State. Here is certainly something which you should
appreciate, Mr. Minister. You are responsible. Are you going to
transmit to our heads of state a draft which you have not yet studied
sufficiently yourself? For my part, when my head of state arrives
here, he will in fact ask which are the questions which have been
elaborated. The files which are to be presented will have to have
substantiating documentation.

Now on this particular question, the study has only just begun; we are only starting our research. We are living here in a
state of fictitious solidarity. We have said that we have not built up
our relations inside the OAU on theories; you know now the hypocrisy
that reigns in the sphere where one follows the principle of washing
one's hands of a thing. But what have you washed your hands of?
After all, it is our interests that are at stake. Is Africa to play this
dangerous game and dabble in hypocrisy? For my part, I do not
believe so. As for me, I hope and honestly think that the idea and the
proposal are laudable, but undoubtedly in the present circumstances
there is some difficulty; and that is why my delegation, while paying
homage to the proposal which has been made to us, suggests that we
take note of it as being one of the future possibilities of the Organization of African Unity. My delegation recommends that this proposal
should rather be registered at the Secretariat. It will be studied when
we have first effectively started off, that is to say, when we have begun the African solidarity, by which I mean the process of unification
of African countries from the beginning and not merely from a legal
point of view.

Togo: ... I would like to translate all these considerations
into a concrete proposal. ... I propose that we refer this question
to the heads of state, as we can but have recourse to them, but that
we accompany it by the opinion, to which the Togo delegation sub-
scribes, which is that, as we have spoken of successive stages, a
commission of experts be constituted to examine what these different
stages should be. Thus, with the results of their deliberations before
us, we may work for the day—which will not be tomorrow, as everybody, including the Togo delegation, admits—when we can establish
the continental government.

Ghana: We are greatly heartened by the fact that it has been
expressed here that, under the general objective of this organization,
our goal is a union government of Africa. Hitherto it has been very
difficult even to discuss this matter with our colleagues. ...

Whatever we do, union government of Africa will come. It has
been said that several generations must come before we achieve
that. I am sure that union government of Africa will come in our own
lifetimes. But if there is a thing which we beleive in, then we must
work for it. It is no use, to think that, where there is a goal, then
the goal may take care of itself. It will never take care of itself.
We need not go to history to find out what can befall this organization
if we just leave things to drift as they are now. Earlier on, I made
mention of the OAS. If we do not take care, tha OAU will go exactly
the same way as the OAS, and what shall we achieve for all the sac-
rifices we are making for the realization of African unity?

In fact, African unity is a general term—we know that what we want specifically at this time is a rapid industrial revolution in Africa and this is a thing which you must think of and plan for. From the very beginning, even before we attained independence as you may remember, even on the very day we achieved independence, we in Ghana always believed that the independence of Ghana is meaningless unless it is linked with the integration of the African continent. . . . We fought for independence and we have gained the riches of experience. Let us make use of what we have studied, let us make use of what we see today, so that this great goal can be achieved.

Tunisia: . . . At Lagos we decided to include the question of African unity and solidarity on the agenda of the next session of the Council of Ministers. . . . But we should refer this problem to the Assembly of the Heads of State, giving them as accurate as possible a description of the discussion that took place at this meeting. That is to say, with the exception of the delegation of Ghana, we are all satisfied that this proposal is a goal to be reached, but its solution is yet not practical.

Assembly of Heads of State and Government

Chairman: We now come to a proposal made by the Ghanaian Government for the formation of a single government of Africa. The Council of Ministers would ask the present conference to declare itself only on the principle. I give the floor to the President of the Republic of Ghana to introduce the proposal and to start the debate.

Ghana (Kwame Nkrumah): . . . I don't think that there has been even one speaker who has gone completely against this idea. Most say that they agree in principle—they agree, but. I will try to explain that but. The point at issue here is that we all agree that this issue is going to face us, is going to face this Assembly throughout our existence, so we must be bold enough to face it now. What I am suggesting is that my whole suggestion has been misinterpreted. . . . I didn't say we should set out on this table and within five minutes establish a union government of Africa. That was not my point. My point was this: that it is a central factor in the political life of the African continent. Since it is going to be a vital issue, let us at least accept in principle the possibility of the establishment of a union government of Africa. . . .

I know Rome wasn't built in a day, but Rome started somewhere before it became Rome, so the only point I am making is this: Let us all agree that some of us, somehow, sometime, shall be faced with this issue. Then what I am saying is: Let us prepare for it. Let's submit this idea to our foreign ministers, who will pass it on to our Jurists' Commission. The jurists will go into it as experts and then

15

have a meeting with the foreign ministers. After that has been done, it can even come before this conference for consideration. That is what I have been trying to put forward.

Mali (Modibo Keita): The comments of the President of the Republic of Ghana give the real problem of the union government, and this problem has been discussed by all Heads of State and Government who spoke during this meeting. We therefore believe that there is a real solution and that the gap that separated our friend the President of Ghana from the majority of Heads of State is narrowing. . . .

The Republic of Mali considers the Organization of African Unity a link and a phase in the historic development of our states. . . . It is for this reason that, since its proclamation, the Republic of Mali has provided in its constitution for the possibility of a partial or total surrender of sovereignty in favor of an African whole, when objective conditions have been fulfilled. It is for these reasons that—the objective conditions not having been fulfilled in 1964—we believe that we have to accept the principle we have affirmed in this Assembly. Having admitted the principle, we have to consider it as the ultimate goal for us all. But a policy, in a well-defined stage, is subject to the aims it wishes to attain. We must therefore define our aim. To form an African government, each one of us will have—subject to that aim and bearing in mind realities—to practice a home policy which would allow progressive steps toward the distant goal. This is why we suggest to the conference not to reject the principle but accept it and ask our distinguished lawyers to study the question. It would be a first step we have taken, but only a first step, bearing in mind the present contradictions in our political, economic, and social systems, as well as the fact that we possess different governments, even if we share the same concern in ensuring a better life for our people. I recapitulate: The Republic of Mali agrees on the principles and also agrees on the principle of entrusting African friends with the responsibility of studying the possibility of submitting to us a concrete plan. This plan would be the goal that we strive to reach each day, each month, each year.

Dahomey (Sourou Migan Apithy): . . . I would first like to recall the Pan-African Conference held in London, 17 years ago in 1947, at which our friend Nkrumah was Secretary-General. It was during this conference that was born the dream of African independence. Who, at that time, would have believed that 17 years later we would be here, 35 independent nations of Africa? What was thought of as a dream then has become reality today, and in the same spirit, what is just a dream today can—bearing in mind the rapid evolution of history—become the reality of tomorrow. The people of Dahomey associate themselves with all efforts tending to consolidate our union. Accordingly, in our constitution of 1958, as our friend Modibo stated,

16

the Dahomean people drafted an article according to which they have the right to give up a part or all of their sovereignty for a valid and coherent African whole. So we are in agreement on the principle. . . .

But while agreeing on the principle of the draft submitted to us, we ask that it be subjected to a thorough study and that a factual report be presented, pointing out the difficulties that we might encounter, as well as the possibilities, and also giving us direction on the manner in which we should proceed. The delegation of Dahomey urges that this draft be immediately taken into consideration. As has been suggested by President Nkrumah and by the President of Mali, Modibo Keita, we would like these texts to be entrusted to a qualified committee for detailed study. Consequently, we strongly support what President Nkrumah and President Modibo Keita have said, namely, that the Assembly take the draft submitted to us into consideration.

Nigeria (Tafawa Balewa): I think this idea of an African government is a dream. When I was asked about it somewhere, I said that nobody can tell whether the dream might not come about. It is a dream or a nightmare. As far as Nigeria is concerned, I must make it absolutely clear that we, on our own free will, shall never surrender our sovereignty to any organization. This statement is indirectly a vote of no confidence in the Organization of African Unity. When we started this Organization only a year ago, we were working, progressing, and now we are trying to impose something. Well, if we want a union government to replace this organization, then it means that after only one year's experiment we find that this organization is failing; that is what it means.

All of us have said there might be a union government, it might come about. Nobody knows when. The proposer even said that he doesn't mean it will come today or tomorrow. He doesn't know when it will come, but these are ideas in his head. Of course there are other ideas, too. For years there has been a group of people who want to have a world government; it might come about—we don't know. And so I am one to make it clear to the conference: This is a dream and Nigeria will not be associated with this dream. Therefore, even in principle, I think it is merely a waste of time, a waste of effort to go into this question.

Madagascar (Philibert Tsiranana): . . . I completely associate myself with the President of Nigeria. . . . We must be frank. There are many here among us who do not want, under the present circumstances, to lose their sovereignty. We Malagasy people have just achieved our independence. Well, we are jealous of this independence. If we are replaced tomorrow by a world government or even by a continental government, the Malagasy people will refuse. This does not mean that we do not want, that we do not like union, but that is our sentiment. We all fought to achieve independence for our countries,

17

and I repeat what I said last time: Madagascar is among those who fought for a long time.

We once had, as you must know, an ancestral government. We had kings who had embassies in the countries of the big powers, and our fathers fought for our independence. They failed because we were an island and did not receive any help. We fought again in 1945. We failed because nobody helped us and we were an island. And now that we have achieved independence—and just a few years after we acceded to it, this independence for which we shed our blood—we are told that there will no more be a Malagasy government but a union government. This is difficult for the Malagasy people to grasp. . . . Therefore, we will never subscribe to a union government.

Our descendants may do so. That dream may become reality tomorrow, but I believe that for our generation this dream is far from becoming reality. But we are ready to work with all Africans, just as we do in the OAU, on in order to defend Africa and defend all our states. But as far as fusing our states into a union state, I am not saying that my friends are being demagogues but I am being frank. I cannot subscribe to it.

Ethiopia (Haile Selassie): When we speak of African unity, the word unity implies many things. To achieve unity, much work must be done and many steps must be taken. But we all wish to achieve this complete unity. Obviously, when we meet here it is to exchange free and sincere opinions; otherwise our meeting would have no results. We agree on certain principles. We have our ministers of foreign affairs who can study everything in detail, make proposals, and then we either adopt or reject them. Everyone here will sincerely advance his views, even if his views are considered, for the moment, daring.

Our friend President Nkrumah has submitted his views, and they are in the same spirit as everybody else's. They tend to establish an African union. As the name Organization of African Unity denotes, we are always advancing toward unity. When will we reach it? What shape will it have? How much longer will it take? There is so much to say about the subject, as the speeches and our exchange of views have largely proved. As has been said by our friend Modibo Keita, why should we, from the start, reject the ideas of one of our brothers? Consequently, we support the idea of submitting, without delay, the draft, the ideas of President Nkrumah, for study, either to our ministers or to lawyers. And we will discuss it again, because in the long run we are all going toward unity. Besides, it would not be wise, it is not our duty to reject anything before a detailed study of it is made. Examination will tell us whether such or such an obstacle is insurmountable; that this step can be made in certain conditions and another cannot. Our ministers of foreign affairs are here. Therefore, our proposal is to examine the draft, not to reject it.

Cameroun (Amadou Ahidjo): . . . The idea of a union government at the level of the African Continent is most generous, as has been said. Those who have spoken have all declared their wish to see Africa more and more united. Why should we not, one day, constitute one state, one nation? But even if we believe—and I believe—that those who said it were sincere, I personally believe that there is a difference between wishes formulated in a speech and concrete study of a problem by responsible heads of state and government. In fact, I believe that we have to constantly bear in mind that we are responsible people, that we are a conference of responsible heads of state and government and not a party congress.

Everything we decide here, the studies we recommend . . . as soon as we take a decision, our peoples rightly expect it to be implemented within six months or a year. I believe that it would not be the right thing to decide on a principle, and entrust our ministers of foreign affairs to study the implementation of this principle, when we very well know that, in spite of our wishes, the principle could not be implemented before five, ten, fifteen, or even twenty years. I believe that such a mistake would be a disservice to Africa.

On the other hand, there is not a question of forming two or three governments, but one, on the level of the African continent. We must not forget that there are African territories which are not yet independent. We all wish to see them free as soon as possible. But their liberation could take years. We do not know what the actual leaders or the future leaders of these territories will do once they become independent, of the idea of establishing a government, one government for the whole continent. For these reasons, I believe it might also be wise to wait for these states to gain independence, so that their representatives, in their sovereign capacity, could air their views on this important problem. . . .

I will go even further, if we agree on a union government, I sincerely do not know what there is to study. A federal government? Confederal? The world is full of such examples, both in the past and present. The only study to be made, according to me, is to establish that government and to see in practice whether it functions or not. I do not understand what our ministers of foreign affairs could find out other than that the United States of America, the Soviet Union, or the Indian Union discovered when they established their federal governments, or the Swiss government when it established a confederal government. . . . I shall ask my colleagues not to substitute themselves to a committee, but to decide on the principle—for or against—and if they accept the principle, to tell their representatives about it. . . .

Tunisia (Habib Bourguiba): You are all aware of my feelings concerning the very generous idea of African unity, but I said in my speech that it was premature. At the moment, we are dealing with a question of principle. We are told that it is simply a question of requesting that a study be undertaken. I cannot associate myself with President Nkrumah's idea because the idea of a continental government of Africa is immense, but we must not let it become a fixed idea destined to solve all our problems. When it will be known, in the world, that we have entrusted a committee to study the possibility of a government for the African continent, I can assure you that it will not sound serious, when at the present time there are practical endeavors undertaken to establish regional unions. If we come across difficulties: North Africa, West Africa, East Africa are trying to establish some federations, some confederations, and even in this— and I say it with all my experience of North Africa—we are compelled to go very slowly, forging solidarities, economic bonds, pointing out what unites us to countries of the same language, the same religion, the same history, the same fight, and this is already a hard task that we have to broach with a great deal of patience. If now, ignoring all those realities, those objective conditions, it becomes known that we are going to study the possibility of forming a government for the whole continent, I believe this would hurt the prestige of the Organization of African Unity. That is why I am voting against.

UAR (Gamal Abdul-Nasser): The question of unity has always been thorny. Throughout history all over the world unity was never realized in any place without efforts, persistence, and patience.

I greatly admired the speech of my friend President Nkrumah and I shared with him his hopes which he expressed in this speech.

Our people here in the UAR are one of the most enthusiastic peoples for unity. Yet I like to draw your attention to the fact that unity in practice is a very difficult process. Before we speak about unity, we must first realize the makings of unity. Before any unity is put into effect, there must first be a unity of thought.

As regards ourselves, we met last year for the first time and now we are meeting for the second time. Has the past year been sufficient to bring about a unity of idea among us, to get our people to know each other more and to overcome the divergences which existed among us?

I feel, from what has been said by some of the heads, that there are still some contradictions, and even more there are certain doubts and misgivings. We have, first of all, to overcome these doubts and these contradictions. Then we may talk about unity. Without unity of thought and without the existence of complete harmony among us all, we can neither talk nor think about unity.

I believe that my friend President Nkrumah dealt with the subject—I mean the subject of African unity—by presenting the most difficult element or basic factor of unity, namely, the constitutional

20

unity. Constitutional unity always creates numerous problems, particularly if the makings of unity were not there. Let me give an example of the absence of such makings. Each African country has its own currency, which is not recognized by the other African countries, or at least by most of them . . . only 10 percent of African trade is carried on among African countries, while 90 percent of the commercial transactions of Africa depend upon other countries.

If unity is to be achieved, it is imperative that we should look for the makings of this unity, then we should realize these makings. We should endeavor to bring about economic unity for instance, or more and more commercial and economic exchange among the African countries. But first we have to try to conclude economic agreements so that each African state should recognize the currencies of other African states in carrying out transactions, and should not use the sterling, the dollar or the franc. And if we start with a constitutional unity, without laying down as a basis the fundamental elements that can secure its survival, such a unity will only be a source of trouble and instability, which might adversely affect what we have already achieved, within this conference of the Organization of African Unity, of mutual understanding, and our attempt to eliminate existing doubts and contradictions.

I think that any regional African unity is a step toward ultimate African unity. It can even be a tremendous step. Any form of unity, even a regional unity, will meet much trouble, and will need patience and persistence. In my opinion, the unity of the Republics of Tanganyika and Zanzibar is a step toward African unity. We were happy to hear of the talks on unity in East Africa between Tanganyika and Zanzibar, and between Uganda and Kenya, because we felt that this trend would be a step toward the consolidation of African unity. The unity of East Africa has not yet been realized, in spite of the fact that the whole region uses a unified currency, unified services and communications, and can be considered almost as one country. It has all the essential elements required for unity. All leaders and statesmen there know each other quite well. We were happy, too, to hear of the unity of Ghana, Guinea, and Mali, because we thought it was a step toward an African unity; but we were sorry because it was arrested and did not develop as was hoped by every honest aspirant for African unity. We hoped it would be an example to be followed by other African states.

I think that a lack of unity or harmony of thought has been obvious today in the speeches of my friends and brethren, the heads of some states, when some of them rejected the idea when others supported it, and when a third party spoke about the idea as a dream which might be realized five years from now or even in a hundred years' time. I believe it is a very grave mistake to reject the idea of unity. At

21

the same time I believe that it is difficult, or even impossible, for an All-African government to be set up now, because of all the contradictions and the contrasts which we all know to exist among us. Even the unity of thought does not exist, as we all have observed. It is even more than that African states hardly know about each other on the regional level.

Therefore, I think we should refer this proposal put forward by my friend President Nkrumah to one of the committees, so that it can consider the makings of African unity. If we can define the elements which go into the makings of African unity, and if we manage to apply these in the fields of currency, of commerce, of communications, of culture, and every other field—and in all these I stress that of commerce—then well and good. As long as African economy depends on, and is subservient to, some non-African states, then African unity will always be very far and difficult to attain. To establish African unity, the economy of Africa, and the commerce of Africa must be an African business. There should be more and more commercial transactions between the African states, until each African state feels that its own individual interests lie with the other African states.

We refer, then, the proposal presented by my friend President Nkrumah, to a committee to consider the makings of African unity. When this committes reaches any proposals on trade and on economy, we may discuss this in the Economic Council but on a very slow pace, and we discuss this also in the various other committees of culture, of health, etc., but at a very slow and simple pace. We should speed up the process leading to the realization of the makings of unity. The last step in our discussion should then be the constitutional unity. We should discuss first the ways of unifying the systems adopted in our armed forces. Next how to use our own currencies in our internal transactions. It should then be possible for us to use the Ghana currency and for Ghana to use ours, and this applies to all other African states. Thus Ghana would not demand that I pay in sterling or the dollar, and this would apply to all of us. We must also get our people to know each other and put these measures into effect. If we can enforce them, then we can discuss the constitutional aspect later.

But if we started with the constitutional side, we would be faced with great obstacles and major paradoxes and this would be the end of the whole project. I hope that we do not come to that, but I do hope to refer this proposal to a committee that would consider the makings of African unity, without committing ourselves to what is included in the proposal from the constitutional point of view. The committee should submit to our next meeting its proposals concerning the makings of unity. We should insist on carrying out the recommendations of these committees, then we may put if off for one year, and then for another year. Then after four years, as the President of Cameroun said, we may be able to consider the constitutional point of view.

But if we continue to consider the constitutional aspect only in this meeting, then in the next meeting, or the session of the next year or the one following it, we shall never reach definite results. This is obvious in the speeches which have been delivered in this hall.

The Chairman: After the unanimous approval on this intervention, I believe that the debate is now clear. We should entrust a committee with, not the task of establishing a constitution on the institutional foundations of African unity, but with the study of the concrete bases, the concrete and objective fundamentals. . . . Now you have just applauded an idea. I agree, you are enlisted, you are twelve speakers enlisted, but I see that the last intervention is almost unanimously agreed upon. Are you against the proposal?

Senegal (Leopold Sedar Senghor): No, but we must make it more precise.

The Chairman: Then, I ask the President of the UAR to make precise the points which I shall put to vote and thus the debates shall be closed. The President of the UAR has the floor.

The UAR (Nasser): I would like to repeat my proposal that the concept of unity should not be put to vote lest it should be rejected while it is the hope of all African peoples. Therefore, I propose that Ghana's suggestion be referred to a committee to be formed for the consideration of the makings of unity, provided that the constitutional aspect should be the last element to be considered—after the investigation and the realization of the makings of unity. The committee should present to us, during our forthcoming sessions, its report on what it arrived at concerning the makings of unity. Then we should approve what we are then in a position to approve. Thus we approach unity step by step and the concept would not be rejected. . . .

Ghana (Nkrumah): I think that the point of view which has been put forward by my colleague and friend President Nasser is no different from the matter I have been trying to put before the House. My point is this: This idea, whether it is a dream or not—because most ideas that are bred throughout the whole world first come out of the brain of a man—so it must be a dream before it comes down to earth. What I am putting forward is this: Refer this matter to a committee as President Nasser has said and let them study. I am quite sure that with the studying of the fundamentals, the economies, it will lead eventually to what you people call political economy; you cannot divorce and tell the fundamentals from economy. There are cultural problems, social problems, and all these problems which must be studied. If you begin from the economic and cultural side, before you get to the end you are in the political implications of the whole problem. And so the idea which I put forward is this: Let us refer this to a committee, let them study. And the report that will come out of it will be the only thing. They might even say "we have found out, after we have studied the project, that you must study the economic situation first." So I think let them study it and report to us.

The Chairman: I put the proposal of the United Arab Republic to a vote. Those in favor of it should please do so by acclamation. It is now adopted.

PROHIBITION OF INTERVENTION AS A NORM

Fifth Extraordinary Session of the Council of Ministers
of the Organization of African Unity, Lagos,
10-13 June 1965

Nigeria (Tafawa Balewa): Let me say straightaway that I have not the limited objective of placing before you at this meeting the outline of a complex problem which now confronts our Organization. I want to do much more than that. I want you to examine the very foundations and the principles of the Charter of our Organization. I want you to search for a realistic and lasting solution to the prevailing serious crisis. I want you to speak your minds frankly and honestly during your deliberations. The African is well-known for his ability to settle quarrels after sincere exchange of views. . . .

It was our hope that after the historic meeting in Addis Ababa in May 1963, narrow national or personal objective would lose its primacy among the factors that shape our decision on African problems. We know from experience that there would always be problems in Africa. . . .

It was in the month of February that I learned with grave concern that fourteen of our member states had decided to boycott the second ordinary session of the Assembly of Heads of State and Government scheduled to be held next September in Accra. Subsequently on 22 April, a delegation of six member states of our Organization, led by my august friends, the distinguished Presidents of Niger and Upper Volta, came to Lagos and expostulated with me along the same line. . . .

In subscribing to the principles of the Charter, as Ghana and the other member states did, every single one of them pledged not to interfere in the domestic affairs of one another. They also pledged that they would not allow their capitals to become headquarters of subversion against one another.

But contrary to the undertaking, the fourteen states had found that Ghana has become the headquarters of subversion against several African states; that Ghana had established training camps for subversive elements from African states; and that Ghana provided very generously every possible facility to dissident elements from African

24

states to overthrow the legitimate governments of their home countries. Opposition elements from African states were being sent to train abroad and they were returning to training camps in Ghana, to further their subversive interests. In realization of this, the fourteen heads of state resolved at Nouakchott that, as long as Ghana continued to harbor these dissident and subversive elements and to promote in concrete terms their subversive intentions, they would not go to Accra.. . .

I think the chief value of your discussions should be that they would form the basis of healing the wounds that now exist in our relations.

The central point of your deliberations must be how to save our Organization from its present difficulties, without leaving many scars in the place of old wounds. . . .

You have a commanding responsibility under our Charter to implement the decisions of the Assembly of Heads of State and Government. One of such decisions is the meeting scheduled for Accra next September. You are to prepare the grounds before it can hold. But being human you can only do so within the framework of reason and realism. You cannot ignore the serious threat of a boycott of that meeting. This is the task before you. You must perform it within the context of our Charter. . . .

Niger: The delegation of Niger is pleased to avail itself of this opportunity to bring to our august Assembly a full explanation and the very details of the grievances we hold against Ghana. . . .

At the time of independence we were very proud to applaud the independence of this brother country which has more than 400,000 people from Niger as a second father country. Such links show how much we in Niger feel it is our duty to do everything we possibly can to maintain and to consolidate the links which existed between our country and Ghana. . . .

Furthermore, we know that Ghana was one of the first African countries with which Niger exchanged diplomatic missions. Commercial agreements and agreements of cooperation were also signed between the two countries in 1963. Nevertheless, during that period, we knew that Ghana was harboring the leader of the opposition of the legal government of the Republic of Niger, Djibou Bakary.

After that time we knew that the opposition was an integral part of the CPP—that is the party of Dr. Kwame Nkrumah. After that period, we also knew that this party was giving membership cards to the members of the opposition party of Niger. . . .

It is not the promises of violence by Djibou Bakary that we are very worried about. In view of the popular support of the masses, we do not feel that there is any real danger against our country. We do not really believe in the subversion which is organized, trained, and financed by Ghana against our country. However, we are very

25

much astonished to find that after having violated the countries of Togo, Dahomey, Nigeria, and Upper Volta, the supporters of Djibou Bakary coming from Ghana arrived on 4 October 1964 at 5 o'clock in the morning, crossing a distance of more than 2,000 kilometers from Nigumu to Tera, and attacked the following places in our national territory: Bosso, Nadawansa, and Bone in the extreme west of Niger. These terrorists coming from Ghana assassinated a man in a dispensary in Bosso and another man in the village. They killed the director of the village school, Bibossa, in the district of Bone.

After this incident, on 19 October 1964, in view of the evidence available, I wrote to the Ambassador of Ghana in Niger and asked him to intervene with his government so that an end could be put to such bloody incidents. . . .

The President of Niger himself wrote to President Kwame Nkrumah asking him to stop providing support for the killers of Djibou Bakary. After these two steps, Dr. Kwame Nkrumah answered as follows on 3 November 1964: That Djibou Bakary did live in Ghana and also other political refugees from Nigeria and Ivory Coast who were planning to overthrow their governments. He pointed out that a solution could only be found to these problems on the formation and in the constitution of a continental government. Also in this letter, he pointed out to President Hamani Diori that he was still expecting the pair of giraffes which the President had promised him for the zoo in Accra. . . .

A letter of 16 November 1964, written by Dr. Kwame Nkrumah and sent to President Houphouët-Boigny, reads as follows:

> So as to restore the continued harmony and mutual understanding and further promote understanding in the suspicion among Ghana, Ivory Coast, Upper Volta, Niger, and the Federal Republic of Cameroun, and in the interest of our mutual wish and effort to accomplish unity and solidarity in Africa, the following orders have been taken and the measures should be taken immediately:
> * Concerning Niger, Ivory Coast, Upper Volta and Ghana, Djibou Bakary must leave Ghana.
>
> * * * *
>
> * Samoe, Irie, Bibby, and Fatu Aligen must leave Ghana. Others will live peacefully in Ghana and can continue to live in Ghana peacefully and return home whenever they wish to do so.

But after this time there was another letter from the President of Ghana dated 14 January 1965, written to President Houphouët-Boigny which closed the door to all hopes:

That was why I decided to allow these refugees to stay in Ghana with the condition that they will not undertake any subversive activity against their governments. I received a very solid promise from all the refugees concerned, and I accepted their words of honor.

After this discussion, it is possible for us to tackle the actual problem or to study the problem here, and I should move on to the facts now.

I would first of all speak on the commandos and their profession of faith. This faith is based on an oath which is a blood oath in the following terms:

I swear never to hesitate to punish or to have the enemies of the people of Niger punished no matter who they may be without any sentiment or consideration.

I swear to obey the Secretary General and all people who have been called upon by circumstances to assume responsibilities and to observe without restrictions all directives of my Party, and to act without hesitation in order to achieve the objectives completely.

I swear to spare no effort in order to be worthy of my Niger homeland and never to betray the confidence of my leaders and to accept any punishment which may be undertaken against me if I fail.

One would notice that these ideologies come from Kwame Nkrumah's Institute in Winneba. This ideological training of the terrorists was organized and provided with the means of carrying out crimes against my country.

Now the document of material existence given to the terrorists by Ghana was recovered in my country. A letter was written which explained the financing of Niger subversion by Ghana. This is a memorandum on a revolutionary operation by the elements of a revolutionary party in Niger. It is a letter from the terrorists written to the head of the Africa Office in Ghana, and it reads as follows:

The Committee of the Revolutionary Staff has the pleasure of pointing out, in reference to your certificate for a military revolt in Niger, the arrival of our commandos in Niger in November 1964, and that you promised us all

military assistance necessary. We are now able to put
into operation the services of 25 men who have come from
China and Cuba to complete our ideological training both
in political and military fields.

As you know, our aim is to vanquish the neocolon-
ialists in order to establish the People's Republic of
Niger and to achieve an African Union.

This is no time for us to discuss. It is now time
for us to act, and we hope you will contact us in Dahomey
and in Lagos so as to send to us as early as possible
the men we need in Kano, Fwatua, Katsira, Magaria,
Gumei, Kikwa, Bida, and Horin, and to know whether to
go to Niger, or stay in Gaya, or go to the Republic of
Dahomey.

Ghana: We have met today at a very grave moment in the history
of the African unity movement, grave because by our actions we can
either kill all the efforts we have together been making to build a
strong, united Africa or we can once again prove to the detractors
of African unity, those who call our unity "paper unity," that they are
wrong and that we are determined to consolidate and strengthen our
forces despite the vicious machinations and slanderous utterances
of the enemies of African unity.

Ghana came to this meeting to help in removing any misunderstanding about Ghana's position and her preparedness to ensure that
her guests who attend the Summit Conference in Accra later this year
will be well cared for. Our President, Osagyefo Dr. Kwame Nkrumah,
has written to his brother Presidents that they have nothing to fear
about coming to Accra.

Obviously, Ghana did not come here to take part in any discussion or meeting which will lend itself to an illegal or dangerous act;
that is, to review the decision of the Assembly of Heads of State to
hold their next meeting in Accra. I am sure that all member states
are aware that the supreme organ of the OAU is the Assembly of
Heads of State and Government, and its decisions are not subject to
a review by any other body. . . .

It is not the intention or policy of the Ghana government to
impose its socialist policy on any country. But Ghana cannot be blamed
if the people of some countries see merit in this approach to national
reconstruction.

We are therefore at a loss to understand why some member
states are trying to boycott the conference because of Ghana's
attitude. What is inconsistent about the policies I have outlined and
the OAU Charter? None!

There has been a string of attacks, of abuses, of calumnies, and of insinuations all against Ghana, and in particular against our President, Osagyefo Dr. Kwame Nkrumah because it is said that we are harboring people engaged in subversive activities against our neighbors. . . .

No country can, on very serious grounds, refuse to accept people who for one reason or the other disagree with their governments and therefore decide to leave their countries. . . .

Therefore, far from charging Ghana as being a haven, a harbor for refugees, one should rather compliment and congratulate Ghana for its humanitarian decision to open its doors to people who say they have genuine fears for their lives and are fleeing from their countries. . . .

Let me take a particular instance of one refugee whose presence in Ghana has been objected to: Djibou Bakary. Djibou Bakary, it is well known, was once Prime Minister of Niger. In the French referendum of 1958 he urged his country to vote no. The result was that he was thrown out of his country and, afraid for his life, he took residence and asylum in Ghana. Are honorable gentlemen here saying that Ghana should have handed Djibou Bakary back to the French? What is wrong in asking Djibou Bakary to stay in Ghana and refrain from using Ghana to attack his country?

Djibou Bakary has been accused of operating commando attacks from Ghana, and every attack on any village in Niger has been attributed to Djibou's men coming from Ghana across three or four countries.

I would like to say that when Djibou Bakary left his country, naturally some of his supporters stayed behind, and some of them fled into territories just across Niger borders. Why is it that the government of Niger does not consider that those commandos could have come from these countries or even from Niger itself?

I began my speech by indicating that we are at a very grave moment in the history of the African unity movement. We shall have to decide here and now whether the seeds we sowed many years ago and which have germinated into a tree with full promise of blooming would have been sown in vain. We have to decide here whether we want to go back to the position before the Summit of 1963 when we had various splinter groups in Africa fighting each other and giving the wrong impression that we were not mature.

This is Africa's finest hour. Let us show the world that we are united; let us show the world that we are capable of solving our differences. Let us rise above such squabbles and with the object of a great meaningful and strong Africa in view decide to resolve our differences in a true spirit of African brotherhood. . . .

Congo (Leopoldville): I am not used to speaking on little issues. I believe that we have reached a point that is very serious. If we try to remember what was said by the Prime Minister of Nigeria when he spoke to the Council, he said we must look the problems in the eye because if we do not look them in the eye we will propose false solutions and we will be wasting our efforts. Now it appears that we have not borne this thing in mind.

There was a head of state who spoke to us on the proposed boycott by some members of the Organization. They gave a motive for it. It is Ghana, which for the moment is the future site of our conference. However, we have heard the accusations made against Ghana and we have heard the defense made by Ghana. We have found that our methods should be that there would be no debate, that we would establish a committee which would seek measures acceptable to all the parties.

For two days this Committee has been working and it has not managed to find in itself measures which can be acceptable to all the sides. Now it is understood that all the measures will be submitted to the Council if they are found acceptable. Thus we find that a situation has arisen in which we will democratically submit to the vote, and with regard to which we will not be able to convince our heads of state about so as to make them change their decisions, either because the political guarantees which have been requested have not been given to us, or because we ourselves will have to admit that we have got into a deadlock, and that we are ending in a fiasco. . . .

We must find a measure or measures which will get our heads of state who have refused to go to Ghana to change their minds and go to Ghana. But none of the measures which have been put down on paper here is acceptable.

The Chairman: I think we will all be very happy to hear that both parties have come to an agreement and there is no enmity now on the Resolution.

Credit for this is due to the two parties who, on our appeal, gave way in the interest of African unity. I think we must commend them very highly for this very courageous and very bold step they have taken to compromise in order to reach a solution. . . .

The Chairman (at a later, final session): We have reached the end of our deliberations and I must say that we have had a very successful meeting. I suppose there were skeptics outside hoping that we would fail at this meeting. But we have passed a Resolution unanimously on the purpose of our meeting here in Lagos. . . .

The Council of Ministers of the OAU, meeting in its
Fifth Extraordinary Session, at Lagos, Nigeria, from
10 to 13 June 1965.

HAVING heard the opening address by the Rt. Hon. Alhaji Sir Abubakar Tafawa Balewa, Prime Minister of the Federal Republic of Nigeria;

HAVING heard the statements made by certain delegates and particularly those from Ivory Coast, Niger, Upper Volta, and Ghana, concerning the problem arising from the venue in Accra of the meeting of the Second Assembly of Heads of State and Government of the OAU;

BEING anxious to comply with the fundamental principles of the Charter of the OAU which have been freely accepted by all the Member States;

RECALLING Resolution No. AHG/Res. 22 (1) of the First Ordinary Session of the Assembly of Heads of State and Government held of in Cairo, UAR, from 17 to 21 July 1964, worded as follows: "having taken note of the generous invitation by the Government of Ghana to hold the Second Ordinary Assembly in Accra, accepts this invitation with pleasure, decides to convene the Second Ordinary Session of the Assembly at Accra, on 1 September 1965."

SANCTITY OF BOUNDARIES AS A NORM

Report of First (Political) Committee, Seventh Session
28 February 1964

Ethiopia: I think we should first of all hear the two sides before we go to committee. . . .

Somalia: The 300,000 or so Somalis who live in those areas under Kenya's jurisdiction which are contiguous with the Somali Republic declared before an independent Commission of Inquiry in October 1962 that they wished to exercise their right to determine their political future and reunite with the Somali Republic. This human right was denied to them by the British government with the support of Kenya's leaders. This constituted a miscarriage of fundamental justice which has naturally caused the greatest resentment, not only to the Somali Republic but, more important still, to the Somali inhabitants of this area.

The resentment of the Somali Republic does not stem from any desire for territorial aggrandizement. Indeed, the territory in question is wholly uneconomic, as the Kenya delegation pointed out in Dar-es-Salaam. But the economic implications of the issue have no bearing whatever on our policy. It is guided solely by a desire to reunite the Somali people as one nation-state on the principle of the right to self- determination—a principle firmly entrenched in the Charters of the Organization of African Unity and of the United Nations. . . .

On the attainment of Kenya's independence in December last year, a general amnesty was granted to all political prisoners in Kenya, but this amnesty was provocatively and quite unnecessarily denied to the Somali leaders, who to this day remain in detention without trial. It is because of the suppressive measures and the continued denial of their legitimate aspirations that the Somali people have revolted against the local authorities. As the revolt gathered impetus, the government of Kenya declared an emergency in the area on 25 December, placing the Somali-inhabited northeastern region under martial law. . . .

In a recent letter to Kenya's Prime Minister, the Somali Prime Minister gave an assurance that instructions had been issued to the responsible authorities, in those Somali regions adjacent to the Kenya border, to prohibit, as far as possible, any armed person crossing from Somalia into the territory of Kenya. I hope that delegates at this conference will accept this assurance.

My government has attempted on a number of occasions to settle its dispute with Kenya peacefully. As far back as August 1962, Mr. Kenyatta, the Prime Minister of Kenya, was invited to visit Mogadishu expressly for this purpose. . . .

We must also invite the Council's attention to the recent Kenya-Ethiopia defense pact, announced in November. It is claimed by these two countries that the pact is for the defense of their respective territories. Why then was this pact negotiated secretly as far back as June of last year? This was many weeks before the Kenya government met my government to discuss our dispute formally around a conference table. Does this not throw doubt upon Kenya's sincerity in wishing to find a just solution to her border dispute with the Somali Republic?. . . .

Kenya: First of all I want to say at the outset that there is no military conflict between the Somali and Kenya armies. Our main trouble with Somalia is the continued invasion of Kenya territory by armed bandits known as shiftas who come into Kenya, loot, kill, and then run across the border into Somali territory.

Another root of the problem is the claim by the government of Somalia to be the spokesman of the Somalis in Kenya who are, in fact, Kenya citizens. The northeastern region is patrolled for security reasons by the Kenya police and the Kenya tribal police. We said in Dar-es-Salaam that, because of the activities of these shifta terrorists, a state of emergency was declared on Christmas day last year and that my government declared a five-mile no man's zone on the Kenya side of the Somali-Kenya border. The Somali government refused to take a similar step. The shifta terrorists still continue terrorist activities in Kenya.

Yesterday's Daily Telegraph referred to the intensification of these shifta activities. We have repeatedly requested the Somali government to declare a similar five-mile zone on its side of the border. This request has not been accepted. We have, since our meeting in Rome, constantly invited the Somali government to reopen the talk on the problem, and more than three times our government has approached the government of Somali through the distinguished representative, the Minister of Foreign Affairs, but we have had no reply. The only response we have received is continued attack—raids and attacks into Kenya, subversive propaganda attack against Kenya from Radio Mogadishu. . . .

As has been stated, a five-pointed star is incorporated into the flag of Somalia, each point representing an area in that part of Africa which Somalia claims as belonging to her. One of these points to the Northern Frontier District (NFD). Thus, it will be seen that Somalia has written its territorial expansionist ambition into its constitution. To achieve this aim, Somalia uses the shifta terrorists to terrorize and kill the peaceful people of Kenya inside Kenya territory. After committing these acts the shiftas flee across the border into Somalia. The Kenya security forces by observing the Somali border and respecting her sovereignty are compelled to give up the chase to avoid violation of the territorial right of Somalia. . . .

While that remained the stand of my government Somali government has not desisted from rhetoric and radio propaganda against Kenya, nor has it done anything to stop the murderous activities of the shifta gangs against Kenya.

I will now proceed to explain this. Referring to the Kenya elections which are shortly to take place in the northeastern areas, Radio Mogadishu broadcast as follows, 6 p.m., and I beg to quote:

An unwanted election is to be held in the NFD. To the NFD people we say that they should be on their guard against elections. If anybody stands for the elections, the colonialists will say that the Somalis are willing to join Kenya. Whatever they are, in the NFD they the Somalis, should enter into the struggle to back the elections. . . .

The principle of self-determination which the Somali government adopts cannot be applied to free people living in an independent sovereign country. Kenya is a mixed society of which Somali and NFD are a part. I have already shown that in spite of intimidation and vile propaganda by the Somali government, the Somalis in the

33

NFD have of their own accord thrown in their lot with the Kenya
government by taking part in the elections in which six candidates
have already been returned unopposed.

It is common knowledge that the colonial boundaries in Africa
cut across many ethnic groups throughout the continent. There is
not a single African country here or outside this hall which would
remain unaffected were this conference to sanction what would virtually mean the redrawing of territorial boundaries to conform to ethnic
grouping. . . .

Uganda: We of the Uganda delegation have listened to the arguments put forward by both Kenya and Somalia, and since we are quite
close to the two territories we are naturally concerned by the situation
which has been created by the dispute between the two countries.

Now last night we got a map in a book called The Somali
Peninsula, a New Light on Imperial Motives. In this book one would
find on Map number 2 that Uganda is now brought more or less into
the arena. Now, we are not going to rush, but I feel that the Somali
government will in the future be called upon by my government to
explain why Uganda is being brought into the arena. We have heard
that some 300,00 Somalis live in Kenya. That may be true. We do
have also a few Somalis in Uganda who have migrated to Uganda.

Now the present need arises today—and this is very important—
and the question is: Are we going to destroy all the countries of
Africa firstly and start to reorganize anew in order to find that each
country has got only one language and only one appearance? This is
vitally important, because when once we come to the conclusion that
once one walks around Nigeria and one finds a group of people speaking
a language which resembles one's own, one must lay claim on
them. . . .

I say this because the argument I have heard brings me to only
one conclusion, and that is, there is no such country as Kenya because
the whole north is now being claimed by Somalia. According to the
argument, the whole south must go to Tanganyika because the Massais
live both in Tanganyika and southern Kenya. If they must be united,
they must go back to Tanganyika. As we all know, up to 1923 part
of western Kenya was in Uganda. We in Uganda have not decided to
claim the territory which was conscribed to Kenya in 1923 because
we want to live together as brothers. Now, if we claim the west,
Somalia claims the north, and Tanganyika claims the south, there
will be no Kenya.

Now let us take a country like Uganda. We have got my own
tribe in Uganda, and some of them are in Sudan. A section of a tribe
called Alur is in Kenya while another section is in Uganda. Some
Banyaruandas are in Rwanda while some are in Uganda. How are we
going to recollect them to form one nation? So, I think this

34

argument—that since the Somalis perhaps used to be one people at one time, and since they look alike (although I cannot distinguish them from the Ethiopians), that they should be collected together and brought into one state—should be rejected. This is not because I dislike the Somalis, but I think that it is a dangerous principle which is going to undermine the integrity of our states. . . .

Nyasaland: Africa has been left behind. Africa has been a neglected continent. We cannot afford to concentrate our energy into the negative of our political, or even social life. We should channel our own enthusiasm of nationalism and our funds, energies, and talents to rebuild Africa so that it will occupy its rightful place in the world community. What I would have thought is that this is a problem which concerns this conference and the whole of Africa. By this I mean the removal of barriers between ourselves—linguistic, political, or geographic barriers—so that we can all utilize our talents and potentialities to build up, as I have said before, the gigantic continent which this continent is bound to become. But as long as we concentrate all our time quarreling among ourselves, destroying the very talents that can help us to build our countries, so long will the ex-colonial powers sit in their metropolis and laugh at us.

It is therefore the hope of my delegation, the appeal of my country, that very soon we shall see the end of these quarrels and condemn those who have left the quarrels for us. One means of doing this is the removal of these barriers. We should be thinking of methods and ways and means of bringing about African unity. We should think of the construction of transport systems so that we can move between African countries more freely and more easily than we are doing at the moment. We can think of our inter-African trade, the exchange of scholars so that we can share the knowledge in Africa in order to rediscover ourselves. . . .

Somalia: I am sorry to take the floor again, but with the permission of my Foreign Minister, I would like to say just a few words. At least the impression may have been left that Somalia is trying to expand its territory at the expense of other neighboring countries. Somalia has no desire to extend its territory. The point at issue is that, because of ancient history, certain Somalian populations have been left within the borders of other countries. This is a human problem. It is not only a question concerning a piece of territory; our territory is large enough and we are quite content with it, but this is a human problem. It concerns those people who want to be free. . . .

Kenya: I want to make only three points. The first is that it is true that Ethiopia and Kenya have actually gone into this military pact. It was in fact announced in Dar-es-Salaam and the copy of the announcement is here. So the action is not a secret. If you look at

35

your Charter Article 2 (f), you will see that you have allowed cooperation for defense and security. Therefore, in view of this, Ethiopia
and Kenya were doing just as any other group of countries could do.
That is the first point.

The second point is this: To train an individual to take law into
his own hands and move from one place to another to kill and terrorize is to disorganize an otherwise organized society. And any
person who trains such persons to do that is dangerous to that organized
government.

My final point is this: We are anxious, and it is true that we
are anxious to cooperate with Somali. In fact, our Prime Minister
has received the Minister of Foreign Affairs of Somali at the airport.
Jomo Kenyatta has gone to meet the Somali Minister of Foreign
Affairs in order to discuss and press the importance of this question
of getting together. We are in fact anxious that that thing should come
through. But as regards the question of territory, Kenya will never
allow an inch of that territory to be taken away by anybody. . . .

NONALIGNMENT AS A NORM

Report of the First (Political) Committee, Council
of Ministers, Organization of African Unity, Lagos,
26 February 1964

Tunisia: Item Seven on our Agenda is the declaration of the
nonaligned foreign policy of the African continent and the coordination
of African policy as regards future nonalignment and Afro-Asian
conferences.

I would like to make some clarification on the proposal which
was made by the Tunisian delegation.

The government of Yugoslavia, after having had contacts with
the countries present at the Belgrade Conference, decided to join
together with the government of the UAR and the government of Ceylon
in order to prepare a conference of nonaligned countries. In the report which we had to make for the preparation of the conference, we
had wanted to stress from the very beginning that when the first
Belgrade Conference took place in July 1961 a number of African
countries were not yet with us, the Organization of African Unity had
not yet been formed, and the Addis Ababa Conference had not taken
place. All the African countries ratified the Charter (which was
ratified by their respective Parliaments in conformity with the constitutional instrument), and in this Charter all the member states of
the Organization of African Unity have adhered to a policy of nonalignment. Therefore, we told our partner, Yugoslavia, that we are of

36

the opinion that all the African countries will have to be invited to this conference.

I must say that the reply of the government of Yugoslavia was affirmative and was not against the presence of all the nonaligned African countries in the next conference. This is the first question.

The second point is that we would have to define, during the preparatory committee which will take place in Colombo on 23 March, the date of the next conference, and I am of the opinion that we will have to take into account the timetable which we have set out within the framework of the OAU in order that there will not be any over-lapping between the various conferences and to take into account certain elements with reference to other international conferences which might be under way.

Thirdly, we would have to decide the venue of this conference, look at the various proposals which might be sent in by either those who attended the Belgrade Conference or those who did not attend. Fourthly, we would have to draft an agenda which would then have to be sent out to all the countries of the former Belgrade Conference as well as to all the countries who will participate in the new con-ference.

I would like to inform my colleagues that one idea was brought forward by the government of Yugoslavia and I would like to have the opinion of the Council on this. The idea was that the next Belgrade Conference could be attended by a number of nonaligned countries which find themselves in other continents than the African or Asian continent. We would like to know what the person who made this proposal had in mind. This is what I have to say as to the next non-aligned conference.

Now, as to the Asian conference, the Tunisian government knows that no formal invitation has been sent out. When Chou En-Lai visited us, he made reference to the Bandung Conference which took place in 1956 and talked about the possibility of an Asian conference like that of Bandung when many African countries were still under colonial rule and therefore none could attend. This is the information at my disposal and I want to inform the Council so that we may per-haps talk about it and in order that those who will find themselves in the preparatory conference of Belgrade will be in harmony with our Organization.

Sierra Leone: I would first of all like to seek clarification on the general principle of nonalignment.

We agreed that we should have on the agenda the question of a declaration of nonalignment by the African states, the member states of the Organization of African Unity, because this is something which is already very decidedly referred to in the Charter of the Organiza-tion, and I thought perhaps the reason why we had agreed to put it on

the agenda was that some kind of a formal resolution should be drawn
up which will point to this fact of decision and agreement which is already in the Charter, and to urge the member states to try to conform in their political external relations to this idea of nonalignment.

It seems to me that we do not all mean the same thing by nonalignment. In the first place, certain of the so-called nonaligned countries set themselves up as judges as to what is nonalignment and they
keep on accusing other people. If one does not accept their particular
idea, he is regarded as being not truly nonaligned. This has to do
with the question of the conference which has been proposed, about
which our distinguished colleague from Tunisia has been giving us
some information.

For some reason or other, and now I speak quite frankly, some
of the leaders of these countries believe that a country like mine which
has an unblemished record on nonalignment is regarded as—I do not
know what English word to use there. They look down on us with a
kind of disdain and sometimes even venture to regard us as a stooge.
I do not know why this is so, when in fact we can point accusing fingers
at them as stooges because they are stooges to certain ideas of nonalignment which cannot be defended, and they refuse to tell us about
their conferences. I am very serious about this, and when we say nonalignment we mean nonalignment, and not alignment to certain ideas
of nonalignment.

If this is a matter in our Charter, I would like us to clarify what,
from the African point of view, we mean by nonalignment.

To go on beyond this, I feel that if we can clarify our minds on
this question, then the question of nonaligned states to me becomes
redundant. I do not see why nonaligned people should be aligned to
any ideas.

As far as the Bandung Conference, the second Bandung Conference, my delegation is 100 percent in line with that, because
just as we have now sought for African unity, we should put more
thought into the idea of Afro-Asian unity. Even when we look here,
we will find that from the various points of view, it is only by meeting
together that we can get the kind of solidarity which we have succeeded
—at least I hope that we have succeeded—in achieving on the African
continent.

I therefore ask you, Mr. Chairman, to direct our attention to
the really careful study and statement of what we mean in the African
context of nonalignment.

Senegal: Nonalignment is an idea which we have had some
doubts about for several years and until now no one has been able
to define what nonalignment is, though one is always nonaligned with
someone or for someone else. I think, therefore, it is a notion which
is fairly vague and which gives the possibility of grouping a certain
number of people who are linked with each other.

However, there is one factor: The conference which should be the second Belgrade Conference of nonalignment should be included in the framework of nonalignment. The Belgrade Conference will have to deal with what is the finished framework of nonalignment, and we are told that there will be another conference which will be that of the Afro-Asian conference, which will certainly deal with nonalignment. Therefore, the question which will arise will be about the Belgrade and Peking conferences. I think we in the Organization of African Unity must not be stooges who could be moved about at will on a kind of chess board, and I think that nothing will stop the OAU from calling a nonalignment conference; that depends on what we call nonalignment. If we can agree on the definition, perhaps, then I think we can avoid being permanent stooges who might be moved about on a chess board.

Madagascar: For us in Madagascar, we do not understand very well what is meant by nonalignment, basing our thoughts on facts and on everyday realities.

Countries in the majority belong either to one bloc, the Western or the Eastern bloc. Some countries which call themselves nonaligned sometimes are in their behavior not only aligned but also engaged, and that is not the case of Madagascar. We are not at all engaged. We often have freedom of movement—I am sorry to be speaking about my country, but some countries with which we are aligned have recognized China. We do not recognize Red China. Some other countries who call themselves aligned have recognized the nuclear test-ban treaty whereas others have refused to recognize this.

We must, therefore, define what this nonalignment policy is. In fact, we are more or less aligned either to the East or to the West. That is a very serious question indeed because in politics there is always a corollary, that is to say, the economic current, the current of changes which take place between friendly countries. In political matters I think we must start upon this question with great reservation, and in any case we should submit to our heads of state that if we are to be considered as nonaligned, we must ask whether we are nonaligned or aligned as to the Conference which has just been perhaps based at Yugoslavia and which they call the Conference of Nonaligned Countries. That is a very bad name and we would have preferred it to be called the Conference for Peace or Conference for Freedom among men.

Tunisia: What the delegate of Sierra Leone has just said as well as the speeches of the delegate of Senegal and some other delegates must be pertinent to me. It is true that the word nonalignment is an idea which is still fairly vague and about which each person seems to believe his own conception.

I am in a greater ease of mind in saying that, as far as the
Organization here is concerned, the policy of nonalignment which we
adhere to is specified—namely, the policy of nonalignment toward
both blocs. That means to say, if I have understood this idea, that
we are not bound by engagements written or oral to be always in
agreement with this bloc or the other for such and such a problem
but that we can adopt our own stand when such and such a problem
arises in the international field, whether it be in the field or international peace and security or in the field of cooperation among nations.

Where a problem arises, we will adopt our own position, not
in trying to agree with this or with that bloc, but we should adopt our
position in regard to the merit of the problem itself. It may happen
that, in taking such a position, we may find ourselves either in agreement with the Eastern bloc or with the Western bloc. Thus, when
certain problems which were mentioned as being the ban of nuclear
tests arose, we in Tunisia saw that it was a most excellent thing and
we adhered to it. Then a large part of the communist or socialist
world with China has not yet adhered to it or is not authorized to
adhere to it. This is another aspect of the problem. And it followed
on matters which occurred in the international field and may thus
go against the United States or against Russia according to the problem
that arises and according to the solution we may choose.

And thus in my opinion should we understand the notion of nonalignment in the way the Charter has explained it.

I would like to read the article or the paragraph which relates
to this. The Charter did not say that we affirm a policy of nonalignment
toward all blocs. It is more precise this way rather than to say toward two blocs. In principle, apart from African unity we are against
the setting up of blocs of an international scale. Such blocs may
little by little create antagonism which may be eminently dangerous
not only to peace but to humanity as a whole. I know that this idea
is not a very precise one as yet. However, it has been a kind of
draft of this policy of nonalignment.

During the first conference of Belgrade in 1961 I think that we
attended such a conference so that we might be able to specify this
thing, considering the experience that we have gathered. We had
what we should understand by nonalignment toward blocs. Now, on
the items which must be discussed by the conference, we should
examine this policy of nonalignment toward all blocs so that we might
perhaps be able to understand what is meant by blocs, the antagonism
involved, and thus contribute toward the maintenance of international
peace and security.

That is the way I see things. We have understood the doubts
that have been expressed by some of the distinguished delegates in
particular by the delegation of Madagascar, Senegal, and Sierra Leone.

Mauritania: It comes to my mind to give you a possible definition of the Charter which might perhaps satisfy some of our friends
who seem to distrust the expression "nonalignment."

I see that Africa has decided not to align itself with any bloc.
When the Organization of African Unity was set up, did the bloc of
nonaligned people not exist yet? Was that not already in existence?
I mean the definition that one may not align oneself with either the
East or the West or to any other bloc that may exist. I do not know
how these things came about, but this is just an idea that came to my
mind.

I think that since some of our friends distrust this expression,
"nonalignment," we might perhaps find something else to call it. We
might say that our policy is one of neutrality. If one does not want
to use the word nonalignment, we can certainly find some other expression which can define African policy, which can show Africa in its
true aspect. And this would show the idea that we belong neither to
the left nor to the right nor to any side.

Guinea: The questions which were proposed on our agenda were
to know first of all how to coordinate our position vis-a-vis the meetings of nonaligned countries, and vis-a-vis a meeting of Afro-Asian
countries. These two meetings have been proposed to certain African
countries.

When Guinea received such an invitation, our government wrote
to the Secretariat of the OAU to tell them to submit this matter to
the OAU so that the members could consult together and decide whether
they should participate and decide the date of the participation and
so on.

Now, as to the declaration of nonalignment which has been
proposed, I entirely agree with the explanation given by the distinguished minister of Foreign Affairs of Tunisia as regards the definition in the Charter.

As to the meaning of the word nonalignment, in our opinion,
nonalignment vis-a-vis all blocs does not signify neutrality. In our
opinion the Organization of African Unity is not neutral. If there are
countries that wish to establish colonial regimes, it will fight against
such countries. It is not neutral. Our countries can go this or that
way. In our opinion, we engage in an action of common policy which
we have defined together within the framework of the OAU. And we
in fact belong to one bloc or another.

But our ties with any bloc are loose. We may agree with the
Soviet Union on this or that policy and disagree with her on others,
just as we can agree with the United States of America or with China
on this or that policy and disagree on other policies of those countries. We agree with any bloc in conformity with the interest of our
countries and our people. What we want is that we should every time

41

coordinate our activities so that some should not go in one camp
while others go in another camp.

We should indeed be a bloc of African countries—that is to say,
an Organization of African Unity. And that is why we should now
examine these questions carefully. We should agree first of all on a
declaration, particularly with regard to the Conference of Belgrade.
There are African countries that have already said that they would
go to that conference and the Council must give its opinion on this.
The Council may either say that they must not go for such and such
a reason or that they may go.

We may say to the country that should go to the second nonaligned conference in Belgrade what our position should be, and if the
majority of the countries agree, they will go and present our stand.
The same is true of the second conference of the Afro-Asian countries. This is the viewpoint of the Guinea delegation concerning this
particular item on the agenda.

Cameroun: Our eminent colleague from Tunisia counted two
blocs—the Eastern bloc and the Western bloc. These two blocs are
not the only blocs because there is already a third bloc. You all know
that between Moscow and Peking there are differences. You know that
Belgrade is a friend of Moscow and you know that Belgrade is opposed
to Peking.

I fear that the two organizations to which we have been invited
are merely a trap, or rather an attempt to get us to be aligned with
one bloc rather than with the other. I think this may harm our Organization and may even kill it. This is the result of the hypocrisy which
we have inherited from European countries or even colonial countries.
We must be frank and I would like to tell you here that we must not
hide the fact. Communist China has not yet proved that it is peaceful.
They keep on sending armaments and warriors to other countries in
order to upset our governments. Is that a proof of peaceful intention?

My last point is this, that I would like to know which African
country is nonaligned. With the exception of perhaps one or two
African countries (I would like to say a single one and that is Ethiopia),
we all have been colonized countries. We have all been colonized
by European countries and now there is rivalry between certain
European countries. I would like to know whether we could not have
our own stand. Can Africa not constitute a school which might inspire other continents? Why should we reply to calls made by either
European or Asian countries? This is a question which I put to all
delegates to be submitted to all governments. Having declared the
principle of nonalignment in our Charter, why should we not have such
conferences called by Africa rather than have them called by Europe
or Asia?

The Chairman: Actually, I have been carrying with me a small
point of view on this question. Africa has about 92 percent of gold
used all over the world, practically all the copper, uranium, now oil,
and we are gaining more and more scientific knowledge. I see that
it is a question of exploiting our natural resources.

That is my personal private belief because of the deepest confidence that I have for Africa and Africans and because I know that
they are not less competent than the rest of the people. You can get
genius in Africa, China, as well as in other parts of the world, and
therefore we who have these potentialities, if we can bend our energies
together and if we can be united—I believe that other people will come
to us. Even now they do come creeping and they do come running.
When you think they come and ask us to come to them, they are plead-
ing that we go to them because they want our natural resources and
our ingenuity.

And then this question of trade. Europe, America, and China
want African resources. We have to apply the relationship of the sell-
er and the buyer. When they are selling to us we are the buyers, and
when we are selling to them they are the buyers. As such, they can
deal with us and we can deal with them, whether they are in Moscow,
in the United States of America, or in China, or anywhere else. What
I would appreciate here is a clarification of what we call neutrality:
whether it is neutrality to destroy our market or to promote our
market; whether it is neutrality to subjugate ourselves completely
to others or to invite other energies for our destruction.

I believe that whatever definition we give or wherever we may
go, either in the United Nations or elsewhere, those people get us
proportionately. They have organized themselves and their natural
resources to our disadvantage. Whether we are in the United Nations,
in China, in Moscow, in America, or in whatever country, if we can
actually put our house to order and see whether we can at least develop
our communication, it will work to our advantage. Communication
is very important. Now, if I want to call Kenyatta, I have first to go
through London, but we have to get direct communication with ourselves and to cultivate the things that will bring us together.

Ethiopia: We did not have the privilege of being present at the
first Conference at Belgrade; therefore, we do not know what happened
there. We hear of the nonalignment conference. What I would like
to know is whether that conference has immediate aims which are of
interest to the OAU. Perhaps the African members who attended the
last conference might be able to tell us what they gained by that conference.

Concerning the Afro-Asian conference it seems at first sight
this might be a conference which might be useful because the colonized
countries of Africa and Asia continue to have the same difficult

conditions as before and they might benefit by the Afro-Asian conference. So I understand the aims pursued by this Afro-Asian conference.

You will excuse me if I do not understand the immediate aims of the conference of nonaligned countries. Therefore, I would like to ask the members who attended that conference at Belgrade to let us have the benefit of their experience.

The UAR: We have heard this discussion, the tone of which, as I understand it, is on the next nonalignment conference and the proposed Afro-Asian conference. So far I have refrained from taking part in the discussion, and I am sorry to say that I will continue to do so.

The two conferences, as I understand it, are conferences to which the heads of state will be invited, and it will be the decision of the heads of state and government. I do not think that I, although leader of the UAR delegation—I am just a Deputy Minister—can comment on matters that would come before the heads of state and government for decision.

Guinea: It will be advisable for the Council to discuss the problems which have been submitted to it. There is already an invitation to the conference of nonaligned states and we are told that on 23 March there will be a meeting at ambassadorial level at Colombo. There are African countries that have decided to take part at that conference. We also have invitations for the conference of Afro-Asian countries, and the conferences of heads of state will not take place before the second half of June, if we follow the request made by Nyasaland that the meeting be held in the second half of June. It will be good, therefore, that the Council have a very clear idea of the whole matter and give instructions to the Provisional Secretariat to inform and communicate with all the African states, or we should prepare a proposal for our heads of state conference, which will take place in June.

Ghana: The first point I would like to emphasize is that, in the matter we are discussing, invitations have already been sent to our heads of state. Whatever we decide here, they cannot take any common action before they deal with those letters or even before the conferences start, so I think we should refrain from taking any decision so that we do not embarrass anybody. But I would like to make this observation—that this is a matter of international importance and in order to give us the standing and status to deal with this international matter it is very important that we observe the part of the Charter in Article 2 which says that one of the chief purposes of this Organization is to harmonize and coordinate our policies with regard to political and diplomatic cooperation. If we are able to do that, then when we go to these conferences we shall have a common stand and Africa's voice will be heard more effectively. That is why it is very important that we adhere to this part of our Charter.

In fact the speeches which have been made here have gladdened my heart because they show unmistakably that we realize the supreme importance of this Organization and the desirability of really trying to realize the objectives for which this body stands. The resources of this continent, if only we can utilize all the potentialities which are open to us, will really make Africa a big continent. We shall benefit and our children shall benefit, too. But in any case there is one point about that item which is very pertinent to us here: that is the question of nonalignment. We have to make it very clear to us what exactly we mean by it and, as has been pointed out, I think we shall take any opportunity to define it as precisely as possible.

However, we have a rough idea of what it is: that we ought not to attach ourselves to anybody, especially to the two main blocs (the Eastern bloc and the Western bloc). But we have the ability to decide on any issue in accordance with the interest of Africa.

The Sudan: The idea behind our thinking is that in the last nonaligned conference there was a lot of controversy as to which African countries should be invited, as to which African countries are really nonaligned or perfectly committed. It was a burning question which was asked by those who extended their invitation for the Belgrade Conference. Since then we have come together, we have drawn a Charter, we have made a small family of nations within the continent of Africa.

It is therefore not in the spirit of the family relations that some people should accept invitations or refuse to recommend others for that invitation; they should not take a stand without going back to their family and telling them, "Look here, my position is that I may be invited to this conference and you may not be invited. What do you think of it?" Or, alternatively, the position may be that those who had received the invitations would have the courage to tell the other people. There is an English proverb which says, "If you invite an Arab, you invite the whole tribe." If you invite an African, you invite the whole tribe. You either invite us all or you leave us all.

I was very much interested in the very eloquent and really interesting comment by the leader of the Camerounian delegation. He seems to say that the whole concept of nonalignment is nebulous, is not clear. To our mind, it is really theory more than practice and, as George Orwell would say—"Some animals are more equal than others," some people are more aligned than others. I would suggest, that you give us the benefit of the services of the committee which was suggested by Ghana, and let us put this question to the little committee which is supposed to help us find ways and means for solidifying Africa. This is one of the contentious principles, this is one of the questions which should be solved, to be clarified for the newcomers and fortified for the old members.

If the distinguished leader of the Ghana delegation would accept the committee's suggestion and also do us the favor of inviting other countries, that would be a great benefit and, furthermore, it will give time for us to cool down, for the atmosphere to clear up and for reason to resume its seat.

I doubt if there is any heart-searching or doubt about the relationship between the African and Asian countries. I think that it is a drawn and acceptable policy of African states to cooperate in international relations, especially at the United Nations, with their brothers in Asia, and if there are doubts about their intentions, I think we must give them time to prove it. Hitherto, they have always had the benefit of the doubt and they have been cooperating very nicely with their African brothers.

As regards the nonaligned question, I suggest that we refer this question of resolution or declaration to the small committee of eleven to advise us on it, and on the other question of our relations with the Asian countries I do not think that is a thorny question at all, it is a straightforward one which was decided a very long time ago.

2

THE LEAGUE OF ARAB STATES AND THE ORGANIZATION OF AFRICAN UNITY

Boutros Boutros-Ghali

How does an international organization function when all its members are underdeveloped countries? How is the balance of power established in a community of poor countries within the framework of an international organization? These are just two of the questions to be examined in this comparative study of the Arab League and the Organization of African Unity.

First we will examine the role of both organizations regarding the decolonization process. Then we will deal with their part in the settling of international disputes. In the third section we will study their action in favor of economic cooperation.

DECOLONIZATION

The Arab League was created in March 1945; the Organization of African Unity was established only in May 1963, some 18 years later. However, the two organizations have many characteristics in common. First, both are anticolonial organizations created to accelerate decolonization. However, the 18 years separating the birth of the two organizations are crucial to their different understandings of the concept of colonialism.

In 1945 the decolonization of the Arab world was not explicitly mentioned among the aims pursued by the Arab League. The Arab world had not yet become fully aware of the scope or the nature of the colonial phenomenon. The only independence of which it could conceive was political independence within the narrow framework of economic and cultural interdependence with the former metropolises.

Moreover, militarily occupied and economically enslaved, the Arab states could not afford to openly antagonize the colonial powers. In the aftermath of the war, these powers seemed to be in a position to maintain indefinitely their domination over Africa and Asia. Thus, colonialism is never mentioned in either the Pact of 22 March 1945 or the Collective Defense Pact of 17 June 1950, and the anticolonial fight is mentioned only indirectly.

By contrast, the Organization of African Unity was born immediately after the completion of the decolonization of North and Central Africa and after the colonized states had reached political maturity either on the battlefields or in the United Nations arena. Moreover, the African states were fully aware of the colonial phenomenon and realized that political independence was only one step in the search for national liberation, and that such a step had to be followed by economic independence. Thus, "the eradication of all forms of colonialism from Africa" is mentioned in the Addis Ababa Charter, and neocolonialism is emphasized by the Charter.

Economically, neocolonialism appears as an attempt by foreign investors to maintain a territory's dependence upon its former metropolis. On the diplomatic level, neocolonialism takes the form of bilateral agreements and the maintenance of military bases. The theme of opposition to neocolonialism, with variations, has now been taken up vigorously by Africans of many shades of political opinion.

The Ghanaian Representative to the United Nations has called neocolonialism "the practice of granting a sort of independence with the concealed intention of making the liberated country a client-state, and controlling it effectively by means other than political ones." To Kwame Nkrumah, the multiplication of artificially created African ministates—in other words, the balkanization of Africa—is a perfect instrument of neocolonialism.

At Addis Ababa in May 1963, President Nasser discussed the effects of neocolonialism in greater detail. He said:

> There exists that insistence on making of the continent
> a mere warehouse for raw materials at prices which fail
> to satisfy the hunger of its people while the total benefit
> goes to the importing countries which try to make of
> their industrial and scientific progress a quasi-
> colonialism of a new form, that of unjust exploitation of
> the wealth of others without a fair share.[1]

It has to be recognized that any relationship between an ex-colonial power and a former colony is inevitably colored by past history. However, while the OAU puts the emphasis on neocolonialism, the Arab League seems less preoccupied by this phenomenon. Two explanations may be proposed to account for this difference in attitude.

First, the common Arab cultural heritage offers a better defense against foreign cultural assimilation and linguistic domination;

consequently, the Arab world is less afraid of the cultural impact of neocolonialism than the African world, which does not have the benefit and defense of a common culture and language.

Second, Zionist colonialism was from the start the immediate preoccupation of the Arab struggle against colonialism. The Arab League went so far as to give this struggle priority over the achievement of the decolonization of its own founding members; thus, Zionism overshadowed all other forms of colonialism.

In spite of this difference in attitude toward the colonialist phenomenon, the two organizations established similar programs of action in order to achieve the total national independence of all Arab and all African countries still subject to foreign domination. These programs include:

● An invitation to the colonial powers to take the necessary measures for the granting of immediate independence to the colonial countries and peoples.

● The sending of delegations to the U.N. Security Council whenever the situation of Arab or African territories under foreign domination is being discussed.

● The severing of diplomatic relations between Arab and African states and the governments giving support and assistance to colonial governments.

● The nonrecognition of new colonialist states (Israel, Rhodesia).

● The total economic boycott of Israel, Portugal, South Africa, and Rhodesia—prohibiting the importation of goods from these countries, closing ports and airfields to their ships and planes, and refusing to grant permission to fly over Arab or African countries.

● The unification of the different liberation movements.

● The creation of liberation armies and volunteer corps on the territory of different independent Arab and African states.

As an example of similar diplomatic action, one can compare the vast campaign by the Arab League in opposition to the payment of compensation by Germany to Israel in 1952 with the diplomatic campaign undertaken by the OAU to obtain British intervention in Rhodesia in 1966. Both campaigns were total failures.

The fight for the decolonization of Palestine has been marked by a series of spectacular defeats with the Zionist state expanding its territorial possession or strengthening its domination on each occasion. The decolonization of southern Africa has equally been marked by stagnation and regression, with the apartheid state strengthening its domination. Nevertheless, the decolonization of all other Arab and African states has been very successful.

It could be argued that the decolonization of the Arab world and Africa would have taken place regardless of the League's action or the OAU's intervention. Such an assumption should be corrected.

The League as well as the OAU provided a framework for expressing the claims of dependent Arab and African states. Within such a framework, the intervention of the Arab states for the decolonization of Arab territories or the intervention of the African states for the decolonization of African territories could not be condemned as a form of Arab or African intervention in the affairs of other Arab or African states.

Moreover, collective Arab intervention or collective African intervention prepared and carried out within the framework of an international organization, and supported by the system and ideology of that organization, gave legitimacy to collective Arab or African action in the face of colonialist dialectic, which views all liberation movements as seditious.

The Arab League and the OAU have contributed to making decolonization a doctrine and principle of international law as adopted by the United Nations. Had this been the sole contribution of the Arab League and the OAU, it would have been a very significant one indeed.

THE PEACEFUL SETTLEMENT OF DISPUTES

In 1946 the ideology that prevailed in the Arab world was "the rule of law." The ruling elites were impregnated with Western constitutionalism and believed that inter-Arab conflicts could be settled by an international judge or an arbitrator. One need only read the minutes of the preparatory meetings that preceded the drafting of the Pact of 22 March 1945 to realize the emphasis certain delegates placed on the principle of compulsory arbitration. However, as a result of the opposition of the delegate from Lebanon, who wished to preserve as much as possible the sovereignty of the future members of the League, a compromise solution was reached. It appears in the Pact under Article 5, which stipulates:

> It is forbidden to have recourse to force in order to
> settle conflicts which may arise among Member States
> of the League. Should a dispute arise between two such
> States, in no way concerning the independence, the
> sovereignty or the territorial integrity of these States,
> and if the parties to the conflict request the Council of
> the League to settle the dispute, the Council's decision
> shall be binding and executory.

And in order to satisfy the delegates who favored compulsory arbitration, Article 19 of the League's Pact states:

The present Pact can be amended by a majority of two-
thirds of the Members of the League. In particular it
can be amended to establish . . . an Arab court of arbitration.

In fact, the creation of this Arab court has been the subject of numerous discussions and even more numerous resolutions. Seldom has
there been a session of the Council of the League at which the matter
of a future Arab court of justice has not been brought up. Despite
all these resolutions, the court has not yet materialized.

Eighteen years later, the same problem of resolving disputes
arose for the OAU. Article 19 of the Addis Ababa Charter stipulates:

Member States pledge to settle all disputes among themselves by peaceful means and, to this end, decide to
establish a Commission of Mediation, Conciliation and
Arbitration the composition of which and conditions of
service shall be defined by a separate Protocol to be
approved by the Assembly of Heads of State and Government. Said Protocol shall be regarded as forming an
integral part of the present Charter.

The August 1963 Council of Ministers, which met at Dakar, set
up a special committee to work out a separate protocol for the Commission. The protocol was adopted in Cairo in July 1964 by the
Council of Ministers (Resolution CM/Res 42/III) and by the Council
of Heads of State (Resolution AHG/22) and became an integral part
of the Addis Ababa Charter, as stated in Article 19 of the Charter
and Article 32 of the Protocol. The 21 members of the Commission
were nominated during the third session of the Heads of State at
Accra in October 1965. However, the Commission was not to meet
before December 1967 at Addis Ababa, and that was its first and last
meeting.

By different roads we reach the same result: the failure of
judicial settlement of disputes in both the Arab League and the OAU.
On the other hand, whenever inter-Arab or inter-African disputes
have been settled, it has been via diplomatic negotiations under the
auspices of the League and the OAU.

How can this similarity be explained?

First, the lack of an international Arab court forced the Arab
states to settle their disputes within the Council of the Arab League.
In the same way, the very long time taken by the African states to
set up the Commission of Mediation, Conciliation and Arbitration
compelled the African states to revert to ad hoc commissions for
the settling of inter-African disputes.

Second, the Arab world and the African world have a certain distrust for international law, which they have come to know only through its colonial aspect, invariably concerned with legitimizing European acquisitions and privileges. Their mistrust of Western-oriented general international law has been transposed to the regional level, and they still have not developed a regional international law that could help them solve their disputes.

Third, judicial settlement is a lengthy and costly process that only wealthy and developed states can afford.

In conclusion, the Arab and African states, in resolving their regional disputes, are still at the stage of diplomatic negotiations, which are more in line with their tastes and traditions. More elaborate or technical procedures might never be put to use, or even worse, might embitter the conflicts.

But this is where the similarities between the Arab League and the OAU in the peaceful settlement of disputes end.

In conformity with the principle stated in article 52 of the United Nations Charter, which provides that members entering into regional organizations shall make every effort to achieve pacific settlement of local disputes through such regional organizations before referring them to the Security Council, both the Arab League and the OAU have repeatedly stated that Arab conflicts should be settled in an Arab context and African disputes should likewise be solved within a purely African framework. But whereas the African states have respected this principle in most of their disputes—for example, the boundary conflict between Algeria and Morocco and the disputes between Ethiopia and Somalia or Kenya and Somalia—the Arab states have rarely observed it. They have always gone directly to the Security Council, bypassing the Arab League—as in the dispute between Egypt and the Sudan in February 1958, the conflict between Lebanon and the UAR in August 1958, and the conflict between Kuwait and Iraq in June-September 1967.

How can one explain this important difference between the attitudes of the Arab states and the African states regarding their respective organizations? How should one explain the inadequacy of the League in solving the conflicts that arise among its members and the success of the OAU in settling inter-African disputes? How can one account for the lack of confidence of the Arab states in their own organization as an instrument for the peaceful settlement of their disputes, and the confidence of the African states in their own organization?

Some have claimed that this situation had its origin in the archaic and obsolete nature of the machinery set up by the League to deal with conflicts. If a court of arbitration existed, then Arab states would be less reluctant to turn to the Arab League.

But in reality this lack of confidence has nothing to do with the system set up by the League. As it happens, the Commission of Mediation, Conciliation and Arbitration set up by the OAU has never functioned either, but still the African organization has managed to settle inter-African disputes within a purely African framework.

We believe that the difference here involves the profound contradictions inherent in the Arab world, contradictions that lead Arab states to prefer intervention by a non-Arab third party (be it a state or an international organization) rather than an Arab one. This crisis has its origins in the predominant role played by Egypt within the League. It is worth noting that in most cases where Arab states have submitted disputes to the Security Council or other institutions, rather than to the League, the conflicts were with Egypt itself or one of its allies. A similar phenomenon can be seen in pan-American practice: States in conflict with the United States or a state having close ties to Washington prefer to turn to the Security Council rather than the Organization of American States, where the U.S. preeminence is unquestionable.

Within the OAU, by contrast, no one African state has a preponderant role. The African states participate in the various forms of collective action and share equally in the decision-making process. Although the Charter of Addis Ababa does not go so far as to state explicitly its rejection of any "leadership," it does in effect debar any single African state from playing the role of leader by stressing the principle of absolute equality. President Habib Bourguiba of Tunisia has said, "The desire for supremacy is the worm in the bud. When one partner wishes to dominate the group, sooner or later that group will fall apart."[2]

In other words, the rejection of the idea of dominant leadership—and the nonexistence, for the time being at least, of any exclusive leadership in the OAU—is the main factor in its success in settling inter-African disputes.

To sum up, a comparative study of different disputes in the Arab League and the OAU leads to the following conclusions.

If the leadership of a particular state in a regional organization is open to doubt, then the member states that are in dispute can afford to reject the competence of the regional organization if they so prefer and appeal directly to the United Nations. This situation appears clearly in the Arab League. By contrast, if the leadership of a particular state in a regional organization is total and unchallenged, the member states will always settle their disputes within the framework of this organization. An example is the case of the Soviet regional system; disputes among the member states are always settled within the system itself and never reach the United Nations.

If the regional organization is not dominated by a single state or a group of states and all states have equal influence within the

53

organization, then the states in dispute will have more confidence in their own regional system for the settlement of their disputes, as in the case of the OAU.

ECONOMIC COOPERATION

The major problem facing the Arab and African states today is that of underdevelopment, and this problem is likely to remain for a long time to come. What are the policies for development and integration that have been adopted by the Arab League and the OAU to remedy this state of affairs?

It may be recalled that the General Assembly of the United Nations has discussed the factors of classification for countries considered "economically underdeveloped." Two criteria of underdevelopment were proposed, one based on national income and gross national product (GNP), the other on utilization of technical assistance from the United Nations. (South Africa is an exception, but it is not in fact an African state within the definition of the Charter of Addis Ababa since it does not conform to the requirement of African legitimacy established by the Charter.)

According to these criteria, every African state, without exception, must be considered economically underdeveloped. However, not every Arab state is underdeveloped and some Arab states are among the richest countries in the world.

Thus the question of Arab underdevelopment has never been posed as a regional problem, while African underdevelopment has been emphasized with lucidity and courage by more than one African Head of State. At the Addis Ababa Conference in May 1963, Leopold Senghor, President of the Republic of Senegal, said: "We have also in common our situation as under-developed countries, characterized by a certain number of traits that can be summed up as under-nourishment and under-productivity because of lack of capital and technically trained personnel."[3]

In the same spirit, Ahmadou Ahidjo, President of Cameroun, declared, "It must be recognised that, in what one calls the 'Third World,' we are among the most disinherited."[4]

The fact that Arab underdevelopment has never been a major preoccupation of the Arab League does not mean that Arab economic cooperation was not one of the aims of pan-Arabism.

After first mentioning political cooperation, Article 2 of the Pact establishing the League adds that the League "also has the objective of assuring, within the framework of the respective regimes and situations of each state, close cooperation between member states in the following matters: Economic and financial matters . . . communication . . . social welfare . . . health."

54

In fact, the anticolonial struggle, and particularly the anti-Zionist fight, forced the pursuit of this objective into the background. It was only after the first Palestine defeat that problems of economic cooperation came to the forefront of the League's activities.

Four procedures, common to all international organizations, were used to lay the foundations of Arab economic cooperation:

1. The adoption of resolutions inviting member states to initiate integration in given fields.
2. The encouragement of meetings, congresses, conferences, colloquia, and seminars devoted to the various fields of economic, social, and cultural cooperation.
3. The creation of relevant specialized agencies attached to the League.
4. The encouragement of the conclusion of technical agreements aimed at institutionalizing Arab cooperation in specific fields such as the transit trade, oil, and communications.

The first procedure was used extensively by the Council of the League, which passed a great number of resolutions concerning the most diverse aspects of cooperation, but these resolutions remained for the most part ineffective.

Use of the second procedure resulted in an incredible number of conferences, congresses, and seminars at all levels and covering the widest range of subjects. One positive aspect of these meetings was that they allowed the Arab elites to become better acquainted. But all too often, the recommendations drafted and adopted at these meetings have been ratified by the appropriate organs of the League, then referred to the governments of member states, then sometimes submitted again by these states to the Council of the League and once more referred to member states in the form of recommendations from the Council—a vicious circle unlikely to lead to any progress in promoting Arab cooperation and integration.

Use of the third procedure gave rise to the establishment of various specialized agencies (the Arab Postal Union, the Arab Tele-communications and Radio-Communications union, the Arab International Institute for the Defense of Society Against Crime, the Arab International Institute for Public Administration, the Arab Organization for Education, Culture and Science (called the Arab "UNESCO"), which operate within the framework of the Arab League but very often compete with the League. On the other hand, many of these specialized agencies—such as the organization of Arab World Airlines (created by Resolution 18, passed by the Economic Council of the League in April 1961) or the Arab Maritime Company (created by Resolution 23, passed by the Economic Council on 17 December 1963)—never actually came into being.

The fourth procedure brought about the conclusion of various international conventions. Chronological priority belongs to the Cultural Convention, approved by the Council of the Arab League at its second session on 27 November 1945 (Resolution 14/2). The Convention on Writs and Judicial Commissions of Inquiry, the Convention on the Execution of Judgments, and the Convention on the Extradition of Criminals (approved by the Council on 14 October 1952) represent a second group of conventions aimed at improving Arab integration in the legal domain.

In the economic field, several conventions have been proposed for signature and ratification. These include a convention to promote and organize trade among the Arab states, a convention on the settlement of payments and the transfer of capital between Arab states, and a convention on the economic union of the Arab states.

It should be pointed out that the procedure adopted for the conclusion of these conventions is a particularly slow one. A draft convention is first prepared by the competent department in the Secretariat of the League; then it is approved by the appropriate permanent commission, which often holds a special meeting in order to give a more solemn character to the convention. In the next stage, the convention is approved by the Council of the Arab League or by the Economic Council. The convention is then signed by an ad hoc meeting of plenipotentiary envoys. Then it still has to be ratified by the various Arab states, and finally the instruments of ratification must be deposited with the Secretariat of the League, which in turn notifies the Arab states when the convention enters into force.

The pointless complexity of such procedures was to a certain extent responsible for the delays incurred in the enforcement of these conventions. Moreover, due to the interval between the drafting of a convention and its application, the convention, once ratified, must almost immediately be amended to make it correspond to the new situation.

As the procedure established for amending these conventions is as intricate and time-consuming as that for ratification, the present approach is inadequate for keeping pace with the Arab world's economic evolution.

It thus seems that this whole structure of conventions is nothing more than a facade intended to hide the crisis of Arab cooperation. It appears that Arab states do not really wish to bind themselves with other Arab states through conventional or institutional obligations. At the same time, however, they wish to show public opinion that they are resolutely heading toward integration. The Arab League is used as a frame for this equivocation, which is deliberately perpetrated with the complicity of its member states. This institutional demagoguery results in a continuous pretense of activity at various levels and masks the stagnation of Arab cooperation.

Having reviewed economic cooperation in the Arab world, let us now see whether African cooperation in the economic fields has been more successful or better managed.

The principle of African economic cooperation is mentioned in the third paragraph of the Preamble and reaffirmed in Article 2 of the Charter of Addis Ababa, which puts among the objectives of the OAU members the desire "to coordinate and intensify their cooperation and efforts to achieve a better life for the people of Africa."

The OAU, however, has not created a special body entrusted with economic cooperation. Whereas the Arab treaty of joint defense and economic cooperation provides for an Economic Council distinct from the other major organs of the Arab League, the Charter of Addis Ababa gives to the OAU's various directing bodies (the Summit Conference, the Council of Ministers, the Secretariat) the task of directly dealing with economic questions. It should nonetheless be noted that, among the five special commissions created in conformity with the stipulations of Article 20 of the Charter of Addis Ababa, the foremost is the Economic and Social Commission, charged with the promotion of pan-African economic cooperation.

At the special session of the African Summit Conference held in Addis Ababa in May 1963, the delegates were so anxious to bring forward the whole question of economic cooperation that they decided, in Point Four of the agenda, to press for the immediate creation of a Preparatory Economic Committee while waiting for the creation of the actual Economic and Social Commission.

The Preparatory Economic Committee never actually met, but the Economic and Social Commission did hold its first meeting in Niamey in December 1963 and considered the major objectives envisaged by the first African Summit and also looked at the problem of coordinating its own work with that of the Economic Commission for Africa. Finally the Economic and Social Commission decided to hold its next annual meeting in Cairo in January 1965. This second meeting was also to be the last, because the majority of African states refrained from sending delegations, and moreover did not even reply to the invitations sent by the Secretariat of the OAU for further meetings.

In order to find some way out of this serious state of affairs, the Secretary General proposed to the Council of Ministers in Kinshasa in September 1967 that the Economic Commission should be bypassed in favor of a direct move to examine economic cooperation.

As the Secretary General's Report indicates, this move is only a makeshift one that presents two major inconveniences. First, it is difficult for the Council of Ministers to deal with the technical details involved in the problems of African economic cooperation. Second, the Council of Ministers of the OAU is primarily a political body, more concerned with questions of decolonization and international politics than with economic cooperation.

The second move was to increase cooperation between the OAU and the Economic Commission for Africa (ECA). An agreement was concluded between the United Nations and the OAU in November 1965.[5] Different methods of collaboration between the two institutions were subsequently implemented, including reciprocal representation and participation at meetings; reciprocal provision of suggestions, recommendations, and comments through resolutions; intersecretariat consultations; exchange and joint use of information; and joint sessions of expert bodies.

Several factors have combined to facilitate OAU-ECA collaboration. In the first place, both organizations are situated in Addis Ababa. Moreover, the OAU, working alone, had been hampered in its functioning by the grave lack of qualified staff and personnel in its Secretariat and this was remedied by cooperation with ECA. Finally, a new division has developed between the work done by the OAU and that done by the ECA. The former is concerned with the political aspects of economic cooperation, the latter with the technical and practical aspects.

In reviewing the net results achieved in the field of economic cooperation after 10 years of work within the OAU framework, several points are obvious. These include the failure of the Economic and Social Commission; the weakness of the different specialized agencies working with the OAU; the lack of interest on the part of the Heads of State Conference and the Council of Ministers of the OAU concerning economic problems; the multiple difficulties encountered by the Secretariat in its attempts to establish a research and study center; and the dominant position of the ECA in the whole field of economic cooperation in Africa.

These conclusions indicate the failure of the OAU's attempts at economic cooperation in Africa, a failure that seems apparent at various levels.

First, at the institutional level, the organizations created for the purpose of promoting economic cooperation have never functioned properly. Second, at what may be called the normative level, those organizations have shown themselves incapable of establishing the necessary basic standards from which to elaborate programs concerning cooperation, and also incapable of agreeing on common policies to be put into practice.

Finally, there is a failure on the level of diplomatic psychology in the sense that the African countries have little or no confidence in African organizations. In fact, this attitude is the principal reason for the lack of success of OAU activity concerning economic cooperation. The Secretariat's report notes with bitterness that meetings attended by non-African states receive the full support of the members of the OAU, while meetings dealing with the same problems but called by the OAU cannot be held for lack of quorum. The report of the OAU Secretariat also is explicit on this point:

> Unless the OAU's Member States wish now to give up to non-African organisations their rights to discuss and decide questions concerning their own social and economic development, unless they wish to transfer their rights and controls to other non-African hands which could make such use of them as would not be in the interest of the majority of Africa's citizens, then it is perhaps imperative that we study the situation as it actually is at present, and that we resolve yet once more to allow the specialised commissions to function with certainty. [6]

Having said this, however, it would be a grave mistake to underestimate the importance of the OAU for Africa and the role it could play in connection with economic and social development.

First, the OAU is the only African organization that deals with economic development on a continental basis. All the other organizations in this area deal with the question either from a point of view that is regional and isolated or from one that is not specifically African. The Secretariat's report refers to "those forces of destruction which are aimed at demolishing this fragile structure of unity which the African states have laboured to build."[7] The OAU wishes, and rightly so, to be the one and only spokesman for Africa, since it is the only organization under which the African states have been able to unite: "It is through the OAU and through it alone, that Africa can choose and effect her own desires."[8]

Second, the OAU enables the African states to present a common front in the specialized agencies and at international conferences on economic development—in Geneva in 1966, Algiers in 1967, New Delhi in 1968, and Santiago in 1970. Most African states have neither the means nor a sufficient number of experts to allow for the proper preparation such conferences necessitate. The OAU gives them the technical and diplomatic assistance that allows them to adopt a common policy and attitude in facing rich countries and non-African partners from the Third World.

Third, the OAU's activities in the field of economic cooperation have enabled a stronger, more mobile cooperation between the African states, on the one hand, and the U.N. and its specialized agencies on the other. The OAU acts as the halfway house between the world organizations and the new African countries. It permits diplomats and experts from these countries to work in these organizations in the interest of Africa.[9]

One is thus confronted by a paradoxical situation. The OAU has failed to promote economic cooperation within the African continent, but it has succeeded in reinforcing the position of Africa in the outside world by successfully promoting economic cooperation between Africa and the outside world.

By contrast, the Arab League has failed to promote economic cooperation either within the Arab world or between the Arab states and the outside world.

The principal explanation may be found in the attitudes of the United Nations, and the majority of its member states, toward the Arab League and the OAU. While the Arab League was never really admitted into the world community, either as such or as the principal organ for Arab cooperation, the OAU was accepted both by the United Nations and by its member states.

In conclusion, the Arab League and the OAU have contributed toward the improvement of the situation of the poor countries within the United Nations and specialized agencies, rather than promoting regional action or continental cooperation.

The Arab League was the nucleus of the Afro-Asian group in the United States, the first institutional voice speaking for the poor nations, face to face with the rich world. Later, the OAU came to reinforce the Arab League when it began to lose its youthful dynamism.

On the other hand, the Arab and African states have obtained more support and aid, in their struggle against colonialism, from the world organization than from their own organizations. The intrinsic weakness of the Arab and African states themselves remains the main cause of the weakness of the Arab League and the OAU. We must add to this weakness the increasing power of Israel and South Africa. Those two dynamic, advanced, and domineering states accentuate the internal contradictions of the Arab world and the African world, respectively, by creating a situation with which neither the Arab League nor the OAU is capable of dealing. This situation has unfortunately pushed the real economic and social problems of the Third World into the background.

And yet, even if the weaknesses of the Arab League and the OAU are further aggravated, these organizations will retain their prestige and their symbolic value because they are the first organizations created and directed by the poor nations, for the poor nations of the world.

Having said this, however, let us not forget that the inability of the Arab and African states to make full use of modern scientific developments and establish a communications network allowing cooperation and awareness of common problems is a phenomenon shared by all the underdeveloped countries.

This inadequacy explains the attitude of the Arab League and the OAU, an attitude characterized by disillusioned impotence and sterile anger. It is responsible for the Third World's distorted vision of contemporary history which leads it to prefer, instead of a technological and realistic approach, the magic of incantation and imprecation. Only an organization which will successfully encourage and spread a politically mature culture—and not simply repeat endlessly partisan propaganda—will render the Arab and African peoples capable of adequately dealing with the regional and worldwide tasks that await them.

Nevertheless, the oil weapon which has recently been used by the Arab countries in a movement of genuine unity of purpose, not only against industrialized countries, but also against South Africa, Rhodesia and Portugal, adds a new dimension to the anticolonial struggle. It offers new possibilities for the underdeveloped countries to engage in a dialogue with the developed world from a position of strength. Bandoeng was a turning point in the struggle for the political independence of the Third World; and the October 1973 Arab-Israeli war is perhaps the turning point in the struggle of the developing world for minimal economic independence.

It can be said therefore, with a measure of emphasis, that the developing countries have undergone a qualitative change—from being the objects of international law and politics to becoming the subjects of a dynamic new relationship with the world of the industrialized rich. The time has come for the regional organizations of the Third World to burst into the political arena of this age of accelerated change.

NOTES

1. SCIAS/GEN/INF/26, p. 2.
2. SCIAS/GEN/INF/8, pp. 5-6.
3. SCIAS/GEN/INF/9, p. 2.
4. SCIAS/GEN/INF/10, p. 7. This paragraph was omitted in the English translation of the speech. See SCIAS/GEN/INF/10, p. 6.
5. U.N. Document A/6174.
6. CM/169, p. 3.
7. Ibid.
8. Ibid., p. 18.
9. CM/157 p. 16.

3

**THE OAU
AND SUB-SAHARAN
REGIONAL BODIES**
Jon Woronoff

To the legal mind, to the student of African affairs, and to many others, it would doubtlessly be more satisfying if there were a clear relationship between the one, all-African organization and the many, smaller regional bodies, particularly numerous south of the Sahara. The ideal would be a subsystem like the United Nations; although there are a large number of regional organizations and even regional groups within the U.N., the relationships are quite distinct, the rules of the game are well known, and these are laid down in the Charter itself or in written agreements. If nothing so clear existed in Africa, it would at least be nice to think of the continent as a solar system in which the Organization of African Unity was the sun and the others dutifully revolved around it. But even this is not the case, and the subregional bodies follow no fixed path as compared with the OAU; there have been many collisions and eclipses, and the force of gravity is frequently defied.

One of the major reasons is quite plain. In the beginning, there was not the OAU but a series of rival pan-African bodies and another series of often rival regional bodies. The continent was born in piece-meal fashion as colonies gradually attained independence. In much the same order, the new states (and sometimes dependent territories) formed units that would strengthen their position and meet the long-stifled yearning for unity. Indeed, it was the sudden outburst of this wish for unity, something that had been welling up over half a century, that created so many fragmentary units. For there were as many ideas on the form and content as there were states and leaders to found such bodies. With no war or external threat sufficiently im-minent to force them to merge, when they did come together it was done freely. Although they and their founders were eventually ready to accept a central organ, the peripheral bodies were not eager to disappear.

The other reason is no less clear, and particularly compelling. Far from being a clean sheet or an inchoate mass on which a simple organizational structure could be imposed, the African continent is one of the richest and most varied in the world. Layers of strong and underlying unity cross or intertwine with other layers of diversity and disunity, and it is natural that these differing lines of force should pull the continent in several directions at the same time.

In the past, Africa consisted of many different ethnic groups, sometimes forming into larger tribes, kingdoms, and even empires. Alliances as well as antipathies have arisen among and between these units, and there was never any political structure to include them all. Over this, the colonial powers imposed a degree of unity within very artificial boundaries. Thus, feeling that after independence the frontiers should not separate them, new unities were created, often bolstered by the older unities. But the earlier divisions were never entirely erased, and some new ones were formed. In addition, Africa is such a broad and variegated continent that, to accomplish specific projects, it is often necessary to form smaller units.

From the very start, there was more than one movement for unity. If we follow this early process in sub-Saharan Africa, we will find that many units were being created and that each of them was based on one or more strong links overcoming certain divisions, but also including and creating other lines of division. Some of the ties were political and ideological, others were geographic and historical, yet others had an economic, linguistic, or ethnic base. Some were created by one state or leader, others by their opponents. As the state system grew and there were new members, it became necessary to accommodate some of them by forming slightly different bodies. Not until most of the countries had become free could one even claim that a broad enough, universal-type organization had been founded.

To provide the proper context and background, it would be wise to remember that even the first so-called "pan-African" bodies were not really continental. In 1958, Kwame Nkrumah, one of the leading fathers of African unity, created two different all-African bodies.[1] The Conference of Independent African States (CIAS) was established at the intergovernmental level and was intended to work out relations and common stands on all matters for all the African states. The All-African Peoples' Organization was to do the same thing at the "peoples" level. But it was not long before the peoples' organization had become so radical that it was criticizing other states and leaders and thus could not be all-inclusive. The fate of the CIAS was the opposite; by including all the new independent states, it gradually became so moderate that it was spurned by its founders. After the second summit conference, it was forgotten.

One reason for the change was the accession to independence, at the same time, of the largest group of African states, the former French colonial territories. Shorn of the few radical members like Guinea, this was a more conservative group led by men such as Houphouet-Boigny and Leopold Senghor, with whom the radicals had trouble getting along. Since, unlike the British colonies, these countries had been formed into various highly centralized groups, it was natural for them to regroup as states. This was both a promise and a danger. For while Senghor was right that they had to avoid any further balkanization, the holding together of some twelve states in even a loose body made them too big a chunk to be swallowed by the others. Seeing this rejection, and also the propaganda and subversion being waged against them, the Francophone states took a step toward unity by forming the Brazzaville Group in December 1960.

Unity may have been the aim, but a front of Francophone moderates only provoked the radicals to further increase their particularism and form the rival Casablanca Group only a month later. This linked states on both sides of the Sahara with a similar ideology. Yet again, as this radical approach proved unpalatable to older countries like Ethiopia and Liberia and the new Anglophone states (including Nigeria), they joined with the Francophones to found by far the largest (although still partial) group remembered for the conferences in Monrovia and Lagos. Each transcontinental unit then proceeded to create some institutions and adopt a charter presenting its claim to speak for the continent. In these years, Africa's voice was shrill and divided as differing leaders and tendencies came out on different sides of issues as controversial as Algerian independence, the Congolese civil war, and unity itself. With relative chaos on the organizational scene, it was not surprising that even more subregional bodies were formed.[2]

First, let us look at the group of Francophone countries. The links between them, whatever their opponents may have thought, were not purely sentimental or only the result of French machinations. For a century, most of them had been undergoing a policy of assimilation in which it was natural that the leaders at least should have gone through much the same schools and training, before they moved on to Paris. In the French National Assembly, these leaders found themselves in opposition to the French politicians and formed their own groups, such as the Rassemblement Democratique Africain. This assimilation and then rejection constituted two experiences they would not readily forget, and despite any differences among them, it was far easier for them to work together and coordinate.

The material reasons were as great. France had divided its empire into French West Africa and French Equatorial Africa. Each had its own capital (Dakar and Brazzaville) and an intercolony infrastructure. Each had hopes for continued unity. There were also such things as established roads and lines of communication, joint services of various kinds, monetary and customs unions.[3]

As the French left, with the help of the peripheral countries like the Ivory Coast, they began dismantling the links. The capital countries tried to hold them together. Thus, Senegal and Sudan (its natural hinterland) tried to keep French West Africa from complete dissolution by forming a four-state Federation of Mali. Those who had already opted out, especially Houphouet, did not mind making it come apart. Once reduced to two, even with leaders who were strongly committed, the Federation found it hard to get started and collapsed.[4] In Equatorial Africa, a similar movement occurred; the four states were only able to rescue some of the common services and customs union and create the Union Douaniere et Economique de l'Afrique Centrale.[5]

Yet no sooner had the old links snapped than the leaders realized that they should not disappear completely, especially not in a less friendly world than they had expected to find. Houphouet, who had helped undermine Mali, had done so partly because he had no faith in such broad unity, and partly because in this particular case the unity was somewhat artificial and the two extra states were the hinterland to his own country. Instead, the Ivory Coast launched a movement for the creation of an entente, a very loose grouping excluding politics as much as possible and building on concrete links such as railroads, similar legislation, and economic relations.[6]

Having once settled their differences and accepted the new regroupings, Houphouet and Senghor were willing to work for the Francophone states as a whole. The ties between them were more tenuous and less material, but they were very real. There was also a shared feeling and approach. That this was not purely a divisive tactic was seen from the growth process. Actually, the Brazzaville Group created no organization until March 1961, and this organization "OAMCE" was limited to economic cooperation. Only when the controversy with the radicals had seriously deteriorated was a political body founded in September, the Union Africaine et Malgache (UAM), as well as a defense organization, Union Africaine et Malgache de Defense (UAMD). Even then, the twelve countries were as preoccupied with their economic links—including such developments as mail and telecommunications and customs—as with politics.[7]

Whereas much was made of divisiveness among the Francophones, there was little talk of this among the Anglophones. They, of course, never went as far. But they did follow very similar trends. In East Africa, there were also real links, rooted in history and the joint services between Kenya, Uganda, and Tanganyika. From the very start, these three states sought to maintain and transform this unity into something deeper. At the same time, the common heritage of British colonies made them turn to other parts of the region. Even before independence, the Pan-African Freedom Movement of East and Central Africa (PAFMECA) was founded to promote the liberation struggle and formed a unique grouping of independent and dependent territories. Slowly it grew and became more diffuse. Its weakness— a lack of concrete links—was also in a way its strength, for it could absorb most of the countries, including Francophones, in Eastern, Central, and Southern Africa, ultimately emerging as Pan-African Freedom Movement of East, Central and Southern Africa (PAFMECSA), [8]

In the heat and rivalry of those days, one final body was created that was primarily political; although it claimed to be a "nucleus" for broader unity, it was in practice as parochial as any. This was founded by Nkrumah in the Ghana-Guinea-Mali Union. Even after it was dressed up with declarations and charters, it did not really draw the states together or have any practical activities. Its main purpose, so it would seem, was as a battering ram against the neighboring Francophone groups first, and then also against PAFMECSA. In theory, it was a regional unit that tried to undermine and destroy regionalism to attain continental unity; in practice, it was just another regional group, and one that by heightening tensions seems to have convinced the others that they needed such partial bodies for protection.

The period before the establishment of the Organization of African Unity was, as we have seen, characterized by considerable flux and disunity. Indeed, a true pan-African body had become urgent because the situation was already so bad that African unity was being scoffed at outside the continent and suspected as a cover for hegemony and imperialism within. Since this feeling coincided with a temporary thaw in the political climate and an end to the major issues dividing the groupings, it was finally possible to bring all the states together in Addis Ababa. To show that the will and desire came from both sides, one need simply look at the major sponsors. They included leading regionalists and antiregionalists: Houphouet, Senghor, Tubman, Nyerere, Haile Selassie, Nasser, and Nkrumah. They all agreed to found the OAU at the Summit Conference. Yet even after May 1963 the situation did not change dramatically.

One might think that, when creating a new organization for the whole continent, the founders would make a tabula rasa and do away with the other bodies. This was not the case. The reasons for this were quite obvious. There were certainly more supporters of regionalism present than opponents. Sekou Toure, like Nkrumah and Obote, thought the old charters should be replaced by a single "Charter of a United Africa." But President Bourguiba again expressed his hopes for a Greater Maghreb, the Emperor of Ethiopia admitted that the regional bodies might subsist, and certain UAM members (including Presidents Senghor and Tsiranana) not only defended their own organization but pointed out the advantages of a regional approach.[9] If the regional bodies were to exist, then one would have expected at least an attempt at defining their scope and limits and working out the relations between them and the OAU. Again, the consensus was lacking and nothing was done. Indeed, this being a meeting for reconciliation, any potentially divisive issue—such as the question of regionalism—was largely ignored. No word in the Charter has any bearing on it, nor are there sufficient indications in the speeches or preparatory documents.

Once the Organization of African Unity was created, however, some leaders did not hesitate to take their stand against regionalism. The first to speak up was Nkrumah, soon by Sekou Toure, who accused the regional bodies of balkanization and demanded that all of them be dissolved. As a token of seriousness, they proclaimed the end of the Ghana-Guinea-Mali Union in June 1963. But this had never been much of a body and had long been dormant, so its passing was hardly noticed. PAFMECSA was a more valid unit, but one whose tasks could readily be assumed by the OAU. A few months later, Nyerere and the other sponsors accepted its demise. But this was not taken as a quid pro quo by the Francophone countries, whose groups were very real and entailed material links. If they were to disband, some said, they would be decreasing and not increasing the sum total of unity.

Thus the battle over regionalism was engaged at the OAU's first Council of Ministers in August 1963. Although it met in Dakar, it was obvious that the Francophones and UAM would come under attack. (Indeed, rather than being seen as a matter for the whole continent, this was largely a sub-Saharan debate. In some ways, that was odd, since one of the strongest groupings was the Arab League, which extended beyond the continent but was hardly considered.) This was the same old battle that Nkrumah had waged from the beginning. However, with the OAU, he now had far more allies. Liberia and Nigeria had joined the Monrovia group in self-defense, not because they wished to form special links with the Francophone community. They, too, were quite willing to urge that the Brazzaville bodies be phased out. In some ways, even members of the Brazzaville group agreed, but would not admit that openly. Their support took another form, namely, sufficient cooperation to adopt a resolution on regionalism.

As the members were still seriously divided on the issue of regional groupings, their resolution was none too strong. They could speak both of the need to end division and the good done by regional groupings. But the conclusion was clear enough: Such groupings were permissible if they were "in keeping with the Charter of the OAU" and met the following criteria:

1. Geographic relations and economic, social, and cultural factors common to the states.
2. Coordination of economic, social, and cultural activities peculiar to the states concerned.

Those that were created before the establishment of the OAU were henceforth, it was suggested, to "refer" to the Charter of Addis Ababa. What this meant in practice was uncertain, but there was no doubt that referral was not a very constraining act. No stronger was the final "request" that member states founding new bodies deposit the statutes at the seat of the OAU before their entry into force. The furthest the resolution went was to invite states to "contemplate the integration of already existing bodies into the specialized institutions of the OAU." [10]

Thus, the new dispensation was not very stringent. The old organizations could continue to exist and new ones could be created if they followed a few simple principles and formalities. The fundamental point was a conformity with the Charter and, although hardly conceivable, any organization that went against it would have been sharply rejected. The others were that the links have some geographic base and economic or technical nature. This was directed particularly against any "political" alternatives to the OAU. Political links were carefully omitted from the list of criteria for forming a grouping; and requiring geographical proximity, as opposed to less concrete ties, implied a certain inacceptability of organization based on political, ideological, or linguistic affinities. With this the resolution had created categories of "acceptable" and "inacceptable" or "good" and "bad" regional organizations. But this did not mean that the OAU would act against the "bad" ones, or that some members would force others to cease such activities.

Similar conclusions were drawn by Boutros Boutros-Ghali. This resolution, he notes, laid down three basic rules for compatibility with the purposes and principles of the OAU Charter. The first, referring to the need for geographic realities and common factors, is that there must be a "real solidarity." Second, the regional groupings must formally declare their compatibility with the Charter, and those already in existence should add such a provision to their statutes. Finally, the new regional groupings must in the future deposit their statutes at the OAU's seat. What does this imply?

There is some doubt as to what, if anything, the OAU could have done with its strict respect of sovereignty and noninterference in domestic affairs. Fortunately, this was a time of great feelings of unity and reconciliation, and some of the UAM members felt that they must sacrifice their organization, or at least its political and defense side. The debate in March 1964 was long and heated. Once again, there was a conflict between Houphouet, who did not wish to remove the political links, and Senghor, who hoped to adapt UAM enough to make it acceptable to the other OAU members and perhaps facilitate its fusion in the larger body. In the end it was decided to cease UAM and UAMD while creating a new organization to deal with the economic and technical matters, the Union Africaine et Malgache de Cooperation Economique (UAMCE).

Let us also look at the statutes and conventions adopted by various sub-Saharan regional groupings created during the years after the OAU's founding and the Dakar resolution. In no case was there any provision for accountability or responsibility toward the main, pan-African organization. There were not even provisions for any form of cooperation or mutual exchange of ideas or information. The most the new groupings did was to refer to the OAU Charter, usually in their preambles, and state that they were established "in the spirit of the Organization of African Unity" (for the Afro-Malagasy Common Organization). Many of these groupings did not even provide for deposit of statutes with the OAU; only the River Niger Commission and the Lake Chad Basin Commission did so formally. A rather interesting innovation, however, was that two of the statutes gave a special and rather significant role to one of the OAU's component bodies. In a very similar provision, both the Organization of Senegal River States and the Lake Chad Basin Commission stipulated that "any dispute concerning the interpretation or application of this Convention which cannot be resolved by the Commission, shall be referred to the Commission of Mediation, Conciliation and Arbitration of the Organization of African Unity for determination."[11] Both also granted staff members the same privileges and immunities as OAU officials of the same level.

Nevertheless, the first years were the high-water mark of the OAU's prestige and influence. It acquired a very strong position as the central organ. The OAU was created with both a universal membership (all "independent" states were permitted to join) and a universal scope since it was to handle not only political but also social, economic, scientific, defense, and other activities. But it was not able to follow this up. It was especially slow with nonpolitical matters of all sorts. Thus there was a broad field open for regional bodies in the economic and technical sphere, which was basically the scope given by the Dakar resolution. Moreover, the continent was too vast for any organization to do all things in all places. Even the Economic Commission for Africa, limited to economic activities, had realized that with a huge continent it was best to form smaller, workable units for concrete activities. It was nonetheless unfortunate that, if regional groupings were to supplement its work, the OAU did not then specify the relations and type of work done by each. This may have

been an oversight in Dakar; it was less understandable that it was not
made up for later.

Thus the decade after the Organization of African Unity was
created, rather then seeing a disappearance of regional bodies, was
one in which regionalism flourished. There was actually a "renais-
sance" of regional bodies: "The institutions that existed expanded
and new ones were created. These bodies sprang up in all parts of
the continent and in the most varied specializations although much of
the activity is now economic and little as yet has been done on a comparable scale in social or cultural fields. Rather than fade away,
African regionalism had been infused with new life."[12] Not surpris-
ingly, most of the new bodies rose up in the place of older ones that
had disappeared, or fit the same political and geographic patterns.
Others that seemed new also followed the deeper and older cleavages
in the continent or the basic rules of power politics. Few things were
more striking than the similarity in the subregional system before
and after May 1963. However, with so many bodies, it is best to take
them by category, starting with the "permissible" economic and technical groupings.

In East Africa, Kenya, Uganda, and Tanzania decided they would
move beyond joint services to form a "common market." After several
false starts, the East African Community was finally created in 1967.
But new problems arose between the members when it came to sharing
responsibilities and benefits and, worse still, with political friction
among the leaders. Meanwhile, with applications for membership or
association and the much broader ECA-sponsored Economic Community of Eastern Africa, there was soon a two-tiered system in which
the threesome had many specific links while the outer groups had
relatively few, and were rather nebulous.[13]

While UAMCE (Union Africaine et Malgache de Cooperation
Economique) provided the broad framework for such activities, its
smaller component bodies also engaged in economic and technical
work (Air Afrique, and so on). The Francophone group also
had other organizations, among the most important of which was the
Entente. The Council of the Entente, in particular, increased its
activities and membership. In addition, there were the central bank
unions and customs unions, later shaped into "economic communities." And other units were forming around other institutions, including the joint projects that gave rise to the Chad Lake, Niger, and
Senegal River groups. There was Senegambia. The ECA also created,
or tried to form, its own Economic Community of West Africa to unite
the former French and British countries of the region.[14]

There was no conflict or trouble between the Organization of
African Unity and these bodies, not because the OAU would not have
liked to form and run the units itself, or at least enjoy some

supervisory rights, but simply because its technical and economic activities had collapsed within the first two years.[15] If anything was to be done here, it would have to be by the states themselves. This was so clearly recognized that the OAU adopted a very different kind of resolution on economic groupings in September 1967. Unlike the more negative one of 1963, this time it actually called upon the members "to encourage the formation of economic groupings by all appropriate means." Although referring only to economic links, it did not exclude and probably implied the social, cultural, and other links that tended to accompany such groupings and were permitted under the Dakar resolution. With this the OAU tacitly admitted that it could not accomplish certain tasks without the aid of regional bodies and gave them a strong legitimacy.

At the same time, the 1967 resolution finally provided some basis for an organized relationship between the central and peripheral bodies. The final objective of these and any other regional units could only be "integrating the continent." And the member states were asked to promote the exchange of information through the OAU's Secretary General.[16] This was a most attenuated form of cooperation and it was never used to the full, but it was a starting point.

The next step was taken several years later. On the eve of the Second Development Decade, in August 1970, there was a renewed interest in one of the OAU's basic tasks that had been least acted upon: "to harness the natural and human resources of our continent for the total advancement of our peoples." There was no doubt that the Organization had not lived up to the promise of its Charter in the economic, social, and technical fields. The Council of Ministers therefore decided to reactivate the commissions responsible for these matters and offered a major role for the subregional groupings. To permit greater cooperation in the future, it was agreed to establish a "system of liaison" with the OAU and ECA Secretariats and to have the administrative heads of these economic groupings meet under the aegis of the OAU to "harmonize and coordinate" the main aspects of their work.[17] That same meeting decided to grant observer status to the Lake Chad Basin Commission.[18]

Thus, the framework for cooperation was more complete than ever, in theory. From year to year, most of the other regional bodies were granted observer status. They were able to attend most OAU meetings, and the OAU Secretary General occasionally attended theirs. There was some increase in mutual understanding and a better working relationship at the level of secretariats. But this cooperation did not affect the policy-making organs, nor did it assume a permanent and effective form. In particular, there were no joint activities or projects to make the central and regional bodies work together. Even this faded as economic regionalism also went into a relative eclipse:

The ECA-sponsored economic communities were never really established, the East African Common Market, and the Senegal River group, among others, ran into political difficulties.

If there was no serious conflict with the economic and technical bodies, there could and indeed was with the political ones. Once the reconciliation was over and there was an important bone of contention between the states, it was natural that blocs should form again and that some of the blocs might become subregional organizations. During the Congolese affair, the states were again sharply divided between supporters of the central government and backers of the "nationalists." Once Prime Minister Tshombe clearly pulled ahead, several of the members went outside the organization to aid the rebels. This was not just verbal assistance; it involved channeling arms and ammunition. The moderates, especially the Francophones, reacted to this by reforming their ranks and creating the Organisation Commune Africaine et Malgache (OCAM) in February 1965. This, they claimed, had been forced upon them because some states had refused to respect the OAU Charter. In fact, since their side was losing, it was the radicals who had violated the rules of the game. And, on the whole, the moderates have been less prone to intervene. At any rate, for the first time in years, there was a group that spoke on the OAU's burning issues and tried to impose its will. There might have been more serious trouble if the war had not ended shortly after.

Once founded, however, the OCAM continued to exist and expand. Most of its activity remained economic—the areas UAMCE had previously looked after, including post, intellectual property, education, the sugar and coffee agreements, and Air Afrique. It also played some roles that replaced the OAU but did not go contrary to it, as when various disputes were settled quickly and peacefully at meetings of heads of state. Thus, especially for technical issues and relations among members, as Cervenka said, Organisation Commune Africaine et Malgache (OCAM) tended to "duplicate" the OAU's field of activity.

On political questions, the approach varied. Actually, little was done about the Biafran episode, even if OCAM made a point of wanting to do something, as opposed to the OAU's apparent indifference. Its members never seemed as concerned about decolonization. But a nasty dispute broke out in public when Houphouet launched his policy of "dialogue." Although not strictly an OCAM policy, since some members were against it and several nonmembers joined with Houphouet, it was commonly attached to OCAM. And Houphouet was clearly using it as he and others had always done, to prepare a position within the OAU.[19]

OCAM, more than any other body, has been accused of splitting the continent, of going its own way, of wrecking the OAU. This is denied by its Charter, which insists that its members be faithful to the principles and objectives of the OAU and stipulates that OCAM itself shall act "in the spirit of the OAU." But the thrust seems to be different, both better and worse for its opponents, as it were. OCAM did not split the OAU; its members did not as a whole either boycott or go against its activities. Even on dialogue, Houphouet did not stay out for good; he merely wished to convince his fellow leaders and attend the OAU when this was purposeful (to his way of thinking). His repeated plea was that first there should be a dialogue on "dialogue" in the OAU. Moreover, complaints were not general but specific, directed to one or two issues at most. Instead, OCAM, as a group of over a third of the membership, has systematically gone into the OAU and tried to influence its policies, or turn them around if they were unfavorable. With this number of members, it was far stronger within than any other group, and it saw no reason to forsake this leverage. Thus ex-President Tsiranana of Madagascar said,

> It has never been our intention to obstruct the work of the OAU, as some have unconvincingly implied, but on the contrary to consolidate it. At present OCAM regards itself, and should be regarded by everyone, as a party in a political assembly . . . . The work of any assembly is based on the mutual concessions of parties moving in the same general direction, and it is in this spirit that we enthusiastically provide the OAU with what is one-third of its effective support.

This made OCAM a party within the OAU or, to quote Houphouet, "a nucleus and a unifying force."[20] But OCAM might more accurately be described as a well-coordinated group of states in a system where its opponents were less organized. This made it a strong organization within OAU.

There was no similar organization among the radicals. They promptly and repeatedly formed blocs and informal caucuses: on the Congo, on Nkrumah's deposition, on Rhodesia and decolonization in general. They met occasionally and talked of forming a group, but this never materialized. It would seem that this was not only due to words of caution from Nasser and others but also because their efforts were too sporadic and because they were only united by political causes that could change. With no economic or technical base to hold them together between confrontations, they had no lasting purpose. On as many occasions as the moderates, they stepped out of the OAU and "boycotted" meetings or decisions. But they also refused to destroy Africa's best, if imperfect tool.

Meanwhile, another politically interested group was being formed in Eastern and then Central Africa. It spread from a small group to one that also had about a third of the membership. Although attendance varied, it was very similar to the old PAFMECSA public. This body was not meant as an "attempt to form a regional grouping or to usurp the functions of the OAU."[21] Yet, more than OCAM, its scope overlapped with the OAU: It dealt with decolonization, liberation movements, economic and social affairs, indeed everything on the OAU agenda. Although not very formal, it has managed to meet regularly, at least once a year, and adopt a multitude of resolutions. It even adopted its own manifesto on decolonization. But there was little conflict since its position was usually in the mainstream of OAU thought and the resolutions could be added to OAU ones. Indeed, the Lusaka Manifesto was promptly picked up by the OAU, although it was a more outward-going one suggesting a basis for understanding and solution, as opposed to somewhat more sterile OAU condemnations. The East-Central group never gone against the OAU as such. But, like OCAM, it has removed some work from its agenda in reconciling members or bypassing the OAU on certain points of decolonization.

As we have seen, the de jure situation of this African "order" is not overly clear. There is nothing in the Charter determining the legality of the regional bodies or their relations with the OAU. Even the one resolution adopted on the subject was carefully hedged, and was obeyed or ignored depending on the circumstances.

The situation today is not that much different from the one before the creation of the OAU. But this does not mean that the OAU is being systematically weakened or undermined. For the de facto situation is quite certain. The OAU cannot carry out many of the activities, and a disbanding of the regional bodies would accomplish little or nothing. The political bodies, although making any confrontation that much sharper, have decided to fight within the OAU and to follow the rules of the game. This, too, is permissible and can be salutary or dangerous, depending on circumstances. At any rate, it cannot be avoided. That some activities are occasionally drawn out of the OAU's field does not matter, for it has more problems than it can handle.

Is this "order" dangerous for the OAU, or for Africa? Probably not. There are advantages to the regional bodies, so they will remain. They are able to make use of the many partial links and forms of unity that have been created over the ages, whether ethnic, religious, linguistic, or other. They are able to bring together a smaller number of states that feel strongly about some issue or are willing to engage in practical work for some limited purpose. They can handle certain concrete tasks that it would be absurd to carry out in larger bodies, such as the improvement of river basins. Technical and economic affairs are particularly amenable to this approach.

The regional bodies also unite countries that are not willing to wait until the others finally agree to do something. By letting each country work at what it deems most important, at its own pace and with its chosen partners, many things can be accomplished that would otherwise not be done. This helps forge further links for a chain that can unite all Africa.

By the same token, there are very strong benefits to having a continental body, and no one would deny that. The OAU has a whole vast scope of its own where there is little overlapping, duplication, or interference from the regional bodies. It has played the major role in decolonization; it has handled most of the disputes on the continent; and it has at least dealt with the continental aspects of economic and technical activities. For example, only it could run the Liberation Committee and Fund, only it could do anything about the Congolese or Nigerian civil wars and the border disputes, and only it could hold an African trade fair or cultural festival. As the one organization bringing all the states together, it is irreplaceable.

And as the one organization that lines the states up toward the outside world, it is equally irreplaceable. Only the OAU could send missions abroad to speak on behalf of the dependent territories. Only it could use every other organization in which Africans are members to increase the role and benefits of Africa. Only it could deal as an equal with the United Nations, or work within it through the African Group. And only it could engage, no matter how haltingly, in protecting the continent either through defense arrangements or by trying to stop interference and promote nonalignment.

Despite the OAU's weaknesses, the regional bodies do not represent a threat to it for another reason: their own fragility. These bodies have remained in flux, being formed, growing, colliding with others and dividing or disappearing. Very few have continued on in their original forms or seem to prosper. The most successful has been the Entente, and also a series of bodies growing out of UAM into OCAM. The East African threesome has always kept some form of organization alive, although even the East African Community has rarely been as endangered as today. But Sekou Toure has frequently destroyed the casing of the Senegal River grouping, although it periodically reformed without him. General Mobutu's attempts at forming organizations around Zaire, rather than joining existing groups, seem to have put an end to UDEAC, without making UEAC a viable alternative. Other "empire builders" are still rather quiet or working behind the scenes. Quiescent since Nkrumah's fall, Ghana can be expected to exert an attraction on neighbors like Upper Volta and Togo, and Nigeria's relations with Dahomey have waxed and waned. It remains to be seen if more recent tries at uniting Anglophone and Francophone in West Africa will succeed. Thus, no regional grouping can look upon itself as definitive in its membership, structure, or purposes.

Since both OAU and the regional groups are weapons for Africa and do not conflict too often, there seems to be little danger either to or from the regional organizations. Is this "order" likely to change in the near future? Again, probably not. What little threat there was from Diallo Telli's remarks—and even he had to bow to OCAM on occasion—has since disappeared. Although appointed by a somewhat marginal Francophone and OCAM member, the new Secretary General, Nzo Ekangaki, probably will be more scrupulous in sticking to "administrative" tasks and will not go as far in countering any influence. Instead, as someone less unfriendly to the regional bodies, he may be able to increase cooperation and coordination. With the Assembly and Council, it may be possible to accomplish the unfinished work of the Charter by laying down general guidelines for scope and interrelations. Yet even now one can conclude, with Boutros-Ghali, that for all practical purposes "if the Charter of Addis-Ababa was silent regarding the compatibility of regionalism and sub-regionalism with African continentalism, the problem was solved formally and practically by the OAU.[22]

This system may still not satisfy the legal mind. But then, we must remember that the OAU is not run by the jurists and diplomats one finds in most other organizations. If anything makes the OAU special, it is that its delegates are politicians: heads of state, ministers, generals, and senior officials. They are not terribly worried about legal niceties or even precedents. Some of the OAU resolutions, among the most important, when proven unworkable have merely been forgotten.* These are men of action and not reflection, and what is most satisfying to them is what works (or at least seems to work). They prefer having broad leeway in all matters, to decide questions and relationships as they arise, in an ad hoc fashion. Moreover, their primary precept is state sovereignty and each leader's right to determine national policies. No matter what the drawbacks may be, the present system—if it can be called one—will probably be left alone as long as it works.

What can be done, however, is to take advantage of that system even as it exists. For, without going against any rules or the wishes of its governing bodies, the OAU could do much more about supervision and coordination, or at least reporting on what is happening in the whole continent. It should certainly maintain closer contacts with the various regional bodies and keep open channels of communication to see where it would be in their mutual advantage, and that of

---

*One of the most striking examples was the resolution on breaking diplomatic relations with the United Kingdom, implemented by a minority of members that later resumed these relations, but never revoked as such.

Africa, for several or all of them to do something jointly. There could be more informal arrangements for an exchange of documents and reports, there could be consultations on certain issues from organization to organization, the Secretary General could both attend and participate in certain meetings of the other bodies and invite his counterparts to be more active at OAU meetings. There could also be periodic meetings of the heads of all organizations. Much of this, as we have seen, was already provided for in various Council resolutions. So far there has been little follow-up, but the possibilities are certainly there.

In this still formative stage of the African subregional system, some of these links may not seem feasible or even necessary. Indeed, as long as neither the OAU nor the subregional bodies have reached their potential limits, there is not much duplication or overlapping, competition or confrontation. This may change later, and the smaller unities of today can hamper and constrict, if not actually divide and splinter the broader unity of tomorrow. Before that happens, it is essential to create the proper framework. This is certainly a valid task for the second decade of the Organization of African Unity.

NOTES

1. For Nkrumah's career as a "unifier," see W. Scott Thompson, Ghana's Foreign Policy, 1957-66 (Princeton, N.J.: Princeton University Press, 1969); Jon Woronoff, West African Wager (Metuchen, N.J.: Scarecrow Press, 1973), pp. 109-33.

2. For further details of this period, see Jon Woronoff, Organizing African Unity (Metuchen, N.J.: Scarecrow Press, 1970), pp. 28-124.

3. See Ruth Schachter-Morganthau, Political Parties in French-Speaking West Africa (London: Oxford University Press, 1964).

4. See William Foltz, From French West Africa to the Mali Federation (New Haven: Yale University Press, 1965).

5. See A. G. Anguile and J. E. David, L'Afrique sans Frontieres (Monaco: Paul Boru, 1965).

6. See Virginia Thompson, West Africa's Council of the Entente (Ithaca, N.Y.: Cornell University Press, 1972).

7. See Albert Tevoedjre, Pan Africanism in Action: An Account of the UAM (Cambridge, Mass.: Harvard University Press, 1965).

8. See Richard Cox, Pan-Africanism in Practice—PAFMECSA, 1958-64 (London: Oxford University Press, 1964).

9. See Boutros Boutros-Ghali, L'Organization de l'Unite Africaine (Paris: Armand Colin, 1969), pp. 60-62; Zdenek Cervenka, The Organization of African Unity and Its Charter (London: Hurst, 1969), and Records of the Summit Conference.

10. African Council of Ministers (hereafter referred to as CM), Res. 15 (I).

11. Lake Chad Basin Commission Convention, Article 7.

12. Woronoff, Organizing African Unity, op. cit., p. 602.

13. See Joseph Nye, Pan-Africanism and East African Integration (Cambridge, Mass.: Harvard University Press, 1965).

14. For further background on West Africa, see Claude Welch, Dream of Unity: Pan-Africanism and Political Unification in West Africa (Ithaca, N.Y.: Cornell University Press, 1966).

15. See Woronoff, Organizing African Unity, op. cit., pp. 506-86.

16. CM Res. 125 (IX).

17. Boutros-Ghali, op. cit., p. 64.

18. CM Res. 227 (XV).

19. For Houphouet's role and use of regional bodies, see Woronoff, West African Wager, op. cit., pp. 131-56.

20. Journal of Modern African Studies, October 1968, pp. 421-25.

21. The Nationalist (Dar es Salaam), 2 April 1966.

22. Boutros-Ghali, op. cit., p. 64.

4

THE OAU AND
INTERNATIONAL LAW
Romain Yakemtchouk

More than eleven years have passed since the Organization of African Unity was established in May 1963 at Addis Ababa. Historically speaking, eleven years is a very short time, perhaps not enough to draw up a more or less valid balance of an international institution and the place it holds in relation to the positive law of nations. Nonetheless, that is what we are trying to do. Since World War II, and particularly since the 1960s, contemporary history has gone ahead at a much greater rate; some 66 new states have appeared on the chess board of international relations, and political events have assumed such proportions that their topicality and their immediacy argue in favor of rewording traditional legal definitions and make it desirable to adopt new positions of principle, including new value judgments. Anybody concerned with interstate cooperation, any regional organization emerging from the recent decolonization process and working to maintain international peace and security is deserving of particular attention and requires periodic review. Such bodies play an especially important role in international life, both concerning the problem of war and peace and the peaceful settlement of disputes and concerning the establishment, under legal regulations, of mutually advantageous international cooperation.

The various sources of information are of little help in attempting a scientific definition and therefore it is not always possible to be as clear as one would like on the legal development process in Africa; more than once, comments have to be merely approximations. This balance, this appraisal, must first be undertaken from the point of view of legislation, but without neglecting the social and political aspects, since any legal order that did not take into account the

---

Translated from the French.

political realities of its context would be merely academic, insubstantial, and removed from life. It is obvious that these were the main political motives behind the establishment of OAU and they are the basis for its present institutional structure. There was the will of the black continent to confront colonial domination and its consequences, the wish to establish links of political coordination and economic cooperation. Here as elsewhere, in other words, the institutional form is inseparable from its political content.

Our task is not to study the hopes and initial objectives of those who structured the OAU, to see what the latter achievements were and how much of the (long) road still remains to be covered: That is for the political scientists to do. Our approach is rather to deal with the legal realities: It is a matter of defining the contribution of OAU to the regulations of the law of nations at present in force and its effect on the development of such regulations.

Of course, any African state makes an individual contribution, quite independent of OAU, to the establishment of the provisions of international law, and that contribution above all takes the form of a great many bilateral or multilateral treaties concluded both between African states and with non-African countries. However, it is through and within the OAU that this contribution is most obvious, most fruitful, and most institutionalized. OAU is the tangible proof of the legal solidarity of 41 member states, and its drafting of the regulations of the law of nations can be compared to a kind of work of codification, in the broad sense of the word. Codification takes three forms: the official confirmation of certain principles and regulations of the international law in force before independence, opposition to or amendment of others, and the formulation of new legal instruments of specific relevance to the African continent.

It is true that, in more than one respect, the contribution of Africa to a universal legal order is still relatively modest, and the number of legal provisions drawn up by the OAU is still fairly small, insufficiently precise, and lacking mechanisms of restraint. That is hardly surprising: Any valid regulation-drafting process can only be achieved over a relatively long period, and before it can be affirmed, the legal system must stand the harsh test of political contingencies. European powers have taken centuries to forge a certain number of regulations on the positive law of nations, and the capitulation system was extended to Africa from the sixteenth century onward. In the nineteenth century, together with European colonial expansion in Africa, the powers drew up certain principles applicable to Africa; in particular, the Berlin Conference of 1885 proclaimed the freedom of trade and shipping, equality of treatment, neutrality, the effectiveness of territorial occupation, and the frontiers system. Africa did not take part in drawing up those regulations: Africa suffered them, as Africa suffered the regulations resulting from other large international conferences: the Brussels Act of 1890, the colonial regime and the mandate system of the League of Nations, the Treaty of Saint-Germain in 1919, and the United Nations system in 1945. Apart from South Africa, there were only three African countries at the San Francisco conference: Egypt, Ethiopia, and Liberia.

Today, things have changed radically. The old colonial system has been disrupted, the international legal order has assumed greater proportions than before, most of the African nations have acceded to international sovereignty, and OAU comprises 41 independent states. This shows that, in the same way as great human civilizations, legal civilizations are mortal, or at least they call for a constant redefinition of the value judgments and criteria used in their formulation. International law is also subject to this law of evolution: It must take into account the structural changes going on in a continually expanding political world. Seeking to be genuine, it is built on national sovereignty—old and new—but also on the regions and regional bodies; in one sense, its universalism is achieved through regionalism.

It is perfectly true that at the Addis Ababa Conference the heads of state and government took relatively little note of the effect of international law on the new organization and its relations with the United Nations; the text of the Charter holds few direct references to international law. Was this intentional? It is quite possible that there was at Addis Ababa a certain instinctive mistrust, on the part of the African leaders, of any excess of legalism. Independent Africa is mistrustful of formalism since it feels that, before it became independent, the international law then in force was "designed to legalize the privileges of European States or to govern their relations"[1] —it was a kind of superstructure of regulations over the political infrastructure legalizing a system of domination of the black continent by forces external to that continent. In other words, at Addis Ababa only those principles of the law of nations directly concerning Africa were referred to, principles with an immediate political impact on the African continent and accepted as such by the new African states. Solemnly declared at Addis Ababa (Article 3 of the Charter), these seven principles deal with inter-African problems and Africa's relations with the external world; some of them go far beyond the context of law as such and deal more with international politics, where flexibility has greater currency than rigidity. The principles are as follows:

1. The sovereign equality of all member states.
2. Noninterference in the internal affairs of states;
3. Respect of the sovereignty and territorial integrity of every state and its inalienable right to an independent existence.

81

4. The peaceful settlement of disputes, through negotiations, mediation, conciliation, or arbitration.

5. Condemnation, without reservation, of political assassinations and subversive activities carried on by neighboring states, or all other states.

6. Absolute devotion to the cause of total liberation of African territory not yet independent.

7. Affirmation of a policy of nonalignment in respect of all political blocs.

As for other principles—particularly those stemming from the postindependence process—haste was eschewed and time for reflection was agreed upon in order to proceed, in each individual state, to reappraisal and, where necessary, redefinition.

After this brief glimpse of the problem, the general layout of the study is as follows: It is intended to be selective. It limits its research to a few legal problems as we see them, either of particular importance or of particular relevance to the African continent. It deals first with the problem of the African legal order and the conformity of the Charter of OAU to that of the United Nations; the principle of the sovereign equality of the state; the system of the settlement of inter-African disputes; the intangibility of frontiers and the problems of the right to self-determination of the African peoples; problems relating to the decolonization of the black continent, more particularly the legality of resorting to armed struggle for independence. Many other (important) issues should be discussed—for example, international recognition of national liberation movements, the scope of nonalignment, the right to development, disarmament, the position adopted by OAU with regard to the Near East—but they are too extensive to be included here.

THE AFRICAN LEGAL ORDER

The drafting of the principles of international law by OAU raises the problem of the effectiveness and independence of the OAU's legal system, and hence the existence and validity of a specifically African legal order. Clearly, the establishment of a relatively independent legal order presupposes the fulfillment of certain conditions.

It has been stressed that:

in order to establish a legal order, it is necessary to define three consistent types of conditions. First, there should be a set of organs and procedures for the elaboration and promulgation of regulations or individual decisions;

82

second, a body of regulations and decisions taken; and
finally, a set [of] organs and procedures to sanction the body
of regulations. There is a legal order, therefore, if there
is a consistent and lasting set of procedures for promul-
gating regulations, regulations promulgated and sanction
procedures. This whole forms a system insofar as it is
organized, is operational, and is capable of independent
management.[2]

Such a view of the problem shows a great deal of pertinence
and logic and demonstrates the advantage of a certain consistency.
However, a logical order arrived at according to an ideal intellectual
view is not necessarily sufficiently explanatory: It does not take into
account the realities that will be met by any law establishment process. Any regional legal order does not exactly fulfill the requirements laid down in the above-mentioned outline, and if we wanted
(strictly) to apply such criteria to the universal legal order—well,
there probably wouldn't be one.
Whether under the system of the League of Nations or under the
auspices of the so-called United Nations, the functioning of international bodies has always left much to be desired, and sanction
procedures have always been and still are unsatisfactory. The League
of Nations failed dramatically in its sanctions against Italian aggression in Ethiopia, while differences among the great powers in
the United Nations have rendered it completely inoperative and its
many resolutions totally ineffective. Despite this lack and these
serious failings, some regulations of international law have gradually
acquired an existence independent of any purely national institutional
context. This is also true of the Latin American countries, the Arab
countries, the member states of the Atlantic Community, and of
Africa.
The fact, for example, that Africa still manifests some mistrust of international jurisdiction or of arbitration procedures founded
on the strict respect of law is not directly related to the problem
of organs, procedures, or sanctions—it is a social and political attitude
that has emerged more than once; it can be observed and therefore
should be taken into consideration. The lack of formal rules of law
can hardly contribute to establishing a legal order, but the consistent
use of certain practices also has an influence on the establishment
of a kind of parasystem, at least a paralegal order. While rejecting
the legal formulas of arbitration or those of the International Court
of Justice, the African states settle their differences using formulas
that, lacking institutional rigidity, help to regulate certain types of
interstate relationships.

The means here are not very important; what is important is that peace should be safeguarded and conflicts attenuated; hence the purpose of those means would seem largely to have been achieved. That probably does not concord with the institutional scheme we have mentioned. However, if with such means—different and restricted, let us say paralegal—member states of OAU manage to attain some of their objectives, the result will have justified their use. These means are part of a system in the broad sense of the word, of a specific legal order or a paralegal order.[3]

This being so, is it meaningful to talk about the real independence of an African legal order? There are gaps. The application of the OAU's decisions within the continent itself too often suffers from a lack of sanctions. Some resolutions are too verbose or given to political phraseology hardly conducive to effective application; they are adopted for reasons of internal policy or to satisfy the demands of public opinion. As for consistency in bringing certain principles into force, that too suffers from certain insufficiencies. Hence, although part of the (particularly African) doctrine argues that all the broad conditions to create an African international law have already been satisfied, other doctrinal authorities are expressing reservations: The political realities of the black continent seem to them to be too fluctuating to permit the establishment of a real system of law. "In these circumstances, can one talk about a legal system of OAU? The Organization is founded on legal principles, has drawn up some legal instruments and created a practice. But it is easy to show that it is dominated by political problems, that as a result it finds it hard to define the legal consequences of its Charter, to see that its decisions or conventions are implemented, to give consistency to its practice."[4]

All this is pertinent. What regional international organization has not been dominated by political problems? There are hardly any. The difference lies only in the intensity of the political element within the regional legal order.

That means that the real problem does not lie in denying the existence of an African legal order, but elsewhere. Although it is still useful to seek "the first elements of a continental African order,"[5] to define the specific nature of African regionalism, even to define (a much harder task) its "international law in the process of establishment,"[6] it is also timely and indeed essential to consider the means of integrating the evolving African legal system into a general legal order. Universalism is achieved through regionalism, and unity of law does not exclude some diversity and some specificity in the implementation of its regulations: Unity does not necessarily mean uniformity. OAU has the merit of helping to define such specificity: the principle of the intangibility of the frontiers inherited from the colonial powers, the practices that emerge in the recognition of states, governments, and national liberation movements, the affirmation of the legitimacy of armed struggle against colonial domination, and so on. Although the affirmation of these principles and a desire for a measure of independence do not necessarily create a different legal order, nonetheless universal international law must take these factors into account; an affirmation of legal conduct by 41 sovereign states of OAU—out of the sum total of 135 member states of the United Nations—is not to be taken lightly. The importnat thing is to find the means of integrating the specific into the universal legal order. The latter is essentially changing: It is based on the pluralism of values that determines, at least in part, the external attitudes of states and groups of states.

The problem of the independence of regional legal orders and their compatibility with the universal legal order exists since there is—there must be—one single general international law, and not several. Intransigent pluralism in small legal orders—regional, ideological, or national—would endanger the existence of a universal international law. This contradiction is attenuated or disappears insofar as the small legal orders are ready to submit to a process of integration into a higher hierarchical order, if the latter properly takes into account the diversity of values, the pluralism of criteria relating to the fundamentals of law, and certain geographic situations. The problem of coordination and integration obviously raises considerable difficulties that cannot be dealt with here.

CONFORMITY WITH THE CHARTER OF SAN FRANCISCO AND RELATIONS WITH THE UNITED NATIONS

Before turning to the problem of conformity of the OAU Charter with the regional arrangements of the United Nations Charter as laid down in Chapter VIII, Articles 52, 53, and 54, it is useful to give a little background. In 1945, at the time the Charter of San Francisco was signed, the peoples of Africa were living under a regime of colonial dependence, and on that basis they could not take part in drawing up this basic document of the United Nations. Only Egypt, Ethiopia, and Liberia were able to make observations regarding the validity, usefulness, and legitimacy of the regional organizations in relation to the universal organizations. The Egyptian government alone took advantage of that opportunity.

The proposals relating to the establishment of the United Nations, put forward on 7 October 1944 by the four great powers that met at Dumbarton Oaks, included a series of provisions relating to regional organizations, envisaged essentially from the point of view of security, closely linked to the U.N. system and subject to its decision-making organ, the Security Council. Both the Arab countries and the Latin American countries expressed satisfaction at that affirmation of the appropriateness of regional agreements and organs: The Organization of American States on 9 March 1945 adopted the Act of Capultepec setting up a regional security system in "the Western Hemisphere," while the Arab countries were on the eve of constituting the League of Arab States (22 March 1945).

It is in that context that the Egyptian government put forward its amendments to the Dumbarton Oaks proposals, making often pertinent points regarding regional agreements and bodies. The Egyptian amendments stressed the appropriateness of legally defining regional organizations, since the latter should be characterized—contrary to passing military alliances—by the permanence of interstate cooperation, geographic proximity of member states, cultural affinities, and the establishment of common institutions.[7] These proposals had some repercussions at San Francisco, and in varying degrees the Egyptian formulation had some impact both when the League of Arab States was formed and later, in 1963, when preparatory work had led to the establishment of the Organization of African Unity.

Regarding relations with the United Nations, the relative modesty of references in the OAU Charter seems accidental and inconsequential; everybody knows the great attachment that the African states professed (and profess) to the U.N., for it has helped to accelerate the decolonization process. Thus, the Ethiopian draft that served as the basis for the preparatory work of OAU provided that, with regard to relations between the two organizations, nothing in the Charter of the OAU might be interpreted as contravening the rights and duties of member states stipulated by the Charter of San Francisco.[8] But this text was not ultimately adopted, and point nine of the Preamble of the Charter of OAU merely reaffirms the adhesion of the heads of state and government to the principles of the Charter of the United Nations and the Universal Declaration of Human Rights, which it says "offer a solid basis for peaceful and fruitful co-operation between our States."

Another indication is given by Article 2, paragraph (e), according to which one of the aims of OAU is "to favor international co-operation, taking due account of the Charter of the United Nations and the Universal Declaration of Human Rights." However, no direct reference is made in the OAU Charter to the regional arrangements as such, as found in Articles 52, 53, and 54 of the Charter of San Francisco. Should that be seen as a kind of challenge to the world prescribed by the Charter to the Security Council (to the great powers) with regard to surveillance, on behalf of the United Nations, of the activity of regional organizations? Africa is undoubtedly in favor of the United Nations, but it would like to avoid political interference from the powers. Thus, African affairs essentially and primarily must be settled by the Africans themselves, and the role of the universal organization should be only supplementary. In this respect, the Charter of OAU is a kind of Monroe Doctrine for the African continent. But with one reservation: It is not unilateral; it is a multinational document.

Resolution 3, Africa and the United Nations, adopted by the Summit Conference of 22-25 May 1963 at Addis Ababa, gives details with regard to the relations to be established between the two organizations. The conference said it was convinced that the United Nations was an important instrument for the maintenance of peace and security among nations and for the promotion of economic and social progress for all peoples. In that respect, it reiterated its desire to strengthen the world organization and to support it. It reaffirmed its "firm attachment to the objectives and principles of the Charter of the United Nations, of which it accepted all the obligations, including the financial obligations. (Although important, this last detail has no exceptional range, since a great many African countries contribute a total of about 0.04 percent to the budget of the United Nations, i.e., a minimal contribution.)

The Addis Ababa conference also urgently demanded "that Africa, as a geographic region, should be equitably represented in the main organs of the United Nations, particularly in the Security Council and the Economic and Social Council and in the specialized agencies." African governments were requested to take steps and to concert their action to achieve a revision of the regulations in force until that time for the representation of the geographic regions at the United Nations. Finally, African governments were asked to instruct their representatives to the United Nations "without prejudice to their membership and collaboration in the Afro-Asian Group, to set up a more effective African group, with a permanent secretariat, in order to achieve close cooperation and better coordination on questions of common interest."

From then on the African Group in the United Nations effectively contributed to the adoption by the General Assembly of amendments to the initial Charter (17 December 1963) so that the representation of African states in the various organs was considerably strengthened. Since 1966, three African states have been sitting on the Security Council. As for political action, the group has had its ups and downs, and more than once its cohesion has been put to the test. One African observer did not hesitate to say:

the cohesion of the African Group to the United Nations
is a function of the policy of each state. The constitution
of more or less antagonistic sub-groups only reflects the
political constellations emerging outside the United Nations
context. They rather translate a fermentation of the continent, still seeking its own identity in a far from stable
world.[9]

Regarding the means of cooperation between OAU and the United
Nations, institutional contacts have in particular been established with
the General Assembly. Pursuant to the request of 35 African states
submitted by Upper Volta, the General Assembly, on 11 October 1965,
adopted resolution 2011 (XX) establishing the principles governing
cooperation between the two organizations. From then on the Secretary
-General of OAU was present as an observer at sessions of the General
Assembly, on the same basis as the Secretary-General of OAS or
the Arab League. The principles governing cooperation between
the two organizations have been reaffirmed by many General Assembly resolutions; including 2193 (XXI) of 15 December 1966, 2505
(XXIV) of 20 November 1969, and 2863 (XXVI) of 20 December 1971.

The Secretaries-General of the United Nations have stressed
several times the perfect compatibility of OAU with the aims and
principles of the United Nations. Speaking at the fifth OAU summit
in Algeria, on 13 September 1968, U Thant pointed out that the Organization of African Unity seemed to him "the most appropriate
instrument for the reestablishment of peace in Nigeria," thereby
implicitly admitting that the United Nations could intervene in the
solution of the Biafran conflict only on a subsidiary basis, failing a
settlement through OAU. In other words, specifically African problems are in the first instance the competence of the Africans and
their institutions, while problems where the European powers are
implicated—such as the problem of South Africa, where Portugal,
France, and the United Kingdom are implicated—can be dealt with
at the level of the United Nations.

Following this train of thought, OAU takes an active part in
the work of the conferences of nonaligned countries, which accord
it, on the same basis as the United Nations, a prominent place in the
solution of political problems affecting the African continent, more
particularly with regard to the liberation of Africa from colonial
domination.

THE PRINCIPLE OF SOVEREIGN EQUALITY
AND ITS IMPLICATIONS

The principle of the sovereign equality of states has been more strictly formulated in OAU (Article 3, paragraph 1, and article 5 of the Charter) than in the United Nations, in the specialized agencies, or in the context of regional organizations such as the Organization of American States or the European Economic Community.

To say that the present international order is still defining contradictions that some consider difficult to reconcile has today become a platitude. Although the current world order rests on a legal base of egalitarianism, politically it is still inegalitarian and multidimensional. It is made up of state sovereignties of variable political and economic weight, sovereignties that play a differential role in the formulation of the regulations of international law. Insofar as such formulations are imposed or suggested by the great powers, they inevitably lead to the establishment of a law of subordination that is likely in the long term—as was the case for the colonial system —to be contested at the world level on the basis of changes in the distribution of international political power. However, insofar as the formative process properly takes into account the principle of the sovereign equality of states, stressing the reciprocity of their rights and duties to the detriment of any political constraint, it leads to the establishment of a law of coordination.

Contrary to the United Nations, the OAU system has no security council with particular powers in the matter of war and peace, and it gives no privileged position to the "great powers" of Africa. It tries to avoid the formation of any kind of hegemony de facto or de jure, and in no way bases itself on the model of the Organization of American States where the United States continues to play a primary role. It also avoids the weighted voting formulas at present in force in some specialized agencies of the United Nations (International Monetary Fund, International Financial Corporation) and in the European Economic Community, which establish differential voting rights. The OAU formula remains "one state, one vote," and the highest organ of the OAU is the Conference of Heads of State and Government, with a two-thirds majority required to pass a measure.

Thus envisaged by OAU, the principle of the sovereign equality of states has two points worth consideration:

First, in the forum of the United Nations, African states have expressed their will to restrict the prerogatives of the great powers in maintaining international peace and security. They have spoken in favor of the enlargement of the Security Council based mainly on the criterion of geographic regions. Second, they have spoken in favor of a parallel competence of the General Assembly, which would

imply that the majority resolutions of that body—reflecting the point
of view of states of the Third World—would have an almost legal
nature of a restricting scope. All this relates to the difficult problem
of the role assigned to the great powers in the international order,
and is based on the matter of structuring a supranational authority
with the power of sanction: We have not yet come that far.

It is certain that the present (rudimentary) state of international
political relations hardly authorizes the generalization of majority
formulas in the United Nations. All excess is harmful, both with
regard to the abusive prerogatives accorded to the great powers
and with regard to the excessive democratization of the decision-
making machinery of the U.N. organs, which are thus rendered im-
practicable. At this time, the General Assembly, which has gradually
since 1950 become the main body of the United Nations—the functioning
of the Security Council being vitiated by the abusive use of the veto—
enjoys discussing, debating, and voting at an ever increasing rate
resolutions completely lacking in any executory scope. Thus, nobody
takes them seriously. This is not a positive contribution to the work
of peace, and there is in that respect a large measure of political
irresponsibility. Any careless displacement of the world organization's
activity according to the egalitarian principle "one state, one vote"
provokes a reaction from the powers that effectively hold political
power, that finance the United Nations, and without which the United
Nations could scarcely exist. They allege that the General Assembly
is only a means of rhetorical exercise for the delegations, which
have no practical power whose role in the work of the United Nations
is a mere formality. Consequently, the role of the so-called United
Nations in maintaining peace and security, in the peaceful settlement
of international disputes and the solution of serious economic and
monetary problems, is eroding or becoming null and void. The major
decisions are taken not in the United Nations but in the great capitals
of the world: In Washington and Moscow, London and Paris, Bonn
and Peking. All this raises once again the difficult problems of redefining the broad principles on which the United Nations is based
and that of amending its Charter, which dates from the colonial era.
As it now stands, the United Nations system no longer corresponds
to the new structures of international society, which is marked by the
fall of colonialism and the emergence on the international scene of
more than 17 new states in Asia and Africa.

The second point for consideration is closely linked to the
first: It concerns the problem of the accession to independence of
what have been called the minisovereignties—i.e., small or sparsely
populated territories that have just escaped from colonial domination.
This problem is serious in the sense that it is now a matter of seeing
how and to what extent the African formulation of the principle of

90

sovereign equality will resist attempts to generalize certain practices having the effect of limiting egalitarian formulas. Everybody knows that voices increasingly are raised in United Nations to find satisfactory resolutions to the problem of the representation of the microstates; the problem is, of course, a difficult one, but it is important. For example, when the Maldive Islands were admitted to the United Nations (108,000 inhabitants), some states entered reservations regarding the unconditional validity of the concept of sovereign equality that has traditionally prevailed in the United Nations.

In 1967 Secretary General U Thant suggested drawing up an in-depth study in order to define the criteria for the admission of new states to the United Nations. While admitting that even the smallest territories accede to independence by the implementation of resolution 1514 (XV) of the General Assembly, he suggested a distinction should be made "between the right to independence and the full status of member of the United Nations. This status might make microstates subject to obligations that would prove too heavy for them, and might lead to the weakening of the United Nations itself."[10]

It had been suggested that, without any need to modify the Charter, there would be other forms of association than full member state status, and in the perspective of the accession to state sovereignty of all territories at present dependent, this problem could find its application both in the United Nations and in other international organizations including OAU. We might recall that some already independent African states have populations of rather less than a million: Botswana 560,000; Ngwana 430,000; Gambia 370,000; Equatorial Guinea 280,000 and Guinea-Bissau, which has just been made an independent state, 550,000. The same may also be said of dependent territories: Cape Verde Islands 520,000; French Somaliland (the territory of Afars and Issas) 140,000; Spanish Sahara 60,000; Seychelles 55,000. But to repeat, the problem of redefining sovereign equality is a difficult one, concerning the very essence of the international legal order, and its solution presupposes a redefinition of the very concept of sovereignty.

The Settlement of Inter-African Disputes

Three remarks must be made regarding the settlement of inter-African conflicts; the first two are general, the third deals with frontier problems.

First, there is a clear disparity between the official institutional machinery of the Charter of OAU and the practical methods of settlement, to such an extent that the legal elements as such are often reduced to the simplest expression. The mediation, conciliation, and arbitration unit set up at Addis Ababa was found in practice to be inoperative, and again recourse to arbitration or the International Court of Justice has not been favored by the African states. Most of the differences have been settled (or attenuated) through para-institutional procedures, as a result of the moral action of the OAU or through direct political action by heads of state who enjoy particular personal prestige.

More than the letter or the machinery of the Charter, negotiation—there is a temptation to use the African oral tradition—has in this field of conflict undergone some astonishing tests. That, to some extent, relates to the cultural heritage of precolonial Africa. In the absence of written laws, black Africa had forged amazing oral traditions, and its customary law, noncodified but none the less with sufficiently rigid outlines, was a social force exercising unquestionable influence and even moral sanction: It ordered and stabilized. That also shows, yet again, how vain and deceptive it is to limit research on OAU to its formal, institutional aspect, for thus it would be outside reality. Such an approach does not take into account either the psychological context of Africa or its mental structures and ways of thinking, or its concept of justice, which does not necesasrily identify with the concept of essentially logical and rational law so dear to the Western world. Any civilization has its own set of values and its own logic.

Second, although the problems concerning the whole of the black continent—the struggle against apartheid, the struggle for independence in territories still occupied by the powers—are willingly debated in the United Nations, inter-African affairs and conflicts find their priority framework for settlement in OAU. It has been pointed out that "in practice, therefore, the African institution is a privileged context for the settlement of inter-African conflicts. No legal document, however, obliges the African states to regard it as a body of first reference. But the priority is acknowledged in fact by both the African states and the United Nations."[11] This comment is pertinent—through resolution AGH/16/I of 21 July 1964, with the reservation that OAU has recognized "the urgent need to settle, through peaceful means and in a purely African context, all disputes between African states." Although this text is not an official legal obligation, its political scope carries weight.

This moderating action of the OAU has been clear in a great many inter-African conflicts. When, in February 1964, the Security Council was called on to debate the complaint made by the Somalian government against Ethiopia, Secretary General U Thant suggested that both countries seek a settlement of their disputes in OAU. On 10 September 1964 OAU set up an ad hoc committee made up of nine states, its terms of reference being to reconcile Zaire (then the Congo) and to regulate the relations of that country with its neighbors, particularly Burundi and the Republic of the Congo (Brazzaville).

It is true that in this affair the mediating action of OAU came rather late. On 30 December 1964 the Security Council adopted by ten votes and one abstention (France) a text by which it referred to OAU as a regional organization in the meaning of Articles 52 and 54 of the Charter and, in accordance with the OAU resolution of 10 September, considered that mercenaries should immediately be withdrawn from the Congo. It instructed OAU to find a political solution to the Congolese difficulties; in conformity with Article 54 of the Charter of the United Nations, OAU was requested to keep the Security Council fully informed of any action it might undertake in the context of the resolution.

This mission of conciliation and classification was, alas, not accomplished since it was already too late. Between 10 September (date of the OAU resolution) and 30 December (date of the Security Council resolution) an event of capital importance occurred—the fall of Stanleyville. That military operation by the Tshombe government, supported by Belgium and the United States, was to have political repercussions that destroyed any effort at conciliation by OAU. It must also be recognized that the internal divisions and all kinds of divergencies among African leaders in the OAU were not unrelated to that failure.

Among other affairs where the mediation of the OAU came too late is the frontier conflict between Morocco and Algeria: The ceasefire had been announced on 31 October 1963, but OAU set up its ad hoc committee only on 18 November 1963. As for other action taken by the OAU, it is worth noting that, pursuant to the recommendations of the fourth summit of OAU at Kinshasa in September 1967, the governments of Somalia and Kenya agreed to reopen diplomatic relations and resume discussions on the subject of their dispute. With respect to the Biafran problem, the United Nations did not intervene, both because of the refusal of the government of Lagos to accept its intervention and because of the provisions adopted by OAU suggesting a peaceful settlement of the Biafran secession without foreign interference. The abstention of OAU was equally tangible in the conflict between Uganda and Tanzania: "It is noticeable that OAU has not been able to prevent the conflict and no one thought to apply conciliatory machinery."[12] Similarly, when in July 1973, Burundi appealed to OAU to intervene by sending a committee of observers to its conflict with Tanzania, some attenuation was achieved only through the mediation of President Mobuto (Zaire). However, without always achieving the solution of fundamental problems—particularly during the civil war in Nigeria—OAU had the unquestionable merit of attenuating tensions and stabilizing certian conflict situations. Like any international order, African order is in movement, seeking equilibrium, always precarious and never perfect. Nowhere is it ever perfect.

ETHNIC AND TERRITORIAL PROBLEMS

Territorial problems hold a particularly important place in the regulation-drafting machinery of OAU. This machinery has in particular dealt with the problem of the frontiers set up within Africa when the African countries gained their independence. Later, OAU adopted a position of principle on the subject of non-African territorial conflict and strongly approved Security Council resolution 242 of 22 November 1967, dealing with the withdrawal of Israeli forces from all occupied Arab territories. Only the first point will be dealt with here, that relating specifically to African problems.

As is well known, African independence has been acquired in the territorial framework inherited from the colonialists, and that territorial order was clearly not perfect, since it did not take into account—could not fully take into account—the ethnic aspect, which is particularly important in African social and political life. Colonization in the nineteenth century imposed great frontiers on Africa, gathering together ethnic groups that up until then had had no shared community feeling, had even been hostile to each other. Or else colonization divided certain ethnic groups, suddenly separating them by a new territorial order. African frontiers, it is thought, did not usually correspond to the old ethnic demarcations and did not always take into account the historical, geographic, and economic peculiarities of the continent.

It has been said that "in Africa, 44 percent of the frontiers were traced according to meridians and parallels, 30 percent are straight or curved geometric lines, and only 26 percent follow natural lines."[13] This indicates the extent of the territorial problems engendered by colonization—with the reservation that the old ethnic demarcations were far from clear and the very concept of ethnic group raises questions. Some ethnic groups have experienced a long process of maturity and have managed to assert themselves; others have had a troubled development and could not escape all kinds of racial mixture; still others did not survive contact with more powerful and better organized groups and finally disintegrated.

Whatever the case may be, it is certain, for example, that the populations of Lower Zaire and those living near the Sudan frontier [now included in Zaire] formerly had very little or no affinity; it is also certain that the Congo River never served as a frontier between the different peoples of the region that has been shared between the Congo (Leopoldville), French Equitorial Africa, and Angola.

94

It is in this territorial framework inherited from the colonial powers that independence was reached, and it is in this more or less artificial (but necessary) framework that emerged what have been called "the states without nations". In sub-Saharan Africa, the state preceded the nation.

In the beginning, the African leaders were violently opposed to that situation, and the 1968 Accra Conference called for a review of these territorial conditions. Since the first frontier conflicts troubled the African continent at the very moment of independence, the African leaders noted the practical impossibility of taking a step backward in order to achieve the supposedly ideal interstate alliance founded on the principle of ethnic groups, which in Europe would have been described as "on the principle of nationality." The African leader, forcefully proclaimed the tangibility of frontiers, advocated the main tenance of the territorial status quo.

At the conference establishing the OAU in Addis Ababa, several heads of state and government stressed the complexity of the ethnic problem. The African continent is inhabited by a mosaic of peoples and tribes whose particularities are only slowly disappearing in the face of a feeling of belonging to a nation that is taking shape. There are a multitude of races, speaking different languages, whose historical and cultural links have not always been harmonious. At the risk of disintegrating and disappearing, every African state finds itself bound to transcend tribal and ethnic differences at all costs in order to get back to a national consciousness, which is an essential foundation for any state; politically, the African states are too fragile and economically too dependent on countries abroad to undertake the atomization of their minisovereignties. Consequently, at Addis Ababa the African leaders declared a resolve to safeguard and consolidate the territorial integrity of their states (Article 2, section c; Article 3, section 3, Preamble Point Seven). A little later, the Conference of Heads of State and Government, which met in Cairo on 17-21 July 1964, pointed out that "frontier problems are a serious permanent factor of disagreement," considered that "the frontiers of African states, the day of their independence constitute a tangible reality," and solemnly declared "that all member states undertake to respect the frontiers existing at the time of their independence."

The originality of this position, and the interest it holds for the doctrinal development of positive international law, are worth noting. Until that time, international law had not succeeded in clearly formulating principles that should prevail in respect of a state's succession; if the doctrine inclined toward the thesis of the transmissibility of frontiers established by virtue of international treaties, it would be difficult to apply this principle to frontiers resulting from old administrative divisions made by the colonial powers.

According to Article 62, paragraph 2, of the Vienna Convention on the Law of Treaties, "a fundamental change of circumstances cannot be invoked as a motive to terminate or withdraw from a treaty . . . if the treaty in question establishes a frontier."[14]

Admittedly, the principle uti posseditis had already been formulated by the Latin American states when they achieved independence in the 1820s, but there it was a question, with the exception of the frontiers of Brazil, of confirming old administrative divisions established by a single colonial power (Spain), while in Africa it was a matter of essentially confirming old interstate frontiers and, to a lesser extent, old administrative demarcations. It is worth pointing out that, out of 104 African frontiers, 77 were established through international treaties, 25 originate from an administrative regulation of the colonial powers, 2 are of a mixed character; in other words, out of 79,000 kilometers of frontiers, 59,000 kilometers are based on international treaty and 20,000 kilometers on the internal legislation of the former colonial powers.[15] It is to be hoped that, on the basis of stability in the Latin American territorial order, which has been enforced for a century and a half, the African continent will have the wisdom to steer toward a long period of territorial calm and stability.

PROBLEMS RELATING TO DECOLONIZATION

The problems relating to decolonization on the African continent are the main concern of OAU. According to OAU, no African country can feel free and safe while colonialism subsists on any part of the black continent. This thesis is enshrined in many resolutions of the United Nations, most of which, alas, have remained dead letters. This is a striking example of the enormous disparity still existing between the verbiage of the international organization, which is devoid of the power of sanction or coercion, and the harsh political realities which take no account of, indeed flout, the desires of the majority. Further, it is a matter of the issues relating to apartheid in South Africa, the status of Namibia, the problem of the accession to independence of the Portuguese colonies, or the Rhodesian affair. In all these matters, the decolonization process has met with obstacles that, so far, have not been overcome by either OAU or the United Nations. The power of world public opinion to change outdated political structures and establish a more just and humane international order, one less enmeshed in considerations of economic advantage and political domination, remains illusory, indecisive—in a word, insufficient. World public opinion is powerless to impose on states a system of legal norms and ensure their eventual effectiveness, this aim remains a function of political contingencies, which are ever predominant, to the detriment of the demands of reason and justice.

OAU again took up the principle of the self-determination of peoples, (as outlined in Article 2, paragraph 2, and Article 55 of the Charter of the United Nations) in the General Assembly resolutions of 5 February and 16 December 1962, the declaration of the Afro-Asian Conference of Bandung of 24 April 1955, and the Declaration on the Granting of Independence to Colonial Countries and Peoples adopted on 14 December 1960 by the fifteenth General Assembly of the United Nations. Under the terms of that Declaration, "all peoples have the right to self determination," and by virtue of that right they freely determine their political status and freely pursue their economic, social, and cultural development. OAU contributed an important supplement to the formulation of this principle.

According to the OAU doctrine, the right of peoples to self-determination is a categoric demand for which there shall be no exceptions, a sort of natural right valid in all places and for all time, taking priority over all other provisions of the Charter of the United Nations, particularly those relating to recourse to the threat or use of force (Article 2, paragraph 4); the settlement of international disputes by peaceful means (Article 2, paragraph 3); and the "reserves" of the powers (Article 2, paragraph 7). According to this concept, most of the member states of the international community can legitimately impose a political solution—independence—despite the resistance of the administrative power; in other words, the decolonization process falls outside the realm of matters that "are essentially with the domestic jurisdiction of any State" (Article 2, paragraph 7).

Little by little, the African leaders have come to feel that the refusal of the administrative power to bow to the will of the people who demand independence, supported by the majority of the member states of the international community, implies and justifies the legitimacy of national liberation movements and their armed struggle. Thus, if it is not granted peacefully, independence must be wrested away by force. This is not an entirely new attitude, since the history of nations shows many examples where political independence was conquered by ferocious struggle that broke the old legal framework. That was the case, for example, in the United States (a former British colony), Greece, Belgium, and the Latin American states, and many national revolutions in the nineteenth century troubled the work of the 1815 Congress of Vienna. The legitimacy of violence—or of certain forms of violence—had already been proclaimed by the French revolutionaries of the eighteenth century, and later it inspired many theories stressing the ideal of national liberation and political commitment with a view to overthrowing unjust social systems.[16]

On the basis of the heritage of the French Revolution, the Universal Declaration of Human Rights (10 December 1948) proclaimed: "It is essential, if man is not to be compelled to have recourse, as a last resort, to rebellion against tyranny and oppression, that human rights should be protected by the rule of law." What is true for human rights is also true for the rights of nations, and it is in the name of these principles, regarded as imprescriptible, that of some peoples—this was in particular the case in Algeria—have been forced to undertake a long struggle to liberate themselves from foreign domination. On 10 October 1964, the Cairo Conference of the 47 nonaligned countries (including 29 African countries and Angola), noted "with satisfaction that national liberation movements in various regions of the world were carrying on a heroic struggle against neo-colonialism, the policy of apartheid and racial discrimination. This struggle forms part of the general aspiration for freedom. equity and peace." The Conference declared that "colonial peoples may legitimately have recourse to arms to guarantee the exercise of their right to self-determination and independence, if the colonial powers continue to repress their normal aspirations."

That was the attitude adopted by OAU. At the establishment conference at Addis Ababa, President Ben Bella (Algeria) demanded the creation of an inter-African armed force to liberate the territories of the black continent that were still under foreign dependence, and that position was supported by a certain number of other leaders. Although the proposal was not followed up, OAU recommended that member states should receive in their respective territories "the nationalists from liberation movements" and encourage "at the level of each State, the transit of material and the organization of volunteers in various fields, in order to provide national African liberation movements with the necessary assistance in the different sectors."

At the institutional level, OAU set the Liberation Committee, with headquarters at Dar-es-Salaam, responsible for organizing direct action with a view to liberating dependent African territories; it is supported by a special fund intended to provide material and financial assistance to the various movements. Financed by OAU, the fund also receives money from some thinking and action organs, for example, the World Council of Churches. The Liberation Committee has operated as best it could, achieving some results but also experiencing some setbacks. Its failures have been due both to misunderstanding among the various liberation organizations and to the poor management of the funds made available to them.

But the idea of direct armed action has nonetheless continued to loom large. At the Rabat Conference in June 1972, President Nguabi (People's Republic of Congo) again brought up the idea of forming African brigades of volunteers to work under the military command of the various liberation movements. All this proceeded in conjunction with action in the United Nations, where the African delegations strongly pleaded in favor of the legitimacy of anticolonial armed struggle demanding the legal recognition of liberation movements. This action found support among the Asian peoples and the countries of the East: "To react against a national liberation movement," said Tunkin, is to violate international law."[17] By resolution 2189 (XXI) of 13 December 1966, the U.N. General Assembly reaffirmed "the legitimacy of the struggle of the peoples under colonial rule to exercise their right to self-determination and independence" and urged "all States to give material and moral assistance to national liberation movements in colonial territories."

On the basis of this development of ideas and events, an African author did not hesitate to support the thesis of a "law of liberation movement." According to Mohammed Bedjaoui, "An outline of a law for liberation movements in the war for independence has thus emerged." Anticolonial struggles have gradually lost their artificial legal character of "internal conflicts" to be seen as international wars, thus transforming the nature and international legal status of insurrectional movements, authorizing the application of the law of war, and bestowing new content on the laws and duties of third states.[18]

On the basis of these considerations, on 23 June 1971 OAU asked the Security Council to apply coercive measures to force South Africa —if necessary by arms—to give up its political and administrative control over Namibia.

This thesis of the preeminence of armed struggle (anticolonial) over any other provision of the law of nations or the Charter of the United Nations—which formally forbids recourse to force, tolerating it only under the auspices of the Security Council or in the case of individual and collective legitimate defense—has not met with unanimous support among either governments or doctrines. Reservations and fears have been expressed, often in a pertinent manner.[19]

In fact, what would happen if tomorrow an African ethnic group or an Asian people, belonging to an independent, decolonized state, demands self-determination? What would happen if—as in the Biafran affair or in Bangladesh—they begin a "war of liberation," this time describing a new state authority as "colonialist"? How will we react if tomorrow the Asian peoples of the USSR demand their independence and begin a national liberation struggle?

Such demands have already been made in the name of the right of peoples to self-determination. Flying the flag of anticolonialism at the tenth congress of the Chinese Communist Party (April 1973) Chou En-lai demanded that the USSR withdraw its troops from all territories north of the Great Wall. In this interpretation, the concept of "colonialism" goes beyond the problem of nonindependent overseas territories or territories under trusteeship. According to this thesis, colonialism exists where one nation imposes its domination on another nation by force, by ideology, by a deceptive mechanism of international law or constitutional law.

The traditional law of nations rejects the legitimacy of recourse to violence and reserves it officially for the universal organization and its organs responsible for maintaining peace and security. That is understandable. Throughout the long history of nations, the most decisive stages for reach state have been marked by war; peace has been only the absence of war. It has been said that between the year 3600 B.C. and today—for roughly 5,600 years—there have been only 292 years of peace; for the rest of the time, i.e., practically without interruption, there have been some 14,500 conflicts settled by bloody war. Therefore, international law has a great deal of difficulty in mastering the phenomenon of violence. The whole existence, the whole future of international law remains closely linked to the regulation of such conflict situations; to leave them to the good will of peoples and governments would be to approve a state of anarchy, and question the validity of an international legal order. The broad interpretation of the "right to war" goes beyond the present provision of the law of nations and the Charter of the United Nations—which, as noted, allow only "the natural law of individual and collective defense," under the control of the United Nations. During the U.N. debate on African territories not yet independent in November 1972, some delegations, particularly those of Latin America, expressed reservations regarding the legitimacy of violence, whether from colonial power or national liberation movement.

There are still diverging points of view, and to reconcile them it would have to be shown that an armed national liberation struggle is just such a legitimate defense. Such an interpretation, we feel, is part of political action; it implies value judgments and in this respect goes beyond the purely legal framework of the law of war. The "licitness" and "legitimacy" in legal terms of armed struggle means that the powers are incapable taking a unanimous decision to authorize it or condemn it. The Security Council has not authorized armed struggle. But it has shown itself incapable of condemning it, and it subsists as a de facto indication of the pluralism of legal approaches.

Given the lack of sanction and constraint, a legal void has been created in the international legal order; in more than one respect, it is shown to be inoperative. The demand for the legitimacy of armed struggle is an attempt to fill that void by new political content, which could later be incorporated in regulations embodying the positive law of nations. Without ignoring the difficulties of such a formulation, it is certain that, in order to be valid and effective,

international law must be built on the basis of the needs of life, to
the detriment of any outdated formalism that is destined to disappear.

NOTES

1. Boutros Boutros-Ghali, Les conflicts de frontieres en
Afrique (Paris: Editions techniques et economiques, 1972), p. 5.
2. F. Borella, "Le systeme juridique de l'O.U.A.," in Annuaire
Francais de Droit International, 1971, p. 234.
3. Gabriel d'Arboussier, "Problemes nouveaux du droit africain," in Afrique-Documents (Dakar), no. 74 (1964):135-46.
4. Borella, op. cit., p. 233.
5. Boutros Boutros-Ghali, L'Organisation de l'Unite africaine
(Paris: A. Colin, 1969), p. 24.
6. R. Yakemtchouk, "L'Afrique en droit international," in
Cahiers économiques et sociaux (Kinshasa), 1969, p. 384; R. Yakemtchouk, L'Afrique en Droit international (Paris: Librairie Générale
de Droit et de Jurisprudence, 1971).
7. United Nations Conference on International Organisation,
vol. IV, pp. 651-52; R. Yakemtchouk, L'O.N.U., la sécurité régionale
et le problème du régionalisme (Paris: Pedone, 1955), pp. 91-93.
8. J. Woronoff, Organizing African Unity (Metuchen, N.J.:
Scarecrow Press, 1970), pp. 151-52.
9. Lazare Nkuba, "Les états africains face au systéme actuel
de l'O.N.U.," Etudes congolaises, May-June 1966, p. 49.
10. Rapport annuel du Sécrétaire général sur l'activité de
l'Organisation (16 June 1966-15 June 1967), 15 September 1967.
11. Mirlande Manigat, "L'O.U.A.," Revue Francaise de Science
Politique, April 1971, p. 382.
12. Georges Lavroff, "L'O.U.A. ou l'impossible désir d'union
politique," Le Monde Diplomatique, October 1972, p. 9.
13. Y. Alimov, "Afrique: règlement des différents territoriaux,"
La vie internationale, January 1973, p. 119.
14. The Rapporteur of the Committee, Sir Waldock, commented
on this provision as follows:

> The weight both of opinion and practice seems
> clearly to be in favour of the view that boundaries estab-
> lished by treaties remain untouched by the mere fact of
> succession. The opinion of jurists seems, indeed, to be
> unanimous on the point, even if their reasoning may not
> always be exactly the same. In State practice in favor
> of the continuance in force of boundaries established by
> treaty appears to be such as to justify the conclusion that

a general rule of international law exists to that effect. The rule here in question, of course, concerns only the issue of the effect of a "succession," as such, upon boundaries established under previous treaties. It does not touch the application of the principle of self-determination in any given case. . . . Nor does it in any way touch the question of what precisely is to be considered the true line of the boundary established under the treaty. It simply prevents any provision of the present articles regarding either the application of the treaties of the successor State or the cessation of the application of the predecessor State from affecting established boundaries.

First Report on Succession of States and Governments in Respect of Treaties Doc. A/CN.4/202; Yearbook of the International Law Commission (1968), Vol. II, Doc. A/CN.4/SER.A.1968/Add.I, p. 92.

15. T. Letocha, "The Problem of Succession of African States in Respect of Post-Colonial Boundaries in the Light of Practice,": Studies on the Developing Countries (Warsaw), no. 1 (1972), pp. 137-38.

16. Friedrich Engels, Le rôle de la violence dans l'histoire (Paris: Editions sociales, 1971); Raymond Aron, Histoire et dialectique de la violence (Paris: Gallimard, 1973).

17. G. Tunkin, Droit international public (Paris: Pedone, 1965), p. 49.

18. Mohammed Bedjaoui, "L'affaire de Namibie: un defi aux Nations Unies," Le Monde diplomatique, December 1972, p. 19.

19. R. P. Anand, "Attitudes of the Asian-African States Toward Certain Problems of International Law," in International and Comparative Law Quarterly, 1966, pp. 55-75.

5

THE OAU
AND INTERNATIONAL
RECOGNITION: LESSONS
FROM UGANDA
Claude E. Welch, Jr.

The 1971 change of government in Uganda posed one of the gravest crises the Organization of African Unity faced in its first decade.

The coup d'etat led by General Idi Amin Dada was not, in and by itself, an unusual event. Nearly half the OAU member states have experienced military intervention in politics. At the time of Amin's seizure of power, 13 of the 40 member states were governed by officers who had seized power unconstitutionally.* Previous eruptions of the armed forces into political prominence had passed without discernible effects upon the OAU. Why, then, did the ouster of President Milton Obote result, among other events, in severe recriminations, in a change of venue for the eighth annual Assembly of Heads of State and Government, and in open dispute concerning the powers and stands of the OAU itself?

The Organization of African Unity became the arena within which an attempt to isolate the Amin regime replayed the division between "radicals" and "moderates" that had marked an earlier period of the OAU's history. The postcoup maneuverings raised, and failed to resolve, the long-standing issue of the role of international or regional organizations in according recognition after unconstitutional changes of government. The open split between the chairman of the Assembly (Zambian President Kenneth Kaunda) and most of the OAU's members brought into question the relative political weight of individual members, since a minority of states felt

---

*Algeria, Burundi, Central African Republic, Congo-Brazzaville, Egypt, Libya, Mali, Nigeria, Somalia, Sudan, Togo, Upper Volta, and Zaire. Dahomey and Ghana were then experiencing what turned out to be brief interregnums of civilian rule.

sufficiently disturbed by the change of government in Uganda to openly question the tenet of nonintervention on which the OAU had been founded.

In analyzing these conflicts, attention must be given the temporal context. The displacement of Obote came at a time of escalating tension about South Africa, and domestic tension in Uganda's neighbor, the United Republic of Tanganyika and Zanzibar (Tanzania). The former Ugandan President was ousted a matter of hours after he forcefully argued against resumed arms sales by Great Britain to the Republic of South Africa. His removal appeared, to many African leaders, as a gratuitous insult to the continent as a whole, and as yet another instance of covert British action against states wishing to alter the balance of power south of the Zambesi. The context of the Amin coup and certain initial acts of the Amin government made it easy to ascribe the change of government to neocolonial machinations against which the OAU should take a strong stand, regardless of its concern for domestic jurisdiction.

This chapter examines the interplay between the domestic politics of Uganda and the Organization of African Unity in terms of three questions:

1. Did the 1971 Uganda coup result from factors primarily internal to Uganda, or primarily from factors inherent in the international context?

2. What accounted for the vehemence with which the coup was greeted by some African leaders, and how did they pursue their opposition to the Amin government?

3. What impact did the dispute have on the OAU, especially with regard to its long-standing unwillingness to become involved in the domestic affairs of member states?

THE CONTEXT OF UGANDA POLITICS

By late 1970, President Obote had developed an image of a political leader dedicated to dramatic political reformulation. This image grew from four major sources. One was his interest in pan-Africanism of a continental rather than regional scope. Reluctant, in the face of internal tensions, to commit Uganda in 1963 to federation with Kenya and Tanganyika, Obote proclaimed his support for an Africa-wide solution. Pan-Africanism thus became, as Joseph Nye has pointed out, a sword that cut two ways—as an argument for achieving regional unity or as an argument for stalling East African federation on grounds it undercut African unity.[1] Obote did support regional consultation, as in PAFMECSA, and regularly participated in OAU activities. His public pronouncements, however, echoed the Nkrumahist argument that political unification should be all-embracing.

The key document in Obote's radical image was the "Common Man's Charter," issued with a flourish of publicity in October 1969. The Charter represented Obote's attempt to forge a new base of political support. In the preceding three years, he had relied upon two main props, having staged what was, in effect, a coup d'etat in February 1966. (He had ousted the figurehead President, assumed all executive power, dissolved all parties save the Uganda People's Congress (UPC), suspended the constitution, and used the armed forces to crush resistance among the Baganda.) The first prop was the armed forces. Obote was sufficiently buoyant to boast in 1968, "I am perhaps the only African leader who is not afraid of a military takeover."[2] The second prop was ethnicity. Support for Obote and the UPC was far more pronounced among northern groups (particularly the Langi and Acholi) than among southern groups. The Charter seemed to portend a shift from control based on coercion and ethnicity to control based on an ideology of ironing out emerging class differentiations. (That the Charter in fact alienated many workers and peasants, as well as privileged groups, was a fact unobserved by most external supporters of Obote.) Certainly the promises contained within the Charter went far beyond the verbal commitments of most African heads of state to economic redistribution.[3]

The image of Obote can, in the third place, be attributed to sheer survival. Time and events had thinned the ranks of militant African leaders. Military coups had silenced Nkrumah, Keita, and Ben Bella by mid-1968. Although some intervening officers (Siyad Barre, Muammer Gaddafy) voiced radical sentiments, most leaders of successful coups adopted moderate stances. Civilian leaders who had survived, such as Nyerere and Toure, sensed that intervention against them was quite possible, unless the army's loyalty was assured. Hence, they stepped up their efforts to ensure control—Toure by a purge of leading officers in mid-1969, Nyerere by wholesale replacement of the armed forces in early 1964, by creation of a national service, and (following the ouster of Obote) by the establishment of a people's militia. Civilian presidents who pressed for dramatic change were thus rare individuals indeed—and Obote by early 1971 had become increasingly prominent within this shrinking group.

Possibly the greatest attention to Obote came through the Commonwealth, within which Obote was an increasingly outspoken leader. From November 1965 on, English-speaking African heads of state railed against the British failure to reverse Rhodesia's unilateral declaration of independence, and against British maintenance of trade and military ties with the Republic of South Africa. The concerns of the heads of state became especially acute after the defeat of the Labour government in the June 1970 general elections. The Conservative victory reversed the coolness that had marked relations between

105

London and Pretoria. After rapid, intense lobbying, the Conservative government avowed its intention of renewing arms sales to the Republic. Despite disclaimers—according to Sir Alec Douglas-Home, "In no circumstances would there be sales to South Africa of arms for the enforcement of the policy of apartheid or internal repression"[4]— African governments felt betrayed. Their concern was not lifted by a 12-0-3 vote in the U.N. Security Council that called for a halt to all forms of military cooperation and for implementation of an arms embargo "fully, unconditionally, and without reservations whatsoever."[5]

The OAU Council of Ministers unanimously condemned Western arms sales to South Africa at its fifteenth session, in August 1970; the following month, the OAU Assembly of Heads of State and Government charged Kaunda with leading a mission to France, Italy, the United States, and the United Kingdom to dissuade them from furnishing military equipment. The mission's success was limited. (France agreed to stop furnishing helicopters; President Nixon snubbed the mission.) Arms sales occupied the center of the political stage at the Singapore conference of Commonwealth Heads of State in January 1971. The sharpest attacks on the British position came from Nyerere, Obote, and Kaunda; in a press conference, Obote warned that British provision of military equipment to South Africa might jeopardize the position of Europeans in Uganda.[6] One week later, Obote was evicted by the coup d'etat. And worse yet, the major Uganda newspaper headlined, "We Won't Quit Commonwealth Over Arms," shortly after the coup.[7]

The military seizure of power was in no direct way connected with Obote's foreign policy stands, however. Like coups in other African states, the Amin coup primarily reflected domestic factors. Amin's apologia for intervention listed 18 factors. Some reflected grievances particular to the military (the alleged creation of a second army largely staffed by Langi; the lack of accommodations, vehicles, and equipment), while others reflected widespread political grievances (detention without trial, corruption, absence of free elections, high taxes, and "the creation of a wealthy class of leaders who are always talking of socialism while they grow richer and the common man poorer").[8] The protection of the armed forces' self-interest thus interacted with broader discontents to bring about intervention.

Michael Lofchie has attempted to explain the coup as the result of "class" action in the face of threatened presidential reduction of perquisites. In Lofchie's words, "The cumulative impression is of an overbearing military establishment, entirely unaccountable to civilian authority, engaged in prodigious misuse of public funds, and involved in immense profiteering at the expense of the society of which it was a part," an argument rebutted by John Chick, Samuel Decalo, and James Mittelman.[9]

Amin initiated the seizure of control without extensive planning, without consultation with senior officers, without direct ties to disgruntled civilian groups, and without reference to foreign policy. However, the timing of the coup d'etat—while Obote was pressing in Singapore for a strong initiative against Rhodesia—led to an easy identification of Amin as a tool of neocolonial interests. To understand this equation, the African context as a whole must be considered.

THE AFRICAN POLITICAL CONTEXT

African nationalist leaders derived few comforts from events during 1970. Construction forged ahead on the Cabora Bassa dam in Mozambique, while the Portuguese stepped up their military efforts under General Kaulza de Arriaga in that colony. Lack of unity continued to hamper the Angolan liberation movement. Although the International Court of Justice agreed to consider the legality of South African rule over Namibia, white domination continued unchallenged on the ground. The call of the U.N. Security Council for immediate rupture of all diplomatic, consular, trade, military, and other relations with the minority government of Rhodesia had no apparent effect on the survival of the Smith government. Within the Republic of South Africa, implementation of apartheid ground inexorably ahead; African National Congress (ANC) members acquitted under the Terrorism Act were again incarcerated; renewed British arms sales, as noted above, seemed likely.

But the sharpest blow came in November, with the Portuguese-backed invasion of Guinea. Strategic points were attacked by 350 to 400 men; the army camp, airport, electric power station, presidential palace, and headquarters of the African Party for the Independence of Guinea and Cape Verde (PAIGC) were damaged or destroyed.[10] The overt action resulted in immediate sympathy for Toure and his government. Emergency meetings of the OAU Defense Committee and the Council of Ministers brought strong verbal support. The brazen invasion made Portugal's determination to retain control of its colonies abundantly clear. Danger from the lingering elements of colonialism thus seemed to hang over all African states.

The year 1970 also witnessed a continuing deterioration of the terms of aid and trade. Agricultural export earnings continued to stagnate. A number of reports came essentially to the same sober conclusions: Increases in food production, in gross domestic product per capita, and in other aggregate measures barely equaled increases in population. As a report submitted to the conference of African planners noted, "for most developing African countries and the bulk of the population, economic growth, as measured by change in real product per head, was slow. . . . In only five of thirty-one plans was the aggregate GDP growth target achieved, or is on the way to being achieved."[11] The vaunted "Development Decade" had clearly started to fail, with developed countries not contributing the 1 percent of GNP requested for overseas investment.

Given this context—impotence vis-a-vis minority regimes in southern Africa, the assault against Guinea, and the deterioration of African economic strength—harsh words might have been expected concerning Obote's ouster. The coup could be interpreted as a blatant instance of neocolonial meddling in African affairs; Amin could be depicted as an agent of forces external to the continent. The vituperative comments of some heads of state must be viewed as reflections, in part, of their grave suspicions. Four examples give the flavor.

Julius Nyerere called the coup

> an act of treason to the whole cause of African progress and African freedom . . . . We do not recognize the authority of those who have killed their fellow citizens in an attempt to overthrow the established government of a sister Republic. . . . [Continued Tanzanian support of Obote] is simply a refusal to allow a treacherous Army leader (who is not even supported by the whole Army), and a few disgruntled politicians, to be heard as if they spoke for the People of Uganda.

Sekou Toure said:

> The dissolution of Parliament and all the other elected assemblies, as well as of the trade unions, the political parties, and all popular organizations immediately after the seizure of power, clearly demonstrates the reactionary and anti-democratic leanings of the authors of the coup d'etat. The Guinea Government refuses categorically to recognize the military junta and strongly and indignantly denounces the usurpers of the Ugandan people's power who are meekly carrying out the directives of imperialism, the sworn enemy of all the African peoples.

Kenneth Kaunda commented:

> We, therefore, strongly condemn the coup as clearly the work of reactionary elements whose only motive is to further their own interests, thereby acting as agents for the enemies of African independence, progress and unity.

Major General Siyad Barre said the events represented

> a repetition of the invasion of Guinea by foreigners, or-
> ganized by the imperialists and their stooges with the
> object of causing confusion in the new African revolution-
> ary era. It is a crime committed by people who stand for
> an evil cause and who seek to retard the development of
> the progressive peoples of Africa.[12]

Did Amin merit such obloquy? The roots of his coup, as noted above,
were in part personal, founded upon rivalries for power and position,
in part a symptom of unrest within parts of the armed forces,[13] and
in part a reflection of profound internal discontents. Foreign policy
per se played no part in the decision to seize power. However, the
pressures were such that, in Mittelman's terms, the coup led to "the
internationalization of political violence."[14] The Organization of
African Unity and the East African Community were the major organizations affected by the spreading ripples of the seizure of power.

THE IMPACT ON THE OAU

The Uganda coup tore at the structure of the Organization of
African Unity because three of its leading officials expressed their
concern in public, despite the long-standing OAU policy of nonintervention in domestic matters. The sentiments of Kaunda, elected Chairman of the Assembly of Heads of State and Government in September
1970, have already been quoted. Criticism came equally from OAU
Administrative Secretary Diallo Telli and from Omar Arteh, Chairman
of the Council of Ministers.
    Since its creation, the Organization of African Unity has side-
stepped involvement in members' domestic matters. Several voices
have been raised against such laissez-faire policies (Nkrumah being
perhaps the most widely quoted). The OAU Charter is abundantly
clear, however. Among the principles (Article 3) are "non-interference
in the internal affairs of [Member] States"; "respect for the sovereignty and territorial integrity of each State and for its inalienable
right to independent existence"; and "unreserved condemnation, in
all its forms, of political assassination as well as of subversive
activities on the part of neighboring States or any other States."
    Prior to the coup in Uganda, close to a score of OAU members
had experienced military mutinies or successful seizures of power
by the armed forces. These passed essentially unnoticed, or at least
undebated, within the halls of the OAU. (The assassination of Togolese
President Sylvanus Olympio in 1963 came prior to the establishment

of the OAU, and clearly figured in the Charter's strong condemnation
of assassination; see the concluding section of this chapter for further
details.) The sole change in personnel that had aroused conflict within
the OAU did not stem from action by the armed forces but from the
election of Moise Tshombe as Prime Minister of Zaire in 1964.
Tshombe flew to Cairo for the first session of the Assembly of Heads
of State and Government, but was forced to cool his heels in the airport. He then diplomatically decided not to attend the meeting, on
grounds the spreading rebellion required his presence in Kinshasa.
The subsequent coup of Colonel Mobutu, and the analogous interven-
tions of Ankrah, Bokassa, Lamizana, and Kouandete, among others,
had no discernible effect upon the OAU. But the Amin coup posed
complex diplomatic issues, owing to the known opposition of OAU
leaders and to the fact that Kampala had been selected as the venue
for the June 1971 sessions.

The first occasion on which the OAU directly confronted the
effects of the coup came a month after Amin's triumph. The sixteenth
session of the Council of Ministers (February 1971) witnessed the
unusual situation of two delegations, one from Amin, the other from
Obote. By that time, Amin had received formal recognition from
Great Britain and Liberia, while Ghana, Kenya, Malawi, Nigeria, and
Zaire had voiced support. Most African states waited cautiously; a
few voiced strong hostility. The views of the last group were seemingly
confirmed by Amin two days before the opening of the sixteenth session, when he announced Uganda would not leave the Commonwealth
over the sale of arms to South Africa.[15] Further, the pro-Amin group
allegedly included six Israeli advisers, whose participation was un-
welcome to many OAU members. The OAU response to the rival
delegations was the exclusion of both, despite the contention by the
Amin group that the change in government was a "purely internal
matter which is not the concern of the OAU," and that, if the OAU
should continue to "involve itself in the internal affairs of member-
States, it is going to destroy itself."[16]

The exclusion from the Council of Ministers constituted both
the sharpest rebuff to Amin and the crest of sentiment against him.
Some observers believed that the intense feelings of a minority (in
particular, Somalia and Tanzania) balanced the more diffuse sentiments of the majority. Given the divisiveness of the issue, action
was postponed and the sixteenth session recessed sine die.

The seventeenth session of the Council of Ministers and the
eighth session of the Assembly of Heads of State and Government
were scheduled for Kampala. As de facto head of the host government, Amin could not be precluded diplomatically from attending.
No Tshombe-style solution would have suited him. But irrespective
of the proprieties of the conference setting, several heads of state

could have been expected to mount severe attacks against Amin. The question was thus whether the sessions should proceed as planned. The long-standing practices of the OAU—that form and personnel of government represented matters for internal jurisdiction—collided with the intense feelings of some member states that Amin had been foisted on Uganda and Africa against the best interests of both. To have held the meetings in Kampala could have jeopardized the future of the OAU. The sole courses of action appeared to be postponing the sessions or changing their venue.

Given the seriousness of the issues confronting the Assembly, OAU officials had little desire to recapitulate the 1965 Accra summit, boycotted by eight French-speaking states because of disagreements with the Ghana government. Postponement was not a realistic alternative. The way was open for conciliation, in which Nigeria played an important behind-the-scenes role. Calling upon the "highest interests of the OAU," Kaunda wrote to all members and proposed to transfer the meetings to Addis Ababa. Thirty-three governments responded favorably, well over the two-thirds majority required for such decisions. Amin criticized the procedure employed by Kaunda, namely, requesting agreement to a change of venue by ordinary diplomatic channels rather by convening an extraordinary session. Given the overwhelmingly favorable response to Kaunda's initiative, Amin's objection became moot.

The Amin delegation at the resumed sixteenth session of the Council of Ministers was seated without dispute; however, it boycotted the seventeenth session and Amin refused to attend the meeting of the Assembly, condemning "any attempt by a few Heads of State to turn the OAU into a private club of their own private property."[17] But Uganda stood essentially alone at this point, with only the Central African Republic joining the boycott. Within a few months, this split had been buried.

Could the dispute have led to any outcome other than a reaffirmation of domestic jurisdiction? In particular, might there have been (as Mittelman suggests) an effort to "collectivize" recognition decisions, and as a result, an enhancement of the OAU's integrative abilities?[18]

Time helped heal the wounds opened by the coup, in three respects.

First, the Amin government could demonstrate its freedom from purported external manipulation. The restrictions put on Asian residents, culminating in the expulsion of more than 50,000 individuals, clearly were opposed by Great Britain. Initial statements by Amin favoring Israel and relations with South Africa were withdrawn or considerably modified.

Second, the passage of time permitted Amin to consolidate his domestic control (even though his bases of support were being eroded by early 1972).[19] The open fighting on the Uganda-Tanzania border between the regular army and pro-Obote refugees from it showed that Amin held the trump of coercive power.

Third, and most important for the OAU, the Uganda imbroglio was overshadowed by the question of "dialogue." In the view of many African governments, the proposal of Ivoirien President Houphouet-Boigny to enter into negotiation with the Republic of South Africa smacked of heresy or of treason. Confronted by this assault on a cardinal principle of the OAU, a majority of member states closed ranks. The heads of state rejected "the idea of any dialogue with the minority racist regime of South Africa which is not designed solely to obtain for the enslaved people of South Africa their legitimate and inherent rights and the elimination of Apartheid."[20] The walkout of the Ivory Coast and its subsequent declaration that it would not be bound by the resolution were more effective in isolating Houphouet-Boigny than in changing OAU policy. But the greatest effectiveness of "dialogue" was the opportunity it gave to bury the recognition issue.

REFLECTIONS

In some respects, the temporary impasse over recognition of the Amin government mirrored the acrimonious debate of January 1963 concerning leadership succession in Togo. President Sylvanus Olympio was assassinated by members of the armed forces, who then invited his former opponents to form a new government. The condemnations of the Togolese soldiers resembled those directed against Amin eight years later; Toure, for example, called the death of Olympio "the tragic consequence of a hideous plot knowingly hatched from outside with which the Togolese people had absolutely no connection."[21] Toure believed the blame could be attributed to extra-Togo influences — not to the real cause of the assassination, Olympio's unwillingness to accede to the demands of job-seeking veterans.

The predecessor of the OAU, the Inter-African and Malagasy States Organization (usually known as the Monrovia Group), convened in emergency session to consider the implications of the killing. A six-part resolution called for: (1) a five-state mission to help clear up circumstances surrounding the assassination, (2) free and democratic elections in Togo, (3) prosecution of those accused of a crime, (4) continued respect for the right of asylum of political refugees, (5) preparation of a draft mutual security treaty to enable collective action against the "danger of internal subversion and foreign aggression which is threatening the territorial integrity and the national independence of all member states," and (6) consideration by the heads of state of breaking diplomatic relations with countries encouraging internal subversion elsewhere.[22] Most of the recommendations were filed, not implemented. The only direct offshoot was the "unreserved condemnation" of political assassination in the OAU Charter. The military-installed government of Togo weathered its brief ostracism and took its place in international groupings.

The Charter of the Organization of African Unity does not incorporate significant mechanisms with which to probe into domestic changes of regime. The OAU does not accredit ambassadors to its members, nor has it a credentials committee (the Assembly of Heads of State and Government serves in this role). The OAU does not furnish economic assistance that could be suspended as a sign of displeasure; there is no provision for expulsion of members, even for nonpayment of dues (the Charter merely notes that member states agree to pay "regularly"). Refusal to seat a delegation, as occurred in the sixteenth session of the Council of Ministers, does not accord with any explicit provision of the Charter.

The roots of the OAU in the Organization of American States (OAS) help explain these gaps. Neither the Rio Treaty nor the OAS Charter provides for expulsion—an absence that led to an acute crisis in the OAS in the early 1960s. Closer Cuban ties with the Soviet Union and Cuban support for guerrilla movements elsewhere in Latin America resulted in efforts to remove Cuba from the OAS. The initiative stemmed from Peru and Colombia, and posed delicate diplomatic problems for the United States.

At the Punta del Este conference of January 1962, the U.S. Secretary of State recommended that the OAS declare Cuban ties with the Sino-Soviet bloc "an ever present and common danger" to hemispheric peace, and accordingly "incompatible" with the inter-American system; he proposed that Cuba be excluded from participating in the OAS and that hemispheric states halt trade with Cuba. The choice of words—incompatibility, exclusion—represents expulsion of the present Cuban regime in more polite words. A resolution declaring such "incompatibility" was passed by a bare two-thirds majority (14-1-6), and Cuba was thereby removed from the OAS. Jerome Slater has aptly noted that these steps "amounted to precious little indeed" in either tightening pressures against Castro or hastening his downfall.[23] The inability of the OAS to effect changes in Cuban policy, even granted the strength of the United States, should give pause to those who feel a regional organization can effectively intervene in domestic affairs.*

---

*This is prior to the diplomatic and political moves undertaken within the OAS without indicating basic trends toward ending the isolation of Castro's Cuba in the Americas.

113

The Cuban issue in the OAS and the Ugandan issue in the OAU point to a basic problem of regional organizations. They derive much of their authority, moral and political, from their claim to represent all states in the particular area. Regional organizations thus differ in kind from organizations founded either for technical or humanitarian ends, such as the United Postal Union (UPU) and the United Nations Educational, Scientific, and Cultural Organization (UNESCO) or for what may be loosely deemed ideological and military ends, such as NATO and the Warsaw Pact Group. The effort to achieve and maintain unanimity within a regional organization necessitates the quest for the highest common denominator of agreement—which may rest at a fairly low level of specificity.

Agreement on two tenets of international conduct marks the OAU. At least until the "dialogue" proposal, the OAU maintained relatively high agreement regarding the achievement of majority rule in southern Africa. The second principle of the OAU has been protection of domestic jurisdiction. The Ugandan crisis resulted from attacks on this latter principle. Inasmuch as close to a score of African states have experienced successful military intervention without complaint from the OAU, the exclusion of the Amin delegation from the Council of Ministers represented both a reversal of a fairly solidly entrenched set of practices and a challenge to a fundamental OAU principle.

The structure and ethos of the OAU make temporizing the most expedient method of treating controversial issues. This tendency is by no means new. As John Markakis noted early in the OAU's history, "controversial issues are skirted, or, if broached openly, they elude determination."[24] The "dialogue" proposal was not avoided, to be certain. However, Houphouet-Boigny's suggestion was supported by only a handful of states (Colin Legum deems them the "dialogue club").[25] Houphouet had not participated extensively in OAU affairs, having boycotted the 1965 summit, and his representative's withdrawal from the Council of Ministers in the resumed sixteenth session had little impact. The debate over acceptance of the Amin delegation, by contrast, was far more divisive, since the key proponents of excluding it held major posts in the OAU. The debate on Uganda was carried out behind closed doors, not in public as was the "dialogue" debate, and indirect measure of its divisiveness. The intense opposition of Arteh, Kaunda, and Nyerere, noted earlier, was sufficient to make the issue controversial, and to make temporizing the solution.

The crisis was resolved in the only way possible: recognition of Amin's fait accompli. The OAU lacks the organizational desire and constitutional prerogative to expel a member. Domestic jurisdiction represented a fundamental principle when the OAU was created, and a decade of experience has not diminished its significance.

114

Military intervention represents a political fact of life in contemporary Africa. To single out a regime for special attention could set a precedent many governments might prefer to avoid. A regional organization, whose strengths derive primarily from its ability to speak for all members, cannot effectively utilize exclusion as an operating principle. The costs of unanimity are diffuseness and principles of sweeping generality.

With the exception of the sanguinary Nigerian civil war, in which the OAU set up a six-member Consultative Committee, the OAU has shied away from involvement in domestic conflict within member states. "Respect for the sovereignty and territorial integrity of each State" can be expressed as support for the incumbent government and unwillingness (as in Burundi, Chad, Ethiopia/Eritrea, and Sudan) to become embroiled in internal blood-letting. The international repercussions of domestic conflicts have resulted in occasional debates within the OAU. However, the OAU has proven far more effective in alleviating interstate tensions than intrastate disputes. Its Commission of Mediation, Conciliation and Arbitration is specifically limited to examination "over disputes between States only" (Article 12), and successes in the peaceful settlement of disputes can perhaps better be credited to the prestige and sagacity of senior heads of state, such as Kenyatta or Haile Selassie, than to the existence of the Commission.

A linear projection provides the safest form of prognostication. The strong rebuff to the "dialogue" proposal indicates no substantial diminution of the OAU's commitment to majority rule in southern Africa. Acquiescence in the Ugandan change of regime added further weight to the OAU's commitment to domestic jurisdiction.

The two basic principles of the OAU were thus tested, and confirmed, in 1971. Sovereignty over internal affairs remains a cornerstone of the OAU. Recognition of a government that has gained control through extraconstitutional means may not be pleasant, but it cannot be avoided by regional organizations.

NOTES

1. Joseph S. Nye, Jr., Pan-Africanism and East African Integration (Cambridge, Mass.: Harvard University Press, 1965), pp. 196-98.

2. A Milton Obote, Myths and Realities—A Letter to a London Friend (Kampala: African Publishers, 1968), p. 30; quoted in James H. Mittelman, "The Uganda Coup and the Internationalization of Political Violence," Munger Africana Library Notes 14 (Pasadena, Calif., 1972): p. 2.

3. According to the Charter, "In our Move to the Left strategy, we affirm that the guiding economic principle will be that the means

of production and distribution must be in the hands of the people as a whole. The fullfilment of this principle may involve nationalisation of enterprises privately owned." Cited in Africa Research Bulletin (Economic, Financial, and Technical Series) 8, no. 9 (31 October 1969): 1481C.

4. Africa Research Bulletin (Political, Social and Cultural Series) 7, no. 7 (15 August 1970): 1824A.

5. Ibid., p. 1824B.

6. Africa Research Bulletin (Political, Social and Cultural Series) 8, no. 1 (15 February 1971): 1967C.

7. Amin's statement shocked many, perhaps most strongly the Sudanese government. He said: "Everybody is talking of South Africa but we have another South Africa in Southern Sudan where Catholics and Protestants are not allowed to go to Church. When worshippers went to Church in [the] Southern Sudan, people with machine guns killed them and burned their houses. This must be solved first before arms to South Africa." Uganda Argus, 24 February 1971, quoted in Mittelman, op. cit., p. 21 (erroneously dated as 24 February 1970).

8. Africa Research Bulletin (Political, Social and Cultural Series) 8, no. 1 (15 February 1971): 1994A.

9. Michael F. Lofchie, "The Uganda Coup—Class Action by the Military," Journal of Modern African Studies 10, no. 1 (May 1972): 25; John D. Chick, "Class Conflict and Military Intervention in Uganda," ibid. 10, no. 4 (December 1972): 634-37; Samuel Decalo, "Military Coups and Military Regimes in Africa," ibid. 11, no. 1 (March 1973): 105-27; James H. Mittelman, "The Anatomy of a Coup: Uganda, 1971," Africa Quarterly 11, no. 3 (October-December 1971).

10. Colin Legum, Africa Contemporary Record: Annual Survey and Documents 1970-1971 (London: Rex Collings, 1971), pp. B369-70.

11. Ibid., p. C258.

12. Colin Legum, Africa Contemporary Record: Annual Survey and Documents 1971-72 (New York: Africana Publishing Corporation, 1972), pp. C61-64.

13. Decalo cites Amin's "involvement in the death of Brigadier P. Y. Okoya in January 1970, the Auditor General's report regarding the possible misuse of defense funds, a long history of friction with Obote, and Amin's contempt for the National Service, the General Service Unit, and the Common Man's Charter." See Decalo, op. cit., p. 112.

14. Mittelman, "The Uganda Coup," op. cit., passim.

15. Ibid., p. 21.

16. Africa Research Bulletin (Political, Social and Cultural Series) 8, no. 2 (15 March 1971): 2008A.

17. Africa Research Bulletin (Political, Social and Cultural Series) 8, no. 6 (15 July 1971): 2125C.

18. Mittelman, "The Uganda Coup," op. cit., p. 30.

19. Legum, Africa Contemporary Record 1971-72, op. cit. p. B226.

20. Africa Research Bulletin (Political, Social and Cultural Series) 8, no. 6 (15 July 1971): 2127A.

21. Helen Kitchen, "Filling the Togo Vacuum," Africa Report 8, no. 2 (February 1963): 8.

22. Ibid., p. 10.

23. Jerome Slater, The OAS and United States Foreign Policy (Columbus: Ohio State University Press, 1967), p. 158.

24. John Markakis, "The Organization of African Unity: A Progress Report," Journal of Modern African Studies 4, no. 2 (October 1966): 149.

25. Legum, Africa Contemporary Record 1971-72, op. cit., p. A71.

6

AN ANALYSIS OF
OAU'S EFFECTIVENESS
AT REGIONAL
COLLECTIVE DEFENSE

B. David Meyers

INTRODUCTION

The founding of the Organization of African Unity in May 1963 ended more than two years of rivalry among short-lived African regional organizations best known by the cities in which they were established—Brazzaville, Casablanca, and Monrovia. The organization was formed despite severe differences among its members on a wide range of issues. It could be formed under such circumstances only because of agreement that it was not intended as a supranational body but rather as a loose association based on voluntary cooperation.[1]

At the OAU's founding conference, the participating heads of state showed considerable awareness regarding the various security concerns with which an inclusive African regional organization would have to concern itself. Consideration was given to such potential problems as internal disruptions, border disputes, allegations of subversion by neighboring states, threats of extraregional aggression, and the need for collective action against the remaining colonial holdings. Articles 2 and 3 of the OAU Charter—which define the OAU's goals and the principles its members adhere to—make clear that the OAU was intended to assist members both in the peaceful settlement of intraregional conflict and in defense against extraregional aggressors. The OAU is thus comparable to the Organization of American States and the League of Arab States in having both internally and externally oriented security concerns.

The author wishes to express his appreciation to Rachel Arthur for her assistance, and to the Research Council of the University of North Carolina at Greensboro for support.

During recent years there has been renewed interest in regional conflict management on the part of both scholars and policy makers. The high costs accruing to the United States from participation in the Vietnam war have been of particular importance in promoting consideration of regionalism as an alternative to unilateral action by the major powers. In 1966, President Lyndon Johnson explicitly stated this idea: "Our purpose in promoting a world of regional partnerships is not without self-interest. For as they grow in strength inside a strong United Nations, we can look forward to a decline in the burden that America has to bear in this generation."[2] Subsequently, President Nixon stated that "it is no longer natural or possible . . . to argue that security or development around the globe is primarily America's concern. The defense and progress of other countries must be first their responsibility and second, a regional responsibility."[3] Such interest makes this an auspicious time to analyze the efficacy of existing regional organizations in order to determine if such institutions have been able to assist in the preservation of international security.

Most of the scholarly research concerning the activities of multipurpose regional organizations such as the OAS and OAU has focused attention on their efforts toward the peaceful settlement of conflicts among members.[4] There has been almost no attention to their efforts to assist in defense against extraregional aggressors. The intention of this chapter is to examine the collective defense activities undertaken by the Organization of African Unity. The responses of the OAU, and of its individual members, to cases of extraregional aggression will then be used to test claims concerning collective defense that have been made by advocates of regionalism.

DIFFICULT BEGINNINGS: THE PROBLEMS OF INSTITUTION BUILDING

Article 2 of the Charter of the Organization of African Unity states that among the purposes for which the members formed the organization was "To defend their sovereignty, their territorial integrity and independence." In order to bring this about, the heads of state agreed that "Cooperation for defence and security" was necessary. Such provisions for collective defense, the only ones found within the Charter, are weak and inexplicit when compared with those of the OAS and the Arab League. The Charter of the OAS, for example, states that an act of aggression against one American state is to be considered an act of aggression against all. Collective responses to such aggressions are detailed in both the OAS Charter and the Inter-American Treaty of Reciprocal Assistance. Arab League documents are highly similar.

119

The OAU was not able to draft equivalent agreements for its members because of the considerable differences in outlook on questions of defense that they exhibited. At the Addis Ababa meeting, there was considerably more expression of concern with the possibility of interference of one African state in the internal affairs of another than with the threat of interference by extraregional actors. Since the majority of the assembled states enjoyed good relations with their former metropolis and were dependent upon it for their defense, extra-African aggression was considered unlikely. Of more immediate concern to them were the threats offered by other, more powerful African states—exemplified by charges of Ghana's involvement in the coup in Togo and Morocco's claim to Mauritania.

Similarly, the OAU Charter says very little about specialized institutions for security concerns. At the founding conference, Ghanaian President Kwame Nkrumah proposed the creation of a "Common Defence System with an African High Command to insure the stability and security of Africa."[5] The Ethiopian draft charter proposed a more modest Defense Board composed of each member's Chief of Staff and empowered to make recommendations to the Assembly of Heads of State. There was little support for either of these proposals as some states mistrusted the intentions of others and feared any sharing of military information. Many states were satisfied with their existing defense arrangements; others simply rejected any compromise of their sovereignty. Rather than risk potentially acrimonious debate and division, the only specialized defense structure that was established was a Defense Commission, one of five specialized commissions responsible to the Council of Ministers. The Charter said nothing about its purpose or responsibilities, deliberately leaving these to be worked out at some future time.

Two meetings were held by the Defense Commission during the first sixteen months following the OAU's founding. If nothing else, they demonstrated the difficulty of reaching any more than the most minimal agreement on security issues. The first meeting of the Defense Commission was intended primarily to define its responsibilities and purpose. No suggestion that involved the creation of any permanent structures received support from more than a handful of the assembled African defense ministers. It was agreed only that the Commission would serve as an "organ of consultation, preparation and recommendation for the collective and/or self-defence of the Member States against any act or threat of aggression."[6]

General unwillingness to institutionalize collective defense, i.e., to establish forces and/or permanent advisory and coordinating bodies, continued to be seen during the following years. In February 1965, the Defense Commission recommended the establishment of an African Defense Organization (ADO) that would have been entirely voluntary and would not have compromised national sovereignty. States that chose to participate could designate forces for ADO service. These forces would only be called upon at the request of a member state, with the approval of the donor state and of the Council of Ministers.[7] This proposal was rejected by the Council of Ministers in March 1965 and by the Assembly of Heads of State and Government in October of that year. The Defense Commission did not meet again for more than five years, and during that period tasks that might logically have been assigned to it were delegated elsewhere.

In 1967, the Organization of African Unity was no better prepared to assist its members in defense against aggression than it had been at its founding. The Israeli occupation of Egypt's Sinai Peninsula and the capture by mercenaries of the city of Bukavu, Zaire (formerly the Democratic Republic of the Congo), presented the organization with two cases of extraregional aggression. On both occasions, African reactions were limited and indecisive.

LIMITED COLLECTIVE RESPONSES: SINAI, BUKAVU, AND CONAKRY

Israeli Occupation of the Sinai

As a result of the war of June 1967, Israeli troops occupied substantial territory belonging to Egypt. At the U.N. emergency session convened to discuss the war, African members divided sharply on most of the major roll call votes. Less than 20 percent of sub-Saharan Africa's votes were pro-Arab, while over 40 percent were pro-Israel.[8]

Although one of the purposes of the OAU is the defense of members against external aggression, the organization has proven unable to initiate collective action on behalf of Egypt. When Somalia requested that an extraordinary session of the Council of Ministers be convened, few sub-Saharan states supported the request and the necessary quorum was not obtained. A number of African states declared that they did not consider the conflict an African concern.

The occupation of Sinai was not discussed within the OAU until the regularly scheduled 1967 summit meetings. There, a concerted Arab effort for a strong resolution of support for Egypt was defeated. Instead, the Assembly passed a "Declaration" that expressed the sense of the membership but contained no operative paragraphs. This non-committal declaration reaffirmed respect for territorial integrity, spoke of sympathy for Egypt, and suggested that the African states would continue to work through the United Nations to secure the evacuation of foreign military forces.[9]

121

During the years 1968-71, Arab-African leaders continued their efforts to use the OAU on Egypt's behalf. There was continued resistance from states favorably disposed toward Israel. The final resolutions adopted at each OAU meeting did little more than continue to express support for decisions made at the United Nations. During this period, only two non-Arab states, Somalia and Guinea, offered material assistance to Egypt. Israel continued trade and normal diplomatic relations with most of sub-Saharan Africa.

At the 1971 Summit Conference, the heads of state adopted a new initiative. A special Peace Committee was established to try to initiate dialogue between the protagonists and improve the general atmosphere in the Middle East.[10] The OAU was unsuccessful in these efforts as it was unable to find a compromise between the Egyptian demand for immediate withdrawal and the Israeli insistence upon negotiations first.

In 1972, the Assembly of Heads of State passed a resolution that explicitly denounced Israel and called for withdrawal from all Arab lands. For the first time, reference was made to the section of the OAU Charter that lists defense of territorial integrity among the OAU's purposes. All members were asked "to give Egypt every assistance."[11] There is little evidence that this stronger resolution had substantial effect. Although a handful of OAU members broke relations with Israel, aid to Egypt was not increased. At the 1973 summit meetings, proposals by Libya calling for direct action against Israel were defeated. Commitment to direct action was again postponed, with the adoption of a resolution calling on African states "to consider taking collective or individual steps . . . against Israel should that country persist in its refusal to evacuate occupied Arab territories."[12]

Despite the continued Israeli occupation of the Sinai, the majority of the African states wished to keep the OAU's role limited. A number of African states have had excellent relations with Israel since independence. Many have not had as good relations with Egypt.* Such states would perceive Egypt, rather than Israel, as a threat to their own security. Other states have had limited contact with Egypt and do not consider that state's conflict with Israel as being of African concern. For these reasons, many OAU members did not wish to

---

*Ethiopia and Zaire have both, for example, received military assistance from Israel. Both have had strained relations with Egypt (Ethiopia because of Egyptian support of Somalia and the Eritrean Liberation Front, Congo because of assistance given by Egypt to Gbenye's Conseil National de Liberation).

extend collective security assistance to Egypt or to involve themselves or the OAU in what was seen as a Middle Eastern conflict.

Thus, for six years the Organization of African Unity failed to respond to the occupation of a member's territory by an extraregional state. During this period, Egypt's most important source of assistance was the Soviet Union. During the years 1955-67, Egypt was the largest recipient of Soviet military aid, getting an estimated total of $1.5 billion worth of equipment.[13] In the first sixteen months following the war, Egypt received a further $2.2 billion in military assistance from the USSR and its East European allies.[14] This increased reliance on one of the major cold war powers was regrettable, as one of the prime purposes for establishing regional organizations is to forestall intrusion by the superpowers.

The Seizure of Bukavu by Mercenaries

The seizure of the city of Bukavu by mercenaries, like the occupation of Sinai, demonstrated the OAU's weaknesses in cases of external aggression. When General Mobutu took over the political leadership of the Congo in November 1965, he inherited the mercenary soldiers who had served Tshombe and Kasavubu. By the spring of 1967, most of the mercenary units had been disbanded and their members expelled from Congo. On 5 July 1967, the remaining mercenaries, supported by units of Katangese militia, seized the city of Bukavu. A military deadlock destined to last for about four months had developed by the end of the first week of the crisis.

In his first public statement, Mobutu labeled the problem as "foreign aggression."[15] This charge became increasingly justified as Portugal and Rhodesia allowed their territory to be used for activities in support of the mercenaries. Mobutu asked the OAU Secretariat to inform all African states of the aggression and ask that they make military forces available for use against the occupied areas. Although a number of African states sent expressions of support, only Ethiopia sent military assistance.

The major reason for this lack of aid was that available military resources were extremely limited. The states immediately bordering Congo had very small armies and extremely limited transportation capabilities. With the exception of Ethiopia, the African states with the necessary logistics capabilities to deliver men or material to Congo did not have such resources to spare at the time of Mobutu's request. Nigeria and Sudan were both involved in civil wars; Egypt, independent Africa's most powerful state, had just suffered great military losses as a result of the June 1967 war with Israel.

Mobutu was considerably more successful in the response given his request for assistance from the United States. At the order of President Johnson, American aircraft and pilots were used to transport elements of the Congolese Army into the Bukauvu area. Although criticism from segments of Congress and the American public forced some of this activity to be curtailed, the United States remained the Congo's major source of military assistance throughout the crisis.

Congo also sought action through the United Nations. On 10 July, the Security Council asked all states not to allow their territory to be used for planning moves against Congo or for the recruitment, training, or transit of mercenaries.[16] At a later date, the Security Council specifically condemned Portugal for allowing Angola to be used as a base for attacks on Congo.[17]

When the OAU met in its regularly scheduled session in September, Mobutu again asked for African aid in ridding Congo of the mercenaries. At his request, the Assembly passed a resolution that guaranteed the mercenaries a safe exit from Africa only if they would leave Congo immediately. If, however, the mercenaries did not evacuate peacefully all African states pledged to assist Congo in removing them by military force.[18]

The mercenaries rejected this offer of safe exit and announced that they would remain in Bukavu until they had effected Mobutu's ouster. Despite the OAU resolution, no further African assistance was forthcoming. Not until early November was the Congolese Army able to force an evacuation of the occupied city.[19]

The prolonged occupation of Bukavu again showed that the OAU was not an effective collective defense organization. When the mercenaries defied the OAU ultimatum, the member states did not send assistance to assure a forceful end to the crisis and maintain their own credibility. Mobutu's request for African military assistance was answered only by Ethiopia. Thus, Congo, like Egypt, was forced to increase its dependence on a cold war superpower.

The Portugese Invasion of Conakry

In September 1968, in response to a series of armed incidents along the borders of independent and colonial Africa, the Council of Ministers resolved that any aggression by Rhodesia, South Africa, or Portugal would be regarded as an attack upon all OAU members.[20] Despite continued incidents, no further decisions were forthcoming until August 1970, when the Council recommended that the Defense Commission be reactivated in order to consider threats of aggression from the colonial areas. This desire to involve the organization in the defense of members threatened by the colonialist-racist powers was augmented by the Portuguese attack on Guinea.

On the night of 22 November 1970, Guinea's capital, Conakry, was invaded from the sea by 250 to 300 uniformed, armed men. The invaders destroyed the city's power station and attacked President Toure's summer villa and the headquarters of the African Independence Party of Guinea and Cape Verde (PAIGC). The majority of the at-tackers were killed in the fighting or taken prisoner; the remainder retreated to their boats within the first 24 hours. The attempted invasion seems to have been a joint venture of Guinean dissidents and Portuguese African soldiers from neighboring Guinea-Bissau; material assistance and officers were provided by Portugal.[21] The intended purpose seems to have been to initiate the overthrow of the Toure government and to deal a serious blow to PAIGC.

On the night of the attempted invasion, Toure appealed to the United Nations for immediate intervention by U.N. airborne troops.[22] When the Security Council met the following day, some members were not convinced by the Guinean delegate's description of events.[23] Rather than sending forces, the Council established a fact-finding mission to study the situation. Toure announced that this was an "inadequate response."[24]

In contrast to the Security Council's response, a number of individual states demonstrated an immediate willingness to aid Guinea. The People's Republic of China announced that it would furnish $10 million to assist the Guinean government.[25] A number of African states sent messages of support to Conakry, and a few offered military assistance. Among those offering military aid were Egypt and Nigeria, both of which had large, experienced armies. As the invaders did not make a second attack, these troops were never called upon.

With Toure's approval, Emperor Haile Selassie called for an emergency meeting of the OAU Council of Ministers and, concurrently, of the Defense Commission. For the latter institution, this would be the first meeting in five years. The Council of Ministers asked all member states to provide assistance to Guinea, both directly and through a special fund to be set up by the OAU.[26] In order that Africa be better prepared to respond to any future aggression, the Defense Commission was called upon "to study ways and means of establishing an adequate and speedy defence of African States."[27]

The widespread consensus that had been exhibited at the extra-ordinary meeting was short-lived; once again, the OAU members proved unwilling and/or unable to back their words with deeds. Despite their agreement at the special meeting, few, if any, states sent financial or other material assistance to Guinea. Within a short time, Toure charged that Senegal and Ivory Coast were harboring and assisting persons who had been involved in the invasion attempt and had broken diplomatic relations with these two neighboring states.[28] These intra-African conflicts disrupted nascent efforts to increase military cooperation among the independent African states.

The OAU members have continued to be cautious, if not reluctant, concerning the creation of institutions for collective defense. More than one-fourth of the OAU membership did not send representatives to the December 1971 meeting of the Defense Commission, where alternative proposals concerning the creation of a high command were discussed. The recommendation coming from this meeting of the Defense Commission—that proximate states create local alliance systems with common information and coordination being provided by an office to be established within the Secretariat—was not accepted by the Assembly of Heads of State. Instead, there was to be a year's delay while a more detailed plan was prepared.

Impatient with this unwillingness to act, a few African states have already made bilateral military agreements with neighbors.[29] The majority of members, however, have made no major attempts to institute military cooperation. Similarly, cases of aggression have been met by words but not by deeds. In June 1972, following a Portuguese attack on a Senegalese village, the Council of Ministers recommended that members put military units and war material at the disposal of states that were victims of such aggression.[30] There is no evidence that any such assistance has been rendered. Thus, in May 1973, at the end of its first decade of existence, the OAU was little better able to assist members against external aggression than it had been at its founding.

EVALUATING AFRICAN REGIONAL
COLLECTIVE DEFENSE

The underlying assumption of almost all regionalist ideas is that states in geographic propinquity are better able to cooperate than are states some distance from one another. It is believed that the conditions found in a particular area of the earth's surface give the nations located there a certain distinct, and unique, community of interest. Cooperation is thought more likely to be evidenced in such a limited area because of the greater cultural, social, and political homogeneity to be found there. According to regionalist advocates, this should lead to the development of highly effective, separate, international organizations based on clearly evident bonds of mutuality.[31]

Working from this assumption, proponents of regional organizations have presented a number of more specific claims concerning the advantages of such organizations in conflict management. This study of the OAU's effectiveness at regional collective defense provides material for testing four of these claims:

1. Local states are more likely to be concerned with aggression against a neighbor than are states located at some distance.

2. Neighboring states are better able to aid one another because geographic propinquity facilitates the delivery of material assistance.

3. Regional organizations can serve their members' defense if appeals to the United Nations prove futile.

4. The existence of regional organizations with the capability of assisting members' defense decreases the probability of involvement by the world powers.[32]

The first of these propositions concerns the attitudes of national leaders to situations of aggression against proximate states. It is difficult to ascertain with any high degree of certainty whether national leaders are concerned with aggression against other states. Individuals may hold such attitudes but be unable to provide material demonstration of their concern. Evidence of at least minimal concern might be identified by the public statements of national leaders and the votes of their representatives in the United Nations. Such expressions of concern and votes in international organizations are useful indicators since they are usually part of the public record and they serve to demonstrate concern without necessitating the outlay of scarce resources.

This minimal test suggests that there was very widespread African concern with the invasion of Guinea and the mercenaries' occupation of Bukavu. Guinea received messages of solidarity and support from most OAU members, including immediate neighbors with whom relations had been strained.[33] All OAU members attended the emergency meeting of the Council of Ministers, where resolutions condemning Portugal and promising assistance to Guinea were unanimously adopted. Concern with the attempted invasion was not as widespread outside Africa. In the U.N. Security Council, for example, France, Spain, the United Kingdom, and the United States abstained on an Afro-Asian resolution that condemned Portugal and demanded that compensation be paid to Guinea.

Similarly, African statesmen demonstrated more concern with the occupation of Bukavu than did non-Africans. Messages expressing widespread regional support were received by Mobutu,[34] and all but one OAU member attended the summit meetings, held in Congo, where the resolution concerning the mercenaries was passed unanimously. With the exception of the United States, few extra-African states demonstrated considerable interest in the conflict.

The Israeli occupation of the Sinai is different from the above cases as unified African concern for the victim was not forthcoming. Before the outbreak of the June 1967 war, a number of African states had maintained friendly relations with both Israel and Egypt. Rather than take positions, a number of these states maintained an official policy of silence and abstention on General Assembly resolutions;

127

other non-Arab African states simply voted pro-Israel.[35] The splits and ambivalence among African states were reflected in the inability to attain a quorum for an emergency meeting of the OAU and in the general unwillingness to commit the OAU to strong positions, to say nothing of action, on behalf of Egypt. In contrast, the concern of the world powers was clear, with that of the Soviet Union being particularly important as it was manifested in material assistance.

The African data, then, provide only limited support for the proposition that concern will be greatest within the region. There was at least minimal-level concern throughout Africa following the aggressions of the mercenaries and the Portuguese, but not on the Israeli occupation of Sinai. This latter case may identify one of the limitations of Africa's sense of continental community, as many states saw the conflict as a Middle Eastern or Arab issue rather than an African one. Historically, one of the divisions among African states has been that between "Arab" and "black" Africa. The sense of community between these two groupings may not be sufficient to create the common concern with aggression that regionalists would expect.

The second proposition, that neighboring states are better able to aid one another because of advantages of geographic propinquity, may be invalidated by the data collected in this study. The ability of the United States and the Soviet Union to respond to acts anywhere on the globe, together with the material weaknesses of the African states, negate this proposition. African states lack substantial military resources and the logistic capabilities to transport men and weapons to neighbors who may be in need. African railroads do not form a continuous network, and air transport capacities are extremely limited. The two world powers have not only men and material available in large quantities but also the logistic capabilities to deliver them quickly to potential recipients. Technology and the abundance of resources available to the superpowers may completely outweigh the advantages of proximity. This was clearly evidenced in American assistance to Congo and the Soviet Union's extensive aid to Egypt.

The third regionalist proposition suggests that such organizations can aid their members' defense if appeals to the United Nations prove futile. The Sinai and Bukavu cases cast considerable doubt on the ability of the OAU to backstop the United Nations. In the former case, the United Nations remained the most important international organization, with the OAU unable to muster strong support for Egypt and unsuccessful in its efforts to initiate negotiations between the protagonists. The same African states that failed to support Egypt at the United Nations also failed to do so in the OAU forums. Congo tried to utilize both the United Nations and OAU while the mercenaries were in Bukavu. Although both organizations passed resolutions favorable to the Congo, neither proved useful in ending the mercenaries' activities.

128

It is possible to speculate that, had events followed a different course, the OAU might have proven useful to Guinea following the failure to get military assistance from the United Nations. Although Guinea proved able to defeat the attempted invasion without assistance, it is believed that Egyptian and Nigerian troops were prepared to intervene if needed. However, the fact remains that in the aftermath of the invasion the African states did not send assistance to Guinea and remained unable to create structures to assist efforts at collective defense.

The final proposition is that the existence of regional organizations with the capability of assisting members' defense decreases the probability of involvement by the world powers. The evidence from this study does not support that claim. In the three cases examined, the OAU did not prove an effective instrument for collective defense and the aggressed-upon states had to increase their dependence on assistance furnished by the major cold war powers. The OAU proved unable to assist its members, and Egypt became increasingly reliant on the Soviet Union, and Congo on the United States. The Guinea case is essentially similar; the largest supplier of assistance was the People's Republic of China. The OAU's effectiveness at insulating intraregional conflicts from intervention by the major powers[36] is not seen in these cases of extraregional aggression.

These four propositions concerning the ability of a regional organization to assist members against extraregional aggression are highly interdependent. Clearly, a regional organization cannot back-stop the United Nations unless its members have the willingness and ability (i.e., desire and resources) to assist in one another's defense. And clearly avoidance of increased reliance on the world powers will have low priority until the effectiveness of the machinery for regional collective defense is substantially increased. Although generalization from the examination of a limited number of cases has obvious limitations, it is clear that the evidence currently available does not support the regionalist propositions.

Lack of mutual trust and shared interests, the low level of African military resources, and the continued availability of extraregional sources of assistance have all contributed to the extremely limited cooperation manifested among OAU members on issues related to collective defense. To date, it remains extremely difficult to identify any contribution the OAU has made to assist members that have been the victims of aggression or to increase the security of the African states against future attacks.

Among the reasons for the lack of military cooperation has been the general shortage of resources available to most African states. Most African armies are small and are particularly deficient in logistic capabilities, especially air transport. This, of and in itself, makes

129

interstate cooperation difficult. With the end to the civil wars in Nigeria and Sudan and the continued growth of the military strength of Zaire and Egypt, it is possible that in the foreseeable future there may be a number of potential military donor states available to OAU members.

The availability of extraregional sources of assistance has helped African states at their moments of need and has reduced any perception of necessity to establish meaningful collective security arrangements at the regional level. A number of African states, especially the former French sub-Saharan colonies, have retained security treaties with the former colonial power and regard these agreements as the basis of their national security. To such states, treaties with powers such as France may seem considerably better policy than attempts to develop military cooperation within the region. Africa is not currently a security community,[37] a region within which it may be assumed that differences between states will be settled peacefully. Lacking such a condition, it is not surprising that many smaller states are hesitant to join in any agreement that might lead to some abrogation of total control over national armed forces and would involve the sharing of military secrets. For smaller states that might feel threatened by neighbors, treaties with extraregional powers—especially the former metropolis, which has already proved its intentions by granting independence—are attractive alternatives to any proposal for instituting regional collective security.

The lack of a strong identification as a community has hurt attempts at instituting military cooperation not only because of lack of trust between members but also because the African states have often not been in agreement on the identity of enemies. The clearest example of this comes in the occupation of the Sinai. Not only were the Israeli actions in Egypt seen as of little concern by many African states but some of them had actually enjoyed better and closer relations with Israel than with their fellow organization member.

Although regional organizations such as the OAU are intended to perform both internal and external security tasks, it may be that these two responsibilities are not compatible. The fact that Africa is not a security community presents the OAU with its intraregional conflict management tasks. And the lack of such community may also limit the willingness of members to institute military cooperation for such purposes as collective defense.

For all these reasons, the OAU members have not been successful at instituting collective security cooperation during the period under examination. Although more military resources may be available in Africa in the foreseeable future, it nevertheless seems unlikely that major progress will be made toward extensive security cooperation because of all of the other obstacles.

130

NOTES

1. The limitations of the OAU's authority and coercive power are analyzed in Yashpal Tandon, "The Organization of African Unity," The Round Table 246 (April 1972): 221-30.

2. President Lyndon Johnson, "Four Fundamental Facts of Our Foreign Policy," Department of State Bulletin 55, no. 1422 (26 September 1966): 453 (address made at Lancaster, Ohio, 5 September 1966).

3. President Richard Nixon, U.S. Foreign Policy for the 1970's: Building for Peace, A Report to the Congress by Richard Nixon, President of the United States, 25 February 1971, p. 14.

4. See, for example, Berhanykun Andemicael, Peaceful Settlement Among African States: Roles of the United Nations and the Organization of African Unity, UNITAR PS No. 5 (1972); B. David Meyers, "Intraregional Conflict Management by the Organization of African Unity," International Organization 28 (Summer 1974); J. S. Nye, Peace in Parts: Integration and Conflict in Regional Organizations (Boston: Little, Brown, 1971), Chapter 5.

5. Kwame Nkrumah, "A Union Government for a United Africa," Addis Ababa Summit, 1963 (Addis Ababa, Ethiopia: Publications and Foreign Language Press Department, Ministry of Information, 1963), p. 47.

6. OAU Review 1, no. 1 (May 1964): 6.

7. Jon Woronoff, Organizing African Unity (Metuchen, N.J.: Scarecrow Press, 1970), pp. 559-60.

8. Fouad Ajami and Martin H. Sours, "Israel and Sub-Saharan Africa: A Study of Interaction," African Studies Review 12, no. 3 (December 1970): 412.

9. AHG/St. 2 (IV).

10. For further information, see Susan Aurelia Gitelson, "The OAU Mission and the Middle East Conflict," International Organization 27 (Summer 1973): 413-19.

11. AHG/Res. 67 (IX).

12. Africa Research Bulletin, May 1973, p. 2850.

13. U.S. Department of State, Director of Intelligence and Research, Communist Governments and Developing Nations: Aid and Trade in 1967, Research Memorandum, RSE-120 (14 August 1968), p. 6.

14. T. N. Dupoy, The Almanac of World Military Power (Dunn Loring, Virginia: T. N. Dupoy, 1970), p. 174.

15. The New York Times, 6 July 1967.

16. The New York Times, 11 July 1967.

17. The New York Times, 16 November 1967.

18. AHG/Res. 49 (IV).

19. The mercenaries crossed the border into Rwanda and accepted a Red Cross offer of asylum. This caused a dispute between Congo and Rwanda, which the OAU was unable to deal with. For further information, see Andemicael, op. cit., pp. 27-30.

20. Africa Research Bulletin, September 1968, p. 1173.

21. For further information, see Margarita Dobert, "Who Invaded Guinea?" Africa Report 16 (March 1971): 17.

22. Africa Research Bulletin, November 1970, p. 1933.

23. Ibid., p. 1934.

24. Ibid., p. 1935.

25. Ibid., p. 1934.

26. Africa Research Bulletin, December 1970, p. 1948.

27. Ibid.

28. For further information on Guinea's conflicts with Ivory Coast and Senegal, see Meyers, op. cit.

29. On 26 March 1971, Guinea and Sierra Leone signed a mutual defense treaty that makes explicit reference to the decisions made at the extraordinary meeting of the OAU Council of Ministers. See Africa Research Bulletin, March 1971, p. 2036.

30. Africa Research Bulletin, June 1972, p. 2496.

31. Pittman Potter, "Universalism Versus Regionalism in International Organization," American Political Science Review 37 (October, 1943): 852.

32. Among the advocates of regionalism who advanced these claims were Winston Churchill, Walter Lippmann, and Edward Carr. See Winston S. Churchill, The Hinge of Fate (Boston: Houghton Mifflin, 1950), pp. 711-12, 804-7; Edward Hallet Carr, The Twenty Year Crisis, 1919-1939: An Introduction to the Study of International Relations, 2nd ed. (New York: St. Martin's Press, 1946), pp. 80-85; Walter Lippmann, U.S. War Aims (Boston: Little, Brown, 1944), pp. 80-85.

33. Africa Research Bulletin, November 1970, pp. 1934-35.

34. Africa Research Bulletin, July 1967, p. 821.

35. Ajami and Sours, op. cit., pp. 409-12.

36. Meyers, op. cit.

37. Karl Deutsch, et al., Political Community and the North Atlantic Area (Princeton, N.J.: Princeton University Press, 1957), p. 5.

7

THE OAU'S SUPPORT
FOR THE LIBERATION
OF SOUTHERN AFRICA
Leonard T. Kapungu

OAU is vehemently dedicated to the eradication of colonialism
in all its forms. The decolonization efforts of the OAU have concerned
South Africa, Rhodesia, Namibia, Angola,* French Somaliland (the
Territory of the Afars and Issas), Spanish Sahara, the Comoro Islands,
the Canary Islands, the Seychelles, and several islands under Portuguese rule around the African continent. However, OAU's most intensive efforts have been directed toward the first six of these territories, and although Guinea-Bissau is not geographically located in
Southern Africa, it is generally included in the generic term that has
come to be identified with the OAU: the liberation of Southern Africa.
Our analysis here is limited to South Africa, Rhodesia, Namibia, and
the remaining Portuguese territory, which would, in certain parts,
relate to Guinea (Bissau) and Mozambique prior to the decolonizing
process of 1973-74.

THE FRAMEWORK OF OAU SUPPORT

The OAU receives its authority to support the struggle for the
liberation of Southern Africa from its Charter, which establishes, as
one of OAU's purposes, in Article 2, paragraph 1 (d), "to eradicate
all forms of colonialism from Africa." To this end, the Charter, in
Article 3, paragraph 6, commits all OAU member states to solemnly
adhere to the principle of "absolute dedication to the total emancipation
of the African Territories which are still dependent."

---

*Guinea-Bissau declared independence in September 1973 and
was recognized by Portugal in August 1974. As for Mozambique,
agreement was reached in late 1974 to declare its independence
under an African government in 1975.

It was very obvious at the Summit Conference of Independent African States at which the OAU was born, in May 1963 in Addis Ababa, that the issue of decolonization of Southern Africa was at the fore-front in the minds of the African heads of state and government who attended the conference. Both in speeches and resolutions, the issue of the liberation of Southern Africa was emphasized. In fact, the issue of decolonization was high on the agenda. It was item 2 on the agenda, and became the first resolution adopted by that august conference. [1] The resolution was further reaffirmed by the first ordinary session of the Assembly of Heads of State and Government (the supreme organ of the OAU), at its meeting in Cairo in July 1964. [2]

The Decolonization Resolution, as it came to be known, defined the role of the OAU in the liberation of Southern Africa. The OAU was to become the conscience of Africa insofar as the denial of human rights to the African peoples in Southern Africa was concerned. It was to pressure colonial powers, especially the United Kingdom, the administrative authority of Southern Rhodesia, and Portugal, the colonial power in Mozambique, Angola, and Guinea-Bissau, to transfer the powers and attributes of sovereignty to the indigenous peoples of their respective territories. The OAU was to serve as the vehicle of direct moral, military, and territorial support to the African nationalists waging armed struggles in their respective territories. Last but not least, the OAU was to mount diplomatic support in the United Nations and other international organizations. Its diplomatic efforts were to be aimed at educating the international public to the ills of the political systems in Southern Africa, where power is ex-ercised in complete disregard of the African majority; at isolating the Southern African regimes and identifying their allies; and at identifying the United Nations with the aspirations of the African peoples in these territories, in the hope that the United Nations could be forced to take direct action on behalf of the oppressed peoples of Southern Africa. [3]

The OAU, realizing how heavy the task before it was, set up a special fund to be raised by voluntary contributions of member states to supply the necessary practical and financial aid to the various African national liberation movements. A coordinating committee, which has come to be known as the Liberation Committee, was es-tablished to propose the necessary fund and the apportionment among OAU member states, and to coordinate the assistance from African states for the liberation of Southern Africa. The Liberation Com-mittee has its headquarters in Dar-es-Salaam. In the beginning, it was composed of nine African states, but it has now been expanded to a total membership of seventeen African states. The Liberation Committee develops the strategy of OAU support for the liberation of Southern Africa and reports to the Council of Ministers, which makes recommendations to the Assembly of African Heads of State and Government. It is this Assembly that is ultimately responsible for deciding what role the OAU should continue to play in the support of struggles for the liberation of Southern Africa.

Nearly ten years after the establishment of the OAU, the Liberation Committee met in January 1973 in Accra to redefine "the objectives and strategy of the liberation struggle" and "to recognize defects and the shortcomings of OAU."[4] This conference did not alter the objectives of the OAU in Southern Africa. It had the experience of a ten-year struggle to rely on, and this experience enabled the OAU to prune its role and tone it to the realities entangled in the problem of the liberation of Southern Africa.

THE OAU AS A UNIFYING INSTRUMENT

Before and shortly after the formation of the Organization of African Unity, the nationalist movements in all the Southern African territories suffered from internal strains brought about by personality clashes, ambitions, and differences in strategy. These strains by and large led to polarization of the movements, and each territory began to have more than one movement claiming legitimacy and supremacy in the struggle for that territory's liberation.

In South Africa there was the African National Congress (ANC) and the Pan Africanist Congress (PAC); in Namibia, the South West African National Union (SWANU) and the South West African People's Organization (SWAPO); in Zimbabwe, the Zimbabwe African People's Union (ZAPU) and the Zimbabwe African National Union (ZANU); in Angola, the Frente Nacional de Libertaçao del Angola (FNLA) and the Movemento Peopular de Liberataçao de Angola (MPLA); in Mozambique the Frente de Libertaçao de Mocambique (FRELIMO) and the Comite Revolucionario de Mocambique (COREMO); in Guinea-Bissau, the Portido Africano da Independencia de Guine e Cabo Verale (PAIGC) and the Frente para a Libertaçao e Independencia de Guine Portuguesa (FLING). All vied for legitimacy and supremacy in the liberation of their territories. Even long after the OAU had been formed, splinter groups claiming to be the legitimate movement of the people emerged in many of these territories. For example, in Angola the Unicio Nacional para a Independencia Total de Angola (UNITA) emerged in 1966, and in Zimbabwe the Front for the Liberation of Zimbabwe (FROLIZ) was formed as late as 1971.[5]

In such a polarized situation, the OAU was faced with a problem of recognition. Which of these movements were to be regarded by the OAU as the legitimate spokesmen for the aspirations of the African peoples in these territories? It was essential for the OAU to determine the legitimate movements because it was on this determination that the OAU could give support. The Conference of Independent African States "earnestly" invited "all national liberation movements to co-ordinate their efforts by establishing common action fronts whenever necessary so as to strengthen the effectiveness of their struggle and the rational use of the concerted assistance given them."[6] This invitation went out in May 1963, and it was repeated time and time again by the organs of the OAU. This was a clear invitation to the liberation movements to find strength in unity and to put scarce resources at the disposal of the OAU for maximum use. But time and time again, the OAU invitation fell on deaf ears.

In 1965 the OAU attempted to utilize the services of some of its member states to urge the liberation movements to unite. The Liberation Committee appointed a Military Commission of Enquiry composed of representatives from Cameroun, Mauritania, and Sierra Leone to determine in the field "the effectiveness of all those Movements which are engaged in the struggle for the Liberation of the so-called Portuguese Guinea (Guinea-Bissau)."[7] A committee of three also was appointed to forge a common front between FNLA and MPLA.[8] The Liberation Committee also invited Malawi, Zambia, Tanzania, Uganda, Kenya, and Ethiopia "to assist ZAPU and ZANU to establish quickly a common front" in the struggle for the liberation of Zimbabwe.[9]

These efforts of the Liberation Committee to unite liberation movements in Southern Africa, especially in Zimbabwe, Angola, South Africa, and Namibia, were to no avail. Each movement hoped that the OAU would recognize it; at times, because of the support given to various movements by some African governments and some non-African states, there was a mood of defiance and even contempt for the OAU in the ranks of the liberation movements. This mood undermined the unifying role of the OAU.

Having failed to forge unity, the OAU decided that, if the liberation movements representing the same territory could not unite, it would give support to the liberation movements that seemed to be waging a genuine armed struggle inside their territories.[10] This decision seemed the most logical in the situation and was made with good intentions. And yet this very decision led to the misuse of resources, to the loss of lives for propagandistic reasons.

The polarized liberation movements, in order to gain the support of the OAU, had to seem to be fighting. So armed men were sent into the territories at precisely the time an OAU organ was about to meet. Guns would be fired and the leaders of the liberation movements would go to the OAU and claim to be waging an armed struggle. Men were sent to fight in areas where there had been no preparation of the minds of local residents. The firing of a gun, with all the noise it makes, was given undue importance in the struggle for the liberation of Southern Africa. In other words, revolutionary effectiveness was sacrificed for propagandistic reasons. Such a situation prevailed in different degrees in all the Southern African territories, although it was greatest among liberation movements in South Africa, Namibia, and Zimbabwe.

The continued support given to various movements by individual African states continued to frustrate the OAU efforts. Member states of the OAU had their own preferences among the contending movements. Some heads of state were long-time friends of leaders of certain liberation movements; other heads of state identified themselves with the ideologies of some liberation movements. As a result, a number of OAU member states supported rival movements. For example, while Zambia openly preferred and supported ZAPU, Tanzania openly preferred and supported ZANU. While Zaïre openly preferred and supported FNLA in Angola, the Republic of the Congo openly preferred and supported MPLA.

Even when the OAU, at one point, seemed to prefer ZAPU in Zimbabwe, FRELIMO in Mozambique, FNLA in Angola, and PAIGC in Guinea-Bissau, the contending liberation movements continued to survive through the aid given to them by individual African and non-African states. In fact, at times, some liberation movements favored by the OAU became complacent, and the movements not so well favored by the OAU began to do better in the struggle than the OAU favorites. These developments led the OAU to reverse itself. It began to favor ZANU in Zimbabwe and MPLA in Angola, although it remained steadfast in support of FRELIMO in Mozambique and PAIGC in Guinea-Bissau. What these OAU reversals in the support of contending movements demonstrated was that the OAU lacked a strategy for unity. The OAU seemed to be satisfied by the victories of the moment and very often swallowed hook, line, and sinker some of the propagandistic reports of the liberation movements. In so doing, the OAU seemed, although unwittingly, to encourage the firing of the gun rather than revolutionary preparedness. In some territories—South Africa, Namibia, and Zimbabwe—these methods led to very little progress in the struggle.

The polarization of the liberation movements was an asset to the regimes they were fighting. The regimes were able to infiltrate the ranks of the movements and obtain vital information. The regimes also encouraged polarization by having agents planted in various parts of the world release leaflets purporting to have been written by one liberation movement, and attacking the contending liberation movement in the most insidious manner. These efforts of the minority regimes demoralized the liberation movements and made unity difficult. In fact, on two occasions the regimes succeeded in carrying

out plans aimed at crippling the fighting forces of the movements.
In 1969 the President of FRELIMO, Eduardo Morrallane, was assassinated; in 1973 the President of PAIGC, Amilcar Cabral, was
gunned down by hired assassins. The OAU Secretary General concluded in his report that these two incidents "prove once more that
the forces of imperialism will stop at nothing in their criminal
intrigues: terror, blackmail and corruption, infiltration by agents,
and hired killers."[11] Such intrigues would continue as long as the
liberation movements were not united in common action against the
regimes.

It was not until 1973 that the OAU at last began to make some
headway in the formal unification of some of the liberation movements.
It threatened to terminate all aid to movements that did not unite.
The targets of the OAU efforts were Angolan and Zimbabwe liberation
movements. Early in 1973, an OAU ad hoc committee composed of
the foreign ministers of Zaïre, Congo, Tanzania, and Zambia was
established with specific instructions to forge a common front between the FNLA and the MPLA of Angola. This time the OAU succeeded in at least making the two organizations sign a formal document setting up a common political organ and a unified military command. With this success behind it, the OAU established an ad hoc
committee composed of the foreign ministers of Zambia, Ghana,
Cameroun, Kenya, and Tanzania, with the specific mission of reconciling ZAPU and ZANU of Zimbabwe. The efforts of the ad hoc committee bore fruit and the two movements also signed a formal agreement establishing a unified military command and a political council.

While the OAU Secretary General has hailed these agreements
as being of great significance,[12] it must be stated that unity of liberation movements does not flow from formal documents signed before
a distinguished gathering of foreign ministers and under threat of
financial penalties. Unity must flow from the hearts of men and women who enter into it with the determination to make it work. Time
alone will assess the nature and depth of the unity the OAU has, after
a decade of failure, at last succeeded in forging among the liberation
movements of Angola and Zimbabwe.

Prior to the independence of Guinea-Bissau and its admission
into the U.N. the OAU was satisfied that FRELIMO and PAIGC were
performing well in the armed struggle and has not seen any necessity
to force them to unite with their contending movements. However,
it is the strongly held belief of the OAU that the liberation struggle
in all these territories has been hampered by factionalism and distrust. The OAU has also been involved in keeping its member states
united behind the liberation movements of Southern Africa. The white
minority regimes have attempted to break the united ranks of the
OAU member states. In fact, they have managed to recruit allies
among the OAU member states, notably the Ivory Coast and Malawi.

In 1971, the Ivory Coast flew a trial balloon, calling on the African states to engage in a "dialogue" with South Africa in the hope that a "peaceful" solution could be arrived at in Southern Africa. The OAU realized that this suggestion was very tempting to African states that were eager to benefit from economic relations with Southern Africa. The OAU also suspected, with reasonable accuracy, that there were some European powers behind this scheme, especially Britain and France, eager to continue their trade with South Africa under the aura of OAU acceptance. Thus the Council of Ministers decided to move fast to deflate the Ivory Coast balloon before it had undermined the efforts of the liberation movements.

The Council, at its seventeenth ordinary session in June 1971, reminded all African states and the world that the OAU had adopted the Lusaka Manifesto, which had been endorsed by the United Nations and the Conference of Non-Aligned States.[13] This Manifesto called for a peaceful settlement of the Southern African problem by means of direct talks between the regimes and the indigenous populations in the territories. The Manifesto stated that the process of dialogue must begin from within the territories themselves. The regimes of Southern Africa had rejected the Lusaka Manifesto. The Council of Ministers, at the June 1971 session, "agreed that no member state of the OAU would initiate or engage in any type of action that would undermine or abrogate the solemn obligations and undertakings to the commitments contained in the charter."[14] And for now the proposal for "dialogue" between African states and the Southern African regimes has been shelved and the African states have outwardly remained united in support of the liberation of Southern Africa through armed struggle.

OAU MORAL AND MATERIAL SUPPORT

There is no doubt that the OAU has wanted to make the African peoples of Southern Africa feel that they are not alone in the struggle against the oppressive regimes. Thus, through resolution after resolution, declaration after declaration, the OAU has sought to identify the whole of Africa with the struggle for the liberation of Southern Africa. The moral support the OAU has given is immense, and in fact decolonization of the nonindependent African territories has become the rallying issue of the OAU. Some authorities, including OAU officials, believe the OAU has survived because of the recognition by nearly all African states that they have a moral obligation to support the liberation of these territories. The OAU is the instrument for the expression of this moral support.

141

But moral platitudes and condemnatory or supportive resolutions and declarations do not liberate an oppressed people. The OAU organs have behaved at times as if their resolutions were sufficient to assist the African peoples of Southern Africa to liberate themselves. But then, such an attitude is commonplace in most international organizations.

The OAU has recognized the need to lend material support to the liberation movements of Southern Africa. From its inception, the OAU established the special fund to which all OAU member states were supposed to make voluntary contributions. It is from this special fund that the Liberation Committee is able to provide funds to the liberation movements, and indeed these movements have benefited from the generous distribution of the funds.

However, it must be pointed out that contributions to the special fund, and its administration and distribution, have left much to be desired. According to the report of the OAU Secretary General, the special fund has suffered from "the non-contribution of numerous member states."[15] Many states refused to contribute to the special fund because they felt the Executive Secretariat of the Liberation Committee was misusing the fund. It is true that there was some reckless management of the fund by the Executive Secretariat, but this mismanagement was used by a number of states simply as a reason to avoid paying. Many African states felt that their responsibilities ended with supporting the establishment of the fund, and they did not contribute a penny to it. The OAU has appealed time and time again for contributions to the fund, but these appeals have fallen on deaf ears. In fact, the default in payment is not only to the special fund but also to the administrative budgets of the OAU. The OAU Secretary General reported that before the twentieth session of the Council of Ministers in February 1973, "The non-payment of arrears of contributions to the OAU budgets nearly paralyzed the General Secretariat's activities."[16]

Thus, the burden of contributions to the special fund has fallen on the shoulders of a very few states whose dedication to the liberation of Southern Africa is unswerving. Unfortunately, such states total less than one-third the membership of the OAU (total membership is 41). The result is that, while the world and the regimes of Southern Africa are given the impression, from the speeches of African leaders, that the whole of Africa is contributing to the special fund, in reality many African states do not follow up their speeches with contributions. The regimes use the resolutions of the OAU to boost their psychological state of preparedness while in reality the liberation movements suffer from lack of funds.

The liberation movements are greatly dissatisfied with the way the special fund is distributed. Every movement must submit its budget and plans to the Liberation Committee, which today has seventeen states represented. The Liberation Committee deliberates on the budgets and plans, and on that basis distributes the funds. But a committee of seventeen is too large a body to deliberate on military budgets and plans. It is common knowledge that some of the states represented on the Liberation Committee hobnob with the Southern African regimes. It also is common knowledge that many African states have peculiar ways of keeping secrets. Thus, it is little wonder that very often the plans of the liberation movements are known to the regimes before they are even launched. All attempts to change the proceedings of the Liberation Committee have failed. In fact, the tendency has been to enlarge the membership of the Liberation Committee because states have refused to contribute to the special fund unless they are represented on the Committee.

One essential support the OAU gives to the liberation movements concerns the request to certain member states to allow their territory to be utilized by the movements. The Council of Ministers, in its fifteenth ordinary session in August 1970, urged "African States neighboring dependent territories to accord to Liberation Movements the facilities necessary for the movement of their men and materials to and from the dependent territories."[17] This statement has been repeated very often in the decolonization resolutions of the OAU.

It is not a light responsibility for a country to have an extra-territorial guerrilla force on its territory. African states, like any other states, are very sensitive to the security situation. But those African states—about six in number—called upon by the OAU to fulfill this responsibility have discharged it with a great deal of selflessness. They have allowed guerrillas to be trained on their soil, military hardware to be stored on their territory.

One would assume that the OAU, having given this heavy responsibility to only six states, would come to the military support of those states when they fall victim to aggressive action by the Southern African regimes. It is known that Zambia, Tanzania, the Congo, Senegal, and Guinea have been victims of aggressive actions by these regimes, which claim that they harbor guerrilla units. In response, the OAU has only offered resolutions of support for these states. Only once did fellow African states offer to send troops to repel such aggression: that was when Portuguese mercenaries invaded Guinea in 1970. But numerous attacks have been made on five of these states, and they have gone unanswered by the OAU.

The Council of Ministers, meeting at its nineteenth ordinary session in June 1972, recommended that:

(i)   concrete assistance be rendered to the [five] above mentioned Member States in order to strengthen their defences;

143

(ii) OAU Member States should endeavor to earmark
national military units or war material to be put at
the disposal of countries requesting such assist-
ance.18

But nothing came out of this resolution. It was filed on the dusty
shelves of OAU Headquarters in Addis Ababa, where many similar
resolutions have been laid to rest. It is therefore a credit to these
five states that, in the face of hostile activities by the racist regimes
of Southern Africa, they have steadfastly continued the discharge of
the responsibility placed in their hands by the OAU. Let it be said
for the record that, although the sixth state, Zaïre, has not been a
victim of these hostile actions, its support of the liberation movements in the neighboring territory of Angola has been as commendable
as the actions of the other five.

The OAU has sought to provide another service to the liberation
movements of Southern Africa. Realizing that there had been little
progress in the liberation struggle, the Council of Ministers, meeting
in its ninth ordinary session in September 1967, decided to establish
an ad hoc committee of seventeen military experts to study ways and
means of implementing the strategy of the liberation struggle.19
This committee became very useful when the liberation struggle
seemed to suffer many setbacks between September 1968 and February 1969. It offered advice to both the OAU and the liberation movements. It issued a study relating to the distribution of means of
struggle, storage of war equipment, and the improvement of transit
facilities, and it is believed this study was very useful to the liberation movements. However, the committee is too large for discussions
of military strategy or the maintenance of secrecy.

THE POSSIBILITY OF OAU DIRECT
ACTION IN SOUTHERN AFRICA

The OAU has been tempted to directly involve itself in the actual
physical liberation of Southern Africa. After all, it is argued that
there are forty-one independent African states and six Southern African
territories under three minority regimes. But for ten years the OAU
did not believe that it was ready to launch a military confrontation
with the regimes. However, it thought it could convince the African
states to apply economic sanctions against the regimes. The Summit
Conference of the Independent African States that gave birth to the
OAU agreed unanimously in May 1963 "to coordinate concerted measures of sanction against the Government of South Africa."20 The
first ordinary session of the OAU Assembly of Heads of State and

Government established in 1964 the Bureau of Sanctions to supervise the implementation of the OAU resolutions calling on member states to apply economic sanctions against South Africa.[21]

In February 1966 the Council of Ministers at its sixth ordinary session was informed by the Bureau of Sanctions that after two years of supposed African sanctions against South Africa there had been no marked progress in the implementation of the OAU sanction resolutions.[22] Many African states simply ignored the resolutions and continued to engage in economic relations with Southern Africa.

In October 1965 the second OAU Assembly of African Heads of State and Government, meeting in Accra, adopted a resolution calling on all African states to impose political, economic, and diplomatic sanctions on Britain if it failed to end the illegal independence of Rhodesia, should it be declared.[23] The white minority regime of Rhodesia unilaterally declared the territory independent on 11 November 1965. The Council of Ministers thereupon met in its sixth extraordinary session on 3 December 1965. It recommended a complete blockade of Rhodesia. Should Britain fail to crush the illegal regime by 15 December 1965, it urged that all OAU member states sever diplomatic relations on that day with Britain. Britain did not terminate the rebellion, but only ten African states implemented the OAU resolution. The rest just ignored it.

Such disregard by the African states of their own resolutions has led many people to the conclusion that the OAU can never mount a successful military operation against any of the Southern African regimes. This conclusion is erroneous and emanates from the frustrations of the moment; it does not have the advantage of any foresight or analysis of the pending crisis in Southern Africa. Many diplomats, both Africans and non-Africans, who attended the tenth anniversary of the OAU in May 1973 in Addis Ababa concluded that if what General Idi Amin Dada of Uganda said had been said by a leader with personal integrity like Julius Nyerere of Tanzania or Leopold Senghor of Senegal, Africa and the world would have spent a moment in thought of the prophetic nature of the words. This is what General Amin said, claiming to be speaking "from the bottom of my heart" and not from "a written speech":

> If you check, physically we are over 400 million, and if you are to take the population of forty thousand in Guinea-Bissau and 250,000 in Rhodesia, is this not very shameful? Today some African countries have modern weapons and we will be in the position to liberate all of Africa.[24]

Africa is beginning to feel the "shame" that Amin spoke about, and countries like Nigeria, Zaïre, and Ethiopia have begun to have large, modernized, and well-trained armies. The gap between OAU resolutions and OAU performance will narrow down. In fact, those who are in the inside of the OAU decision making claim that African states came very close to launching a military operation against the Portuguese in Guinea-Bissau. It is said the plan worked out depended to a very great extent on Amilcar Cabral but that the Portuguese were informed of the plan and thus decided to assassinate Cabral.

However, direct OAU intervention in Southern Africa depends on how the crisis in the area shapes up as the struggle for the liberation of Southern Africa continues. This author does not eliminate the possibility of the involvement of African military operations in direct confrontation with the military operations of the white minority regimes. If white nations come to sustain the minority regimes collapsing in the face of guerrilla attacks, African nations will feel compelled to support the liberation movements by direct action. If the minority regimes continue their aggressive actions against independent African states to frustrate guerrilla units, the other African states will feel obliged to militarily assist the victims of such aggression. In either case there will be a confrontation between Africa and the white minority regimes.

OAU DIPLOMATIC INITIATIVES

When the OAU was formed, many African leaders did not understand how the United Nations worked. They believed that the OAU could pressure the United Nations into taking vigorous action in southern Africa on behalf of the oppressed African peoples. Thus in the Decolonization Resolution adopted by the Conference of Independent States the OAU decided

> to send a delegation of Ministers of Foreign Affairs to
> speak on behalf of all African States in the meetings of
> the Security Council which will be called to examine the
> report of the United Nations Committee of 24 on the
> situation in African territories under Portuguese domi-
> nation.[25]

The foreign ministers of Liberia, Tunisia, Madagascar, and Sierra Leone were appointed to perform this function. It became an established procedure for the OAU that whenever matters of importance in the decolonization field arose, the OAU would send a high-powered delegation of foreign ministers to speak in the U.N. Security Council. This procedure had the effect of dramatizing the concern of the African states and the OAU about the struggle for the Liberation of Southern Africa.

It took almost two years for the OAU and its member states to understand that the U.N. Security Council, as presently structured, is reluctant to take any vigorous action against Southern African regimes. This fact became clear when the OAU tried to pressure the Security Council to act on Rhodesia and Namibia, two of the clearest cases that came under the jurisdiction of the United Nations. Namibia had been a League of Nations mandated territory entrusted to South Africa to administer. Since all League of Nations mandated territories became United Nations trusteeship territories that the United Nations guided to independence, it was logical for the OAU to believe that the United Nations would take vigorous action to see Namibia attain majority rule. But the OAU found the Security Council unwilling to act except to pass resolution after resolution supporting the African majority in Namibia. When the Security Council, after a long delay, determined in December 1966 that the situation in Rhodesia was a threat to international peace and security in the meaning of Article 39 of the U.N. Charter,[26] the OAU expected the United Nations to invoke Article 42 of its Charter and use force against Rhodesia. To the disenchantment of the OAU, the Security Council refused to do so.

By 1966 the OAU had begun to shift its tactics. It had become obvious that the United Nations would not be the machinery for the liberation of any of the territories in Southern Africa. However, the OAU realized that the United Nations would be an excellent platform to appeal to international conscience about the atrocities the Southern African regimes were perpetrating. The aim was to isolate the regimes in international opinion. In October 1966 the African Group, formed by the OAU to coordinate the activities of the African states at the United Nations, sponsored a draft resolution in the U.N. General Assembly establishing a unit in the U.N. Secretariat to deal exclusively with the policy of apartheid in order to give maximum publicity to the evils of that policy. The General Assembly agreed and thus adopted Resolution 2144 (XXI)A.

The OAU decided to continue the efforts began in 1960 by the independent African states in the litigation against South Africa before the International Court of Justice (ICJ) for the violation of the League of Nations mandate in Namibia.[27] When the ICJ, in its decision on 18 July 1966, claimed no jurisdiction over the litigation, the OAU pressed forward, harassing South Africa in every international organization available. Even the ICJ reversed its decision on 21 June, 1971 and declared South Africa's presence in Namibia illegal.

The OAU has steadfastly maintained that economic sanctions against Rhodesia have failed because of the support Rhodesia receives from certain Western states. In a resolution the Council of Ministers, meeting in its nineteenth ordinary session in June 1972, made it clear that the United Kingdom was conniving with Rhodesia while the United States was violating sanctions by importing chrome from Rhodesia.[28] When Rhodesia was invited to participate in the 1972 Olympics, the OAU requested African states to refuse to participate unless the Rhodesian team was excluded. In the glare of international publicity, the Olympics nearly came to a halt and the Rhodesians were excluded.

Regarding the issue of the Portuguese colonies prior to Guinea-Bissau's independence and the Portuguese coup, which brought about an acceleration of decolonization as of April 1974, the OAU had emphasized that NATO powers that provide arms and ammunition to Portugal were contributing to the genocide Portugal was conducting in Angola, Mozambique, and Guinea-Bissau. The OAU had then sought to undermine Portugal by attacking NATO's role in strengthening the military arm of the Portuguese.

Of course the question that has to be asked and answered is: What contribution has the OAU diplomatic initiatives made to the liberation of Southern Africa? One is tempted to say that no contribution has been made at all. But one must consider that, without all these diplomatic initiatives of the OAU, Western support of the Southern African regimes would have been greater and the arrogance of the regimes would have been beyond defiance. These initiatives have indirectly affected the extent to which the Western powers and the regimes can go in pursuit of their selfish aims in complete disregard of the interests of the majority of the people. Furthermore, these diplomatic initiatives have advanced the moral justification for the guerrilla activities of the liberation movements.

However, this is not to say that the world supports these guerrilla activities but at least most states have refrained from condemning them and have chosen to be ambivalent on the general issue of using force to effect change in Southern Africa. If it were not for the OAU diplomatic initiatives, most probably these states would be condemning the liberation movements of Southern Africa.

THE EFFECTIVENESS OF THE LIBERATION MOVEMENTS

The OAU has constantly attempted to evaluate the progress of the struggle for the liberation of Southern Africa. It has been satisfied that the 1972-73 year was characterized by an intensification of the liberation struggle. The OAU noted with pride that, despite the assassination of Amilcar Cabral, PAIGC continued the struggle with even more determination until Guinea-Bissau achieved full independence. The OAU Administrative Secretary General listed in his report some of the successes of PAIGC.[29] PAIGC's military capability includes the ability to destroy Portugal's aircraft, to mount heavy artillery attacks, and to lay ambushes. Its military activities were no longer concentrated only in the rural areas. Urban centers, especially in the south, north, and central regions of Guinea-Bissau, had been frequent scenes of intensive guerrilla operations. The military capability of PAIGC became so high that the guerrilla units were able to capture large quantities of military equipment from Portuguese troops. The OAU welcomed these developments because the captured equipment augmented the scarce resources the OAU and friendly states were able to provide.

In the political field, PAIGC was able in 1972-73 to carry out intensive political activities among the people of Guinea-Bissau and was thus capable of consolidating its hold on the territory. It was able to establish within the country territorial popular power bodies elected in the liberated areas. These bodies were able to elect from among themselves the Guinea-Bissau National Assembly. That Assembly served as the political wing for the struggle of independence.

Prior to the Portugal-FRELIMO agreement on independence which was reached in September 1974, progress had also been achieved in Mozambique. By the end of 1972 FRELIMO had extended its control into the rural provinces of Cabo Delgado and Niassa, and had been able to extend its fighting into Tete province. By 1973 the FRELIMO guerrillas had begun to undertake effective guerrilla activities in Manica and Sofala Provinces from which Mozambique's vital economic interests operate. These operations brought guerrilla warfare to the densely populated heartland of the country. The OAU regarded these developments as "a very favorable factor in guerrilla warfare."30

Since Rhodesia and South Africa were providing many manufactured products needed in the construction of the Cabora Bassa Dam, FRELIMO decided to make the roads and railways linking Rhodesia and Cabora Bassa targets of its guerrilla activities. It is no secret that progress on the dam's construction has been slowed.

The successes achieved by FRELIMO in its struggle against Portugal astonished not only the Portuguese but also the Rhodesian and South African regimes. The successes, especially in Tete province, have posed serious threats to Rhodesia. It is little wonder that Portuguese troops supported by Rhodesian forces have been carrying out mass massacres in Mozambique with the hope of intimidating the people supporting guerrilla units. Portugal also uses herbicides, defoliants, and other chemical and bacteriological products in its antiguerrilla operations. This has caused a great deal of harm to the civilian population.

In Angola, MPLA and FNLA and to a certain extent UNITA have continued the struggle and have also liberated some territory. In

Zimbabwe, ZANU has reactivated its military operations, especially in the northeast part of the country, and FROLIZ and ZAPU have also to a limited extent launched military operations. The liberation movements of Zimbabwe have changed their fighting tactics and have begun to be very effective. The Rhodesian regime has frequently voiced its concern with the security situation in the country, especially after December 1972.

The South African liberation movements, ANC and PAC, have not met with as much success as their counterparts in the other territories. In reviewing OAU documents, one is struck by the absence of any mention of guerrilla activities by the South African liberation movements. In Namibia, the OAU recognizes that SWAPO has been engaged in some military activity although such activity has not yet reached the level of activities that were undertaken in Guinea-Bissau and Mozambique.

In summary, progress has been made in the struggle for the liberation of Southern Africa. The OAU has been satisfied with this progress and has called on all African states to continue supporting the liberation movements. Revolutions cannot be subjected to a timetable. Thus, it is impossible to tell when the liberation movements will achieve ultimate success. But one thing can be said: After more than a decade of struggle, the liberation movements have become confident and convinced that victory is certain. They are today more at grips with the objective conditions that operate in their respective territories than they were ten years ago. The regimes of Southern Africa are today less confident of themselves than they were ten years ago. They are scared, and they are failing to contain the guerrilla activities. It is only a matter of time for the liberation movements and the OAU to achieve the results they have for so long struggled for.

NOTES

1. See CIAS/Plen, 21 Rev. 2, A, Agenda Item II, Decolonization.
2. OAU Doc. AHG/Res. 7(1), AHG/Res. 8(1), and AHG/Res. 9(1).
3. For details of the definition of the role of the OAU, see CIAS/Plen. 2.
4. OAU Document CM/497 (Part 1), p. 17.
5. For details of the polarization of the liberation movements, see Richard Gibson, African Liberation Movements: Contemporary Struggles Against White Minority Rule, (London: Oxford University Press, 1972).
6. CIAS/Plen. 2/Rev. 2, A, paragraph 10.

7. OAU Document CM/Res. 51(iv), paragraph 5.
8. Ibid., paragraph 6.
9. OAU Doc. ECM/Res. 10 (v).
10. See OAU Doc. CM/Res. 75 (vi), paragraph 4.
11. OAU Doc. CM/497, Part II, p. 7.
12. OAU Doc. CM/497, Part I, pp. 12-14.
13. OAU Doc. CM/St. 5 (xvii).
14. Ibid.
15. OAU Doc. CM/497, Part I, p. 17.
16. OAU Doc. AHG/67, Part II, p. 10.
17. OAU Doc. CM/Res. 266(xv).
18. OAU Doc. CM/Res. 271 (xix).
19. OAU Doc. CM/Res. 103 (ix).
20. CIAS/Plen 2/Res. 2, B.
21. OAU Doc. AHG/Res. 6 (1).
22. OAU Doc. CM/111 (vi).
23. OAU Doc. AHG/Res. 25/Rev. 1.
24. Africa, no. 23 (July 1973), p. 12.
25. CIAS/Plen. 2/Rev. 2, A, paragraph 7.
26. U.N. Security Council Resolution 232 (1966).
27. U.N. Press Release, W S/508, 24 June 1971, p. 1.
28. U.N. Doc. CM/Res. 267 (xix).
29. OAU Doc. CM/497 (Part I), p. 12.
30. Ibid., p. 3.
31. Washington Post, 15 July 1973.

INTRODUCTION

The sense of purpose that united the African leaders in their fight against colonialism and apartheid and that gave birth to the OAU in 1963 was soon put to a severe test by a series of crises. Some of them threatened the very existence of the OAU.

The first was the armed conflict between Algeria and Morocco in October 1963, followed by the culmination of the Congo crisis in 1964. The Unilateral Declaration of Independence (UDI) by the white minority government in Southern Rhodesia in 1965 was perhaps the most crucial event in the history of OAU. And OAU was further shaken by coups d'etat in Nigeria and Ghana. The former presaged the Nigerian civil war, while the latter divided the OAU members over the recognition of the military regime that deposed President Kwame Nkrumah. The Nigerian civil war dominated African affairs during 1967-70. In 1970 there was the debate on a "dialogue" with South Africa, proposed by President Houphouet-Boigny of Ivory Coast. In 1971, OAU became directly involved in the troubles in the Middle East, which reached a peak in October 1973 with the outbreak of war between Israel and the Arab states.

Each of these crises had a profound impact on OAU. They shattered the belief of Africans who regarded the "spirit of Addis Ababa"—the atmosphere of brotherhood, solidarity, and understanding in which the Charter of OAU was signed—as a permanent feature of inter-African relations. This in turn provided South Africa, Southern Rhodesia, and sections of the Western press with new arguments about the inability of Africans to govern themselves.

But however damaging these crises were for the political and economic advancement of independent Africa, their effects on the OAU were not entirely negative.

Instead of disintegrating as predicted, OAU became more cohesive in the process. The lessons of each crisis were not lost on the African leaders. They soon realized the usefulness of OAU and did not relax their efforts to increase its capacity to deal with the problems facing the continent. This has been particularly true of the OAU's involvement in the Nigerian civil war, a brief account of which is given in this chapter.

The historical origins of the war between Nigeria and the secessionist Eastern Region, which declared independence under the name of Biafra, as well as the course of war itself, have been treated extensively in a number of books.[1] The purpose of this commentary is to show the impact of the Nigerian war on the Organization of African Unity and on the relationships of its members. Two main principles of the OAU Charter were put to the test:

1. The principle of noninterference in internal affairs (Article 3, paragraph 2), consistently referred to by Nigeria.

2. Respect for the inalienable right to independence (Article 3, paragraph 3), insisted upon by Biafra.

Before examining the Nigerian problem within the context of OAU, recourse will be made to a brief chronology including dates relevant to the scope of this discussion.

CHRONOLOGY

15 January 1966: A group of army officers led by Major Chukwuma K. Nzeogwu executed a coup d'état in the Northern Region of Nigeria. The coup failed in the rest of the country and subsequently in the North, but it resulted in the establishment of military rule in Nigeria from 16 January 1966, when Major-General Aguiyi Ironsi, General Officer Commanding the Nigerian Army, assumed the powers of Supreme Commander of a Federal military government. The Nigerian Premier, Sir Abubakar Tafewa Balewa, was abducted and murdered by the mutinous officers in Lagos.

29 July 1966: General Ironsi's rule came to an end when an anti-Ibo mutiny broke out in the army, in the course of which General Ironsi was killed. The mutinous officers invited Lieutenant Colonel Yakubu Gowon to succeed General Ironsi, whose death was kept secret for six months.

28 September 1966: A wave of massacres of the Ibo swept the Northern Region of Nigeria and did not recede until October 1966. Thousands of Ibo were killed, and the rest fled to the "Ibo homeland" in the Eastern Region.[2] These events were crucial in the subsequent breakdown of the Nigerian Federation.

24 October 1966: The Military Governor of the Eastern Region, Colonel Odumwegwu Ojukwu, refused to attend the resumed meeting of the Constitutional Committee, which was to decide the future constitutional structure of Nigeria.

4-5 January 1966: A meeting of the Nigerian Military Council, attended by all the military governors at Aburi in Ghana, agreed on the principle of collective rule on the basis of concurrence of all military governors on decisions affecting their regions.

17 March 1967: Promulgation of Decree No. 8 (Constitution, Suspension and Modification Decree, 1967) provided for virtual autonomy of the military governors in their regions, with the exception of the right to declare emergency laws "as may appear necessary or expedient for the purpose of maintaining or securing peace, order and good government," which was vested in the Head of the Federal military government. Colonel Ojukwu called Decree No. 8 a breach of the Aburi Agreement.

31 March 1967: Colonel Ojukwu issued Revenue Collection Edict 11, 1967, which in fiscal terms was close to secession. He decided to cease payment of all revenues collected in the Eastern Region on behalf of the Federal treasury. Colonel Gowon retaliated by imposing an economic blockade.

27 May 1967: Colonel Gowon assumed full powers as Commander-in-Chief of all armed forces and Head of the Federal military government with the rank of Major-General, and proclaimed a state of emergency throughout Nigeria. He also issued a decree called the "States (Creation and Transitional Provisions) Decree," creating twelve new states within the Federation.

30 May, 1967: Colonel Ojukwu declared the Eastern Region an independent state to be named Biafra. General Gowon reacted with a general mobilization of troops, described Colonel Ojukwu's act as a rebellion that would be crushed by appropriate measures, and warned all countries not to interfere in the internal affairs of Nigeria but to respect its territorial integrity.

6 July 1967: Fighting started between the troops of the Nigerian Federal Army and those of Biafra, soon developing into a war.

In retrospect, the war between Nigeria and Biafra was from all points of view a catastrophic and protracted struggle. Few people who heard that on 6 July 1967, there had been clashes between the Federal and Biafran troops near Ogoja imagined that the conflict would ultimately result in a war of international dimensions. Indeed, the war lasted 920 days. The number of Ibo and other Nigerians who died in the conflict is unknown. Neither side kept accurate records of the military casualties, and there are no reliable records of the civilian victims of the war, who far exceeded the number killed in

154

in military operations. The number killed is estimated to be between one and two million.

Biafra was defeated for a variety of reasons. Starvation and the superiority of the Nigerian Federal forces in manpower were significant factors. Corruption and dissent within Biafra's ruling elite may also have contributed to its defeat. But the most decisive factor was the massive supply of arms from Great Britain, which by December 1969 had reached a value of £10 million, more than enough to wipe the Biafrans from the face of the earth. Had there not been a surrender on 12 January 1970, that is precisely what would have happened.

THE MOTIVES FOR THE OAU INTERVENTION IN THE NIGERIAN CONFLICT

Despite the attempts of the Federal military government to treat the war against Biafra as strictly an internal Nigerian affair, three elements made it of great concern not only to Africa but also to the whole world:

1. The supply of arms, including aircraft and heavy artillery, by the governments of the United Kingdom, the Soviet Union, Czechoslovakia, and the United Arab Republic to the Federal government, and from undisclosed sources to Biafra.[3]

2. The recognition of Biafra as an independent state, thus according it the status of a full member of the international community, by the governments of Tanzania (13 April 1968), Gabon (8 May 1968), Ivory Coast (14 May 1968), and Zambia (20 May 1968).[4]

3. The condition of Biafra's population, which was cut off from the sea and encircled by Federal troops, and thus became of great concern to the whole world.[5] A worldwide campaign to save the starving women and children of Biafra was launched by the International Red Cross, the Church, and other international bodies.

4. The presence of a group of foreign military observers investigating Biafra's allegations of "genocide."[6]

THE OAU SUMMIT MEETING IN KINSHASA IN SEPTEMBER 1967

The first initiative by OAU on the Nigerian war took place at the OAU Assembly meeting in Kinshasa in September 1967. At that time, the war had already become one of Africa's major problems. The meeting of the OAU Council of Ministers, which always precedes that of the Assembly of Heads of State and Government, did not propose the Nigerian situation for the Assembly agenda. It was felt, however, that if the African leaders had dispersed without a word about the Nigerian conflict, they would have provided the critics of OAU with arguments against its usefulness.

But the decision to discuss Nigeria was very difficult to make. On the one hand, the heads of state and government were faced with the repeated warnings of the Federal government of Nigeria that the war was merely a matter for Nigeria. The Federal government held very firmly to the view that any intervention, even in the form of a discussion at OAU level, would be in violation of Article 3, paragraph 2, of the OAU Charter, which prohibits any interference in the internal affairs of states. On the other hand, the Biafran regime was pressing for "internationalization" of the conflict, which could come about through outside mediation, especially from OAU. Several days before the conference began, Colonel Ojukwu sent to Kinshasa a high-level delegation to acquaint the African heads of state with the Biafran case.

The resolution adopted by the Assembly was carefully drafted to avoid creating the impression that OAU was interfering in the internal affairs of Nigeria. In the resolution, the heads of state and government recognized the situation as an "internal affair, the solution of which is primarily the responsibility of the Nigerians themselves" and resolved to send a Consultative Mission of six heads of state (Cameroun, Zaire, Ethiopia, Ghana, Liberia, and Niger) to the head of the Federal government of Nigeria to assure him of the Assembly's desire for the territorial integrity, unity, and peace of Nigeria. The Mission was later called the Consultative Committee on Nigeria.

The composition of the Mission represented a careful balance of the different attitudes toward the Nigerian conflict. President Ahidjo of Cameroun was known for his sympathies with the Biafran cause and was believed to have cooperated with Biafra in breaking the Federal blockade in the field of telecommunications. Many Ibo trade and work in Cameroun, especially in Western Cameroun, which was once part of Eastern Nigeria. President Diori of Niger, in considering the Nigerian crisis, had to bear in mind the dependence of Niger on the Northern Nigerian Railways as a vital link with the sea. The economic aspect aside, the people of Niger have a natural affection and attachment to Northern Nigerians as fellow Muslims and because they claim the same ancestry. Two other members of the Mission, Emperor Haile Selassie of Ethiopia and President William Tubman of Liberia, were considered to have great influence in African diplomacy, the Emperor being a successful peacemaker in Africa while Tubman, one of the architects of the OAU Charter, had long been the dean of West African politicians. The pressure of General

Ankrah of Ghana on the Mission was justified by the positive role he played at the Aburi meeting and because he personally knew both General Gowon and Colonel Ojukwu. The sixth participant was President Mobutu of Zaire.

The Mission arrived in Lagos on 23 November 1967. In his welcoming address to the OAU Mission, Major-General Yakubu Gowon stated the terms on which he was prepared to listen to the Mission. He said:

> We have always insisted that our friends are only those who are firmly committed to the maintenance of the territorial integrity and unity of Nigeria. Our true friends are those who publicly and genuinely condemn the attempted secession by the few who have imposed their will on the former Eastern Region of Nigeria. The Kinshasa Resolution of the OAU Summit on the Nigerian situation proves that all African States are true friends of Nigeria. I wish to take this opportunity to express formally our appreciation of the brotherly spirit of the OAU Summit in recognising the need for Nigeria to be preserved as one country. It is in the interest of all Africa that Nigeria remains one political and economic entity. The OAU has rightly seen our problem as a purely domestic affair and, in accordance with the OAU resolution, your Mission is not here to mediate.[7]

The communiqué issued by the Mission at the end of its visit to Lagos expressed full agreement with General Gowon's views by reaffirming that "any solution of the Nigerian crisis must be in the context of preserving the unity and territorial integrity of Nigeria."[8]

The terms of reference of the OAU Mission, as well as the Lagos communiqué, were a bitter disappointment for the Biafran politicians. Until the Kinshasa summit, they had advocated OAU mediation, provided that Biafra's sovereignty was not negotiable and that Biafra would be invited to the peace talks as a sovereign state and not as a part of Nigeria. This is why the Biafran reaction to the Lagos communiqué was an outright condemnation of the OAU initiative. An official broadcast by Radio Enugu on 24 November 1968 stated that "by deciding to consult with only one party to the dispute, the Mission has demonstrated its lack of objectivity and doomed itself to failure right from the start." According to Biafra, "the Mission has condoned genocide and has proved itself a rubber stamp by merely endorsing General Gowon's warning that their own countries would disintegrate if they did not rally to his support."

THE KAMPALA PEACE TALKS IN MAY 1968

The Biafran rejection of the OAU attitude toward the dispute was the reason that the first peace talks between the two parties were held under the auspices of the British Commonwealth Secretariat rather than OAU. Most probably, the recognition of Biafra by Tanzania on 13 April 1968 accelerated the preparatory work for the talks.

On 6 May 1968 preliminary talks between representatives of both sides began in London under the auspices of the Commonwealth Secretary-General, who earlier had had separate talks with each side. The Federal military government was represented by Chief Anthony Enahoro, the Commissioner for Information, and the Biafran authorities by Sir Louis Mbanefo. A communique issued by the Commonwealth Secretariat on 15 May 1968 stated that it had been agreed that peace talks would begin in Kampala, Uganda, on 23 May 1968 and that the agenda would be the question of chairmanship, the question of foreign observers, the conditions for ending the hostilities, and the arrangements for a permanent settlement.

The peace talks in Kampala were opened by President Obote of Uganda, who called for an early agreement on the cessation of hostilities as a basic preliminary for a broader understanding. The talks, however, broke down on 31 May 1968. Sir Louis Mbanefo accused the Federal delegation of exploiting the Federal military positions and of trying to dictate rather than to negotiate the terms, using the talks as a propaganda exercise to pin the blame for the breakdown on the Biafran delegation. He further accused the Nigerian delegation of employing obstructionist tactics, of not wanting to talk peace, and of putting forward totally unacceptable proposals.

Chief Enahoro, meanwhile, regretted the departure of the Biafran delegation and claimed that a point had been reached at which there was hope of achieving agreement on a number of matters that might have led to a decision on a cease-fire date. He described the Biafran demand for an unconditional cease-fire as unrealistic, and the further demand for the withdrawal of Federal troops to their positions before the outbreak of war as unacceptable.

The difficulty of reconciling the three objectives implicit in the Nigerian crisis—(1) stopping the fighting, (2) preserving the unity of Nigeria, and (3) giving effective assurances of safety to the Ibo people—appeared in the course of the peace talks held before and during the conflict as the absolutely unsurmountable obstacle to any settlement. Soon after the peace negotiations began, the issue was no longer whether the Biafran Republic could survive or not; the Federal advances into Biafran territory made certain that it would not survive within the frontiers set out on 30 May 1967. The practical question (known as the "permanent settlement") was: On what terms would the Ibo peoples be able to live with their neighbors in the future?

The Federal government's conditions for a settlement could be summed up as follows:

1. The withdrawal of the declaration of independence by the Eastern Region.

2. Public acceptance and recognition of the authority of the Federal military government over the Eastern Region.

3. Public acceptance of the twelve new states.

4. The acceptance of civilians as commissioners in the Federal Executive Council and as members of the State Executive Councils, as a major step in the return to civilian rule.

5. Agreement to the holding of talks on the future of Nigeria by accredited and equal representatives of the twelve states.

The following were the Biafran conditions for a settlement:

1. Internally, the maintenance of order and respect for law must be the responsibility of the Biafran government. Biafra rejected any proposal that gave the Federal government responsibility for the Ibo police.

2. The Biafran Army must swear allegiance to the Biafran government.

3. Internationally, Biafra must be a member of international organizations.

4. Economically, Biafra must be able to conclude international agreements. The country must be able to control its currency, its economic resources, and the rate of its economic development.

While both proposals offered a great deal of scope for maneuvering, there remained a fundamental disagreement, namely, that while the Federal government's principal condition was renunciation of secession by Biafra before a cease-fire, the Biafrans wanted an immediate cease-fire with no such conditions attached.

NEW OAU INITIATIVE: TALKS AT NIAMEY IN JULY 1968

The appalling condition of the population in the battle areas aroused world public opinion and made further African inaction impossible. Humanitarian considerations were behind the initiative of Emperor Haile Selassie to revive the work of the OAU Consultative Mission on Nigeria by convening a meeting of its members in Niamey, Niger, on 15 July 1968. Sensing that the meeting of the Mission was now far more concerned with ending the war than with its original terms of reference, Colonel Ojukwu made it known that he was prepared to come to Niamey, if invited. All six members of the Mission were represented, five of them—Cameroun, Ethiopia, Ghana, Liberia, and Niger—by the heads of state. President Mobutu of Zaire sent a delegation led by a Deputy Foreign Minister.

The assembled members of the Mission first heard General Gowon, who told them that "the rebel leaders and their foreign backers are playing politics with the whole question of human sufferings to their diplomatic and military advantage". He declared that, in military terms, the rebellion was "virtually suppressed already," and that a unilateral cease-fire by the Federal government without any prior commitment from the rebel leaders to give up secession would offer the secessionists the opportunity to regroup and rearm, and prepare for the continuation of the conflict. He added that "a unilateral cease-fire on humanitarian grounds would not, in any way, relieve the sufferings of the innocent victims of our tragic war."[9]

General Gowon did, however, show more understanding for the Ibo fears about safety than his delegation had shown at Kampala, and he agreed to the introduction of outside observers to ensure that Federal troops would not massacre the Ibo. But he was very firm on the terms of reference of the observers: They were not to be concerned with peace-keeping operations but only to observe and bear testimony.

Colonel Ojukwu's speech to the Consultative Mission on Nigeria on 18 July 1968 was not made public, but to judge by the press conference he held at Abidjan, Ivory Coast, on 21 July 1968, he appeared to be impressed by the way OAU dealt with the most important issues of the conflict. Before his departure for Niamey, he had spoken of the obstacles standing in the way of an honorable settlement on Nigeria—among those he cited was the "unrealistic attitude of the OAU." After the meeting at Niamey, he said: "Provided the spirit of sincerity and honesty which was so very evident in Niamey continues, provided Africa is left on its own to grapple with the problems posed by our difficulties, I think there is a hope. Judging from the way the conference started moving, I think there would be permanent peace or at least temporary peace."[10]

The OAU Consultative Mission on Nigeria, although continuing to support the Federal government on the need for preserving Nigeria as one entity, adopted a resolution in which emphasis was put on the relief operations in the distressed areas of Biafra rather than on the reconciliation of the two parties. They were merely invited "to do everything possible to resume the negotiations as soon as possible in order to achieve a peaceful solution to the crisis." Although very little information about the proceedings of the Mission was made public, it seems that arrangements for relief were the main preoccupations.[11]

After hearing both General Gowon and Colonel Ojukwu, the Consultative Mission issued a communiqué that announced that the Nigerian Federal government and Colonel Ojukwu would meet immediately in Niamey under the chairmanship of President Diori of

160

Niger. There would be preliminary talks on a speedy resumption of peace negotiations, to be followed by peace negotiations in Addis Ababa.

The representatives of the Federal government and Biafra met in Niamey on 20 July 1968 under the chairmanship of President Diori of Niger and agreed on the following agenda for the Addis Ababa peace talks:

1. Arrangements for a permanent settlement.

2. Terms for the cessation of hostilities.

3. Firm proposals for the transport of relief supplies to the civilian population.

THE ADDIS ABABA PEACE NEGOTIATIONS IN AUGUST-SEPTEMBER 1968

The peace talks were opened by Emperor Haile Selassie on 5 August 1968. He appealed to both parties not to fail. In closed sessions, the two parties outlined their respective positions. They revealed that a wide gap between them still remained. It soon became evident that an agreement for a political settlement of the dispute between Biafra and the Federal government was virtually unobtainable.

The only area in which the talks could possibly succeed was in regard to relief. The Emperor seized this opportunity to get the two sides to agree on some workable arrangements for getting the relief supplies to the war-ravaged areas. He continued his talks with the delegations in his palace. According to a report on the Addis Ababa radio on 9 September 1968, the Emperor received both delegations on more than 35 occasions. His efforts were commended by Pope Paul, who expressed a wish that, in the Emperor's efforts to mediate for peace in Nigeria, the problems of humanitarian aid should be given priority. This approach to the conflict was strongly supported by the International Committee of the Red Cross (ICIC). The Red Cross special envoy, August Lindt, arrived in Addis Ababa and tried to get the two sides to agree on a "mercy corridor," to speed up relief supplies. Without reaching any agreement, the meeting was adjourned on 15 August 1968 after both parties had accepted the Emperor's invitation to continue the meeting in Addis Ababa on 19 August 1968.

When the negotiations were resumed on 22 August 1968, an agreement seemed to be within reach. On 24 August, both sides had agreed in principle to a compromise proposal, put forward by the Emperor, for air and land mercy corridors to aid the civilian victims of the war. Earlier, the Federal government had requested that the

Biafrans place one of their strategic airfields at the disposal of the terminal already under Red Cross control, since it could receive freighter aircraft from a demilitarized Federal airport.

While the negotiations continued, there were often glimpses of hope, but these always proved to be premature. On 25 August 1968, General Gowon, without waiting for the outcome of the Addis Ababa talks, announced the launching of a "final offensive." As a result, one of the few towns still held by the Biafrans, Aba, fell into Federal hands on 4 September, which in turn put more pressure on the Biafrans at Addis Ababa. But they refused to yield. Finally, on 9 September 1968, after nearly five weeks of negotiations, the Addis Ababa peace talks, which were then concerned with relief operations only, were adjourned. Perhaps "breakdown" would be a more accurate description.

THE OAU SUMMIT IN ALGIERS
IN SEPTEMBER 1968

When the Assembly of Heads of State and Government met on 4 September 1968 at the Club des Pins in Algiers, the significant advances by the Federal troops were not yet over, but the political fate of Biafra seemed to be sealed. The four countries that had recognized Biafra were unable to muster any meaningful support for the Biafran cause.

Although many African leaders sympathized with the humanitarian motives behind the recognition of Biafra by four OAU members, and shared their concern that the misery of the Nigerian war might jeopardize a better future in Africa, they rejected President Nyerere's thesis that unity that is achieved by conquest is worthless.[12] Despite the support of President Nyerere's arguments by President Houphouet-Boigny of Ivory Coast,[13] the fear of similar conflicts in their own countries—many of which had similar tribal and ethnic problems— was a decisive influence on the minds of nearly all the delegates to the Algiers summit.

It must have disappointed Emperor Haile Selassie that he could not report more solid achievements. Although the OAU Consultative Mission on Nigeria had no easy task in trying to help the parties to the dispute to settle their differences in peaceful negotiation, it came closer to solving the problem than had other initiatives made at different times by the Commonwealth Secretariat and other countries, notably Great Britain. In its report to the Summit Conference, the Federal military government maintained its insistence on the principle of a united country but recognized the right of the many minorities in Nigeria to safeguards. The Biafran delegation insisted equally strongly that the Ibo could not live with the rest of the Nigerians and held that secession was the only solution.

The meeting adopted a resolution that appealed to the Biafran leaders to cooperate with the Federal authorities in order to restore peace and unity in Nigeria through the cessation of hostilities. OAU recommended that the Federal military government declare a general amnesty and cooperate with OAU in ensuring the physical security of all the people of Nigeria, until mutual confidence could be restored. The resolution further called on all member states of the United Nations and OAU "to refrain from any action detrimental to the peace, unity and territorial integrity of Nigeria." Finally, it invited the Consultative Committee "to continue its efforts with a view to implementing the resolutions of Kinshasa and Algiers."[14]

Thirty-three delegations voted for the resolution—a great diplomatic triumph for Nigeria. It can be ascribed to several factors.

First, the host country strongly sustained the Federal thesis and would not admit a Biafran delegation, even if the Federal delegation and the conference had been disposed to concede the possibility. President Boumedienne, in his opening address, fiercely denounced "plots from all sides directed against Nigeria, aiming to disintegrate and shake to its foundations this great African State, of the unity and cohesion of which we were and are proud," and this set the course of the conference, which the majority of the delegations followed.[15]

The second factor was the support for the Federal stand from the United Nations Secretary-General, U Thant, who spoke to the conference on 13 September 1968.[16]

The third factor was the desire of most leaders to be on the winning side and thus cement diplomatic relations with Nigeria, which seemed about to reassume a most influential role in Africa.

The feelings of the great majority of states siding with the Federal government were well expressed by the East African Standard of 3 September 1968:

Those readers who have criticised our opinions about
Biafra have misunderstood the motives. Recognising
Ibo concern, nonetheless it should be reiterated that
Biafra took the initiative in secession, though the OAU
specifically supports unity. Even if any hope of success
existed in the beginning, none is left, and for Col. Ojukwu
to continue resistance when the ring is closing is rem-
iniscent of Hitler in his Berlin bunker. Sacrifice of life
and the prolongation of suffering are reasons more potent
than any OAU resolution per se for accusing him of use-
less and callous disregard for his people. Biafra has lost
the war and the terms for a cease-fire should have been

accepted months ago. Every day has added death and suffering—needlessly sacrificed to personal obstinacy in the face of OAU condemnation.

On the question of the independent existence of Biafra, the majority of the OAU members adhered to a policy of nonrecognition of Biafra. Logically, the policy of nonrecognition implies a refusal to admit the validity of change. Whether the change is legal or illegal is another matter; hence the emphasis on the term policy, which should not be confused with law.[17]

A secession from an existing state, although constitutionally a breach of the law and therefore from the point of view of the parent state illegal and an internal matter at that, is not contrary to international law. Some experts on international law go even further and maintain that it is the duty of states to recognize a new state that has come into existence as a result of secession.[18]

To determine the legality of the statehood of Biafra, one would have to examine whether it met all the requirements of international law, namely, independent government, effective authority, defined territory, and a sufficient degree of stability, expressed by the support of the majority of the population. All of these factors underwent a fundamental change in Biafra's case soon after the outbreak of the war. However, Biafra's existence was a fact, however objectionable, as was recognized even by its opponents.

THE OAU MISSION ON NIGERIA MEETING IN MONROVIA IN APRIL 1969

The last meeting of the OAU Consultative Mission on Nigeria was held in Monrovia on 17 April 1969 and was attended by President Tubman (Liberia), Emperor Haile Selassie (Ethiopia), President Ahidjo (Cameroun), and I. K. W. Harlley of Ghana. The OAU Secretary-General, Diallo Telli, also was present.

The Mission ended its three-day meeting on 20 April 1969 without breaking the deadlock in the war between the Federal government and Biafra. In a statement issued on 20 April, the Mission proposed that "the two parties of the Civil War accept in the supreme interest of Africa, a united Nigeria, which ensures all forms of security to all citizens." It also proposed that "within the context of this agreement, the two parties accept an immediate cessation of fighting, and the opening without delay of peace negotiations." Furthermore, the Consultative Mission offered its good offices to facilitate negotiations. The Mission "noted with satisfaction that the Federal Government of Nigeria accepted the proposals" and expressed regret that the Biafran delegation did not.

164

The Biafran delegation was later reported to have stated that, if the words "a solution" had been used in place of the words "united Nigeria," it would have been willing to accept the declaration in principle. The Biafran delegation was not prepared to discuss an OAU concept of territorial integrity without some bilateral discussion about what this would entail.

THE OAU SUMMIT MEETING IN ADDIS ABABA IN SEPTEMBER 1969

Another initiative by OAU for a settlement of the Nigerian conflict was made at the sixth Assembly of Heads of State and Government in Addis Ababa on 6 September 1969. The conference adopted a resolution urging both sides in the Nigerian civil war to call a cease-fire and negotiate for a united Nigeria. The four countries that had recognized Biafra (Gabon, Ivory Coast, Tanzania, and Zambia) abstained, as did Sierra Leone. The resolution appealed

> solemnly and urgently to the two parties involved in the civil war to agree to preserve, in the overriding interests of Africa, the unity of Nigeria and accept immediately the suspension of hostilities and the opening without delay of negotiations intended to preserve the unity of Nigeria and restore reconciliation and peace that will ensure for the population every form of security and every guarantee of equal rights, prerogatives and obligations."[19]

LAST PEACE EFFORTS

Colonel Ojukwu, in an address to the Biafran Consultative Assembly on 1 November 1969, reiterated his preparedness to meet Federal representatives at any place and any time. He excluded OAU as a possible forum, however. He said that Biafra had lost faith in OAU "due to its lack of foresight, objectivity, courage and conviction."[20]

A few days afterward, a Biafran policy statement was issued by the Markpress Agency in Geneva (acting as public relations office for Biafra). Indicating a major concession by Biafra, it said:

> Since our attachment to sovereignty is functional and not sentimental, Biafra will be prepared to accept, at the suggestion of no matter who, any alternative arrangement that can guarantee the non-recurrence of the massacres of the past 25 years.

165

This announcement was taken to mean that Colonel Ojukwu was prepared to abandon his hitherto unyielding demand for secession from Federal Nigeria. Twenty-four hours later, however, the head of the Markpress Agency, William Bernstein, declared that the statement had been completely misinterpreted. He said that it was

> absolutely ridiculous to say that Biafra is prepared to give up her independence. Biafra has always demanded safety guarantees for the Ibo people, whose mistreatment was the principal cause of secession. But this would have to be done within the framework of an economic federation of autonomous states. Sovereignty can be interpreted in many ways. The way it is understood by Biafra is an economic federation of independent States, with Biafra keeping her Army.

Colonel Ojukwu's attempts to secure mediation in the conflict through Switzerland, Austria, Sweden, and Yugoslavia, in preference to OAU, did not yield any positive results. No official approach was made to the Federal government, and the Federal authorities stressed repeatedly that OAU was the only body authorized to mediate.

The last round of peace talks between Biafra and the Federal government was about to take place in December 1969. Both parties were invited to Addis Ababa by Emperor Haile Selassie. The question of whether the Emperor's initiative was a private one or that of the Chairman of the OAU Consultative Mission on Nigeria gave rise to some controversy. The Biafran interpretation was that it was a private initiative, as Biafra had refused to have anything more to do with OAU. The Nigerian Ambassador in Addis Ababa, Olu Sanu asked for clarification and on 17 December 1969 he publicly announced that he had received assurances from the Ethiopian Foreign Minister, Ketema Yifru, that the talks were organized by the Emperor within the framework of the OAU. As a result of this impasse, the talks never took place and the Biafran delegation (led by Pius Okigbo), which had already arrived in Addis Ababa, returned home on 18 December 1969. By that time the war was practically over.

THE COLLAPSE OF BIAFRA

After the end of 1969, the morale of the Biafran Army was rapidly declining and desertions reached alarming proportions. The famished soldiers threw away their arms and disappeared into the bush or into the crowds of distressed refugees. By the end of 1969, what was left of Biafra's territory was filled with refugees clogging the roads and overcrowding the refugee camps and villages. The frequent strafing of the retreat routes by the MIGs of the Nigerian Air Force added to the panic, which was increasing from day to day. According to an official Federal announcement on 11 January, Owerri fell on 9 January 1970.

On the morning of 10 January 1970, the last meeting of the Biafran Cabinet was held. Colonel Ojukwu announced that he would leave Biafra "in search of peace" and appointed his Chief of Staff, Colonel Phillip Effiong, to administer the government.

Meanwhile, Federal troops had gotten to within three miles of Biafra's only remaining airstrip at Uli. One of the last to use the airport was the Biafran leader, Colonel Ojukwu, who arrived at the airfield at about 3 A.M. local time on 11 January.* The following day, 12 January, Colonel Effiong offered to General Gowon an unconditional surrender of Biafra, and it was accepted.

The surrender ceremony took place at Army headquarters, Dodan Barracks in Lagos on Thursday, 15 January 1970. Colonel Effiong formally presented a document to the Head of State, Major General Yakubu Gowon, before members of the Supreme Military Council, the Administrator of the Central Eastern State, A. U. Asika, and top-ranking military and government officials. The declaration stated that the so-called "Republic of Biafra" had ceased to exist and that:

1. The authority of the Federal military government of Nigeria was accepted.

2. The existing administrative and political structure of Nigeria was accepted.

3. In the future the constitutional arrangements would be worked out by the representatives of Nigeria.

General Gowon concluded his speech by calling on the Biafran delegation: "Gentlemen, let us join hands to rebuild this country, where no man will be oppressed."[21] Then the two soldiers, General Gowon in uniform and Colonel Effiong in civilian clothes, posed for photographs, embracing each other several times. Thus the Nigerian and Biafran military, which started the war, ended it with an embrace.

––––––––––––––

*The whereabouts of Colonel Ojukwu were not known until 24 January 1970, when it was announced that he had been granted asylum in the Ivory Coast, on condition that he not engage in political activities.

CONCLUSIONS

Ojukwu grossly miscalculated the impact of the Biafran case on the international scene, where he hoped for both recognition and material assistance. Biafra did not obtain recognition soon after secession, owing to three main factors:

1. The assumption by the Federal government of the political initiative in the crisis, following the creation of twelve states.

2. The Federal government's firmness in the west and its gaining the support of Chief Awolowo, who became a member of the Federal Executive Council.

3. The rapid and effective institution of an economic blockade of Biafra.

By these three moves, plus a very sharp warning to the outside world not to interfere in what was described as a purely internal problem, the Nigerian Federal government rapidly showed its determination to oppose the secession. The Portuguese connection and the help Biafra received from South Africa lost the Biafrans a great deal of African goodwill.

The recognition of Biafra by Gabon, Ivory Coast, Tanzania, and Zambia strengthened Biafra's claim to independent existence and its demand to be treated on an equal basis with the Federal government at the peace talks. But this never amounted to anything more than moral support of the Biafran cause—support given for purely humanitarian reasons. There is no need to go deeper into the recognition of Biafra by the four African states or the effect of the implied recognition by France, which was believed to have provided Biafra with more than moral support.

Within the context of the Nigerian crisis, Biafra's existence depended above all on the outcome of the armed conflict between the two sides and not on the legitimacy of the Biafran cause. The significance of the policy of nonrecognition of Biafra, which was endorsed by the OAU Summit Meeting at Algiers when it called upon "all member states of the United Nations and OAU to refrain from any action detrimental to the peace, unity and territorial integrity of Nigeria," was that it upheld the principle of African unity. This might be seriously undermined if secessions of the Biafran type were allowed to happen.

Support for the Federal military government, even by those who realized the inhumanity of their decision, was justified by the argument that the break-up of Nigeria would spell the break-up of every other African state. Since the boundaries of African states are artificial, and since the states contain different tribal groups that have often been in conflict in the past, it has been argued that the secession of one tribal group in Nigeria would encourage the

Somalis in Ethiopia and Kenya, the Ashanti in Ghana, the Baluba in Congo, the Ewes in Ghana, Togo, and Dahomey, and so on, to make similar attempts. This fear of disintegration had a decisive effect on the majority of OAU members.

In Africa, there are strong feelings about secession. For loosely united states, some still economically and politically unstable, to admit the validity of Biafra's cause would have given rise to trouble and reopened the disputes on the definition of boundaries and the re-grouping of ethnic and tribal groups. This eventuality would have multiplied the difficulties of the continent and jeopardized its economic development.

It was because the African states were only too well aware of their own predicaments that they were inhibited from fully expressing their deep concern over the Nigerian war. Their support for the Nigerian Federal government stemmed from the expediency of practical politics.

This is not just a reflection of the conservative outlook of most of Africa's heads of government. The leaders of Guinea, Algeria, and the UAR were among the most vociferous of General Gowon's supporters. One of the errors of Colonel Ojukwu was to suppose that such states would rally to his support after secession because of the "progressive" nature of the Biafran regime, in contrast to the "feudalistic" nature of the Federal government.

The Federal military government never asked for U.N. intervention. Biafra's plea for U.N. mediation was ignored, and U.N. involvement was limited to the humanitarian relief carried out and organized with the consent of the Federal military government. In the absence of a Federal request for U.N. help, there was no legal basis for the United Nations to adopt any measures aimed at restoring peace in Nigeria. The consent of a legitimate government is the only basis on which the U.N. peace-keeping force can operate in a country. This applies not only to military operations but also to "humanitarian intervention" for relief of the civilian victims of war. The dilemma of those who, deeply moved by the mass starvation of the Ibo, were urging their governments to mount an airlift to Biafra against the wishes of the Federal military government, was that such action would constitute a violation of Nigeria's sovereignty.

The loss of almost two million lives was the most horrible aspect of the Nigerian war. However, two important lessons emerged from the conflict:

1. The Nigerian experience convinced all OAU members to accept the authority of OAU concerning the settlement of their disputes of whatever origin and magnitude.

2. The outcome of the Nigerian war was that 60 million Nigerians found a common political and economic future within the framework of twelve states. The functioning and prosperity of such a large federation demonstrates the advantages of close cooperation on an interstate and regional basis.

NOTES

1. For guidance on books about the Nigerian war and its background, see Ch. Ch. Aguolu, Nigerian Civil War, 1967-70 (An Annotated Bibliography (Boston: Hall, 1973). Excellent documentation on the conflict has been provided by A. H. M. Kirk-Greene, Crisis and Conflict in Nigeria- A Documentary Sourcebook, 1966-1970, 2 vols. (London: Oxford University Press, 1971). The best coverage of the war in the author's opinion, is John de St. Jorre, The Nigerian Civil War (London: Hodeer & Stoughton, 1972). Military operations, peace efforts, the roles of the great powers and the relief organizations are also described in Z. Cervenka, The History of the Nigerian War, 1967-70 (Frankfurt: Bernard & Graefe, 1971), which contains over 1,200 bibliographic entries.

2. The number of people who died in the pogrom was at first put by the Eastern Region at 7,000, at the Aburi meeting at 10,000, and by Lieutenant Colonel Ojukwu in his address to the OAU Consultative Committee on Nigeria at Addis Ababa on 5 August 1968, at 30,000.

The number of refugees has varied, the highest figure given being about two million. The Federal government figures for the victims of the September-October disturbances were 5,000 only.

The main point about the September killings was that they affected the mass of the people and created the sort of emotional climate in which secession was possible. The argument about numbers (whether it was 5,000 or 30,000 killed or whether there were 700,000 or 2 million refugees) is irrelevant. Whatever the number, it was sufficiently large to create a trauma of considerable proportions, because it affected so many families and stretched right down through society.

See K. Whiteman, "Enugu: The Psychology of Secession (20 July 1966 to 30 May 1967)," in Nigerian Politics and Military Rule: Prelude to the War, ed. by S. K. Panter-Brick (London: Athlone Press for the Institute of Commonwealth Studies, 1970).

3. Le Monde of 17 October 1968, in an article entitled "Des armes seraient acheminees chaque nuit du Gabon au Biafra," reported on the delivery of arms of French and German manufacture by mercenary pilots from Libreville to Biafra. France, however, made an

official denial of giving any military assistance to Ojukwu. The French embassy in Lagos issued a statement on 10 November 1968, quoted in the following way by Lagos Radio on 11 November 1968: "It says there is no truth whatsoever in the report recently carried in some sections of the Nigerian press to the effect that France has supplied jet planes and other military equipment to the rebels. France has been widely accused by both the local and foreign press of supplying arms to the rebels for the prosecution of their ill-fated war against their fatherland."

4. President de Gaulle, too, said at a press conference in Paris in the first week of September 1968 that French recognition could not be excluded in the future. In de Gaulle's words, 'France in this affair has assisted to the extent of her possibilities. She has not taken the step of recognition of the Biafran Republic, because she thinks that the gestation of Africa is above all a matter for the Africans. Already there are some African States of West and East Africa which have recognised Biafra. Others also appear to be moving in this direction. This means that for France the decision which has not been taken cannot be excluded in the future.' See West Africa, 14 September 1968, p. 1086.

5. In The Observer of 22 September 1968, Colin Legum wrote: "By next Sunday another 10,000 people—many of them children—will have died in Biafra. And many thousands more will have become victims of kwashiorkor, a terrible protein-deficiency disease, and will also die unless the right kind of food and medical supplies reach them in time." John de St. Jorre of The Observer wrote from Lagos on 28 September 1968: "Now over 5,000 die each day in Biafra."

6. The word genocide has often been used in relation to Nigeria's war with little realization of its meaning. According to the 1948 Geneva Convention on the Prevention and Punishment of Genocide, acts of genocide are those committed with intent to destroy, in whole or in part, a national, ethnic, racial, or religious group, to cause serious bodily or mental harm to members of the group, deliberately to inflict on the group conditions of life calculated to bring about its total or partial destruction, to impose measures intended to prevent births within the group, or forcibly to transfer children of one group to another. For the text of the Convention, see American Journal of International Law 45 (1951). At the end of August 1968, the Federal government had invited foreign observers to visit the battle areas and observe the conduct of Federal troops. An invitation had been extended to the U.N. Secretary General, the OAU and the governments of Britain, Poland, Canada, and Sweden to send one observer each. The team of observers was given full facilities to visit the areas of military operations and observe the conduct of Federal troops as they advanced into Biafran territory.

171

There were two representatives of the OAU—General Nega Tegegu of Ethiopia and Major Slimane Hoffman of Algeria; Colonel Olkiewitz represented Poland; Nils Gussing represented the U.N.; Major-General Arthur Raab, Sweden; Major-General W. A. Milroy, Canada; and Major-General Henry Alexander the United Kingdom.

All observers' reports concluded that there was no evidence supporting the allegations of genocide by the Federal forces against the Ibo people. For the text of the reports, see Z. Cervenka, op. cit., pp. 87-92.

7. Press release by the Federal Republic of Nigeria, 23 November 1967.

8. Ibid.

9. Africa Research Bulletin 5, no. 7, p. 1122.

10. Ibid., p. 1124.

11. Ibid.

12. Nyerere stated: "Unity can only be based on the general consent of the people involved. The people must feel that this State, or this Union is theirs and they must be willing to have their quarrels in that context. . . . We in this country believe that unity is vital for the future of Africa. But it must be a unity which serves the people and which is freely determined upon by the people . . . it seemed to us that by refusing to recognise the existence of Biafra we were tacitly supporting a war against the people of Eastern Nigeria—and a war conducted in the name of unity. We could not continue doing this any longer." See Julius Nyerere, "Why We Recognized Biafra," The Observer (London), 26 April 1968.

13. President Houphouet-Boigny, in his declaration on the recognition of Biafra on 9 May 1968, said, "Unity is the fruit of the common will to live together; it should not be imposed by force by one group upon another. If we are all in agreement in OAU in recognising the imperious necessity of unity, unity as the ideal framework for the full development of the African man, we also admit that it should not become his grave. We say yes to unity in peace, unity in love and through brotherhood. Unity is for the living and not for the dead." The statement by Houphouet-Boigny is reproduced in Afrique Express (Brussels), no. 161 (25 May 1968), p. 7.

14. AHG/Res.51 (IV), 1967.

15. West Africa (London), 21 September 1968, p. 1091.

16. U Thant called on OAU to bring about a settlement and warned that the continuance of the crisis would endanger African unity. He said that the Nigerian conflict had already "created difficulties in relations between African States, and its continuation is bound to affect badly needed co-operation and unity among African countries." In his view, the 1967 OAU summit resolution, pledging faith in the Nigerian Federal government and recognizing Nigeria's territorial

integrity, was the basis for his approach to the problem. "I believe that OAU should be the most appropriate instrument for the promotion of peace in Nigeria," he said.

17. There is a consensus among states that recognition is basically a political right each state reserves to itself, and that such objective criteria as exist—such as that the government recognized should have de facto control over the country and, for de jure recognition, expressed support of the masses of the population—are no more than a minimum guide for the governments according recognition. These criteria have no mandatory force. It is also generally understood that, where a government refuses to recognize a regime on some seemingly objective grounds, such as the refusal of the United States to recognize Communist China—on the ground, among others, that the regime was forced upon the people and not democratically elected—the reasons for nonrecognition are really political. See Y. Tandon, "Military Coups and Inter-African Diplomacy," Africa Quarterly 6, no. 4 (January-March 1967): p. 279.

18. "Although rebellion is treason in the eyes of municipal law, it results—when followed by the establishment of an effective government wielding power over the entity of national territory, with a reasonable prospect of permanency and with the consent or the acquiescence of the people—in a duty of other States to recognise the change and to treat the new government as representing the State in international sphere." See Lauterpacht, Recognition in International Law (London: 1947), p. 409.

19. AHG/Res. 58(VI), 1969.

20. G. O. Ojukwu, Biafra: Selected Speeches with Journal of Events (New York: Harper and Row, 1969).

21. The surrender ceremony, statements, and documents are contained in a pamphlet published by the Federal government of Nigeria in 1970 under the title "Victory for Unity."

9

THE SOUTHERN
SUDAN SETTLEMENT
AND ITS AFRICAN
IMPLICATIONS
Mansour Khalid

National unity is one of the major challenges facing they nascent states today. Those states are almost all beset with problems of ethnic fragmentation, tribal dissidence, and regional disaffection, all factors that severely tax their ability to resolve the handicaps that militate against national integration. Such problems pose the constitutional question of loyalty to one system of authority.

The lack of a sense of nationhood leads to varying ideas of social justice among ethnic groups, which in turn leads to clashes, sometimes deteriorating into civil wars.

It is precisely for this reason that the problem of Southern Sudan has been regarded as having grave implications for Africa. And it is precisely for this reason that the peaceful solution of that problem had a reverberating effect on Africa. Without presuming to inflate our achievement, one can confidently put forward the thesis that the Addis Ababa Agreement, and the legislation ensuing from it, represent a landmark in Africa's march toward unity. But our experience, despite common denominations, should not be taken as a prototype answer to similar situations in many parts of Africa. In dealing with such cosmic issues as nationalism, people should avoid

---

The southern Sudan problem exemplifies to some extent the indirect role which may at times be played by the OAU not as an organization per se, but as an environment or an umbrella facilitating conflict resolution, hence the cogency of this chapter. In this connection, see also, Yassin El-Ayouty, "Settlement of the Southern Sudanese Problem: Its Significance and Implications for the Future," Issue: A Quarterly Journal of Africanist Opinion, Vol. II, no. 1 (Waltham, Massachusetts, The African Studies Association, Spring 1972), pp. 10-12.

the temptation of resorting to facile comparisons and simplistic
abstractions.

SUDAN'S EXPERIENCE

The conflict in the Sudan was not untypical of conflicts in other
African countries, although it had its own peculiarities. To understand the nature of the conflict, it is worthwhile giving an account of
the factors that gave rise to it. A historical background is therefore
in order. The problem has roots in history as well as culture. It is
the typical colonial situation emanating from arbitrary divisions
cutting across linguistic and ethnic groupings, whether through the
accident of conquest or the expediency of politics. And it also is the
typical postcolonial situation of pressures to assert ethnic identity
and articulate (often inchoate) ethnic convictions opposed to counter-
vailing pressures to centralize authority as a focus of common
identity and allegiance.

A combination of factors was at work in keeping the North and
the South apart. On the cultural level, the pluralistic Sudanese society—
a veritable microcosm of Africa—embraces a great span of population
ranging from the Nubians (widely presumed to be descendants of the
ancient Pharaohs of Egypt) to Hamitic, Arab, and Negro elements,
as well as a substantial proportion of mixed races containing in their
blood two or more of those ethnic groups.

Some uninitiated political writers have tried to depict the Sudan
as a biracial country consisting of "black" Negroes and "white" Arabs,
the one set against the other. This is indeed an oversimplification
that many, unfortunately, found convenient to accept. The explanation
for this state of affairs lies in the heterogenous racial composition
of the so-called Arab North. A more exact terminology than Arab
may be the French term "arabisant," or the equally popular term
"Afro-Arab."

The 1955 census reveals that the Arab population of Sudan
makes up 39 percent of the total, mainly residing in the North. That
figure might as well be taken with a grain of salt since the census
accepted professed ethnic allegiances at face value and without
verification. Nevertheless, the North had 31 percent non-Arab
population, largely people of Negroid and Hamitic stock. The Southern
Provinces, combined, with their 597 tribes grouped into 56 tribal
groups, made up the remaining 30 percent of the total population.

But Arabism to us is not a racial concept—it is a culture. It
is a way of life expounded in prevalent values, convictions, and
attitudes. On this account, the statistics are interesting. To take
the figures provided by the much outdated 1955 census, we find that

51 percent of the Sudanese population was Arabic-speaking and a much higher proportion in the country belonged to the Muslim faith. The fact that almost two decades have passed since 1955 militates for the possibility of large increases in those figures. In saying this, however, I must add that the diffusion of the Arabic language was never achieved forcibly, nor at the expense of local languages and dialects. Arabic was accepted all over the country as an intertribal "lingua franca," and not as a substitute for local languages and dialects.

The dichotomy is therefore not as heightened as some authors would like to suggest. Some of these authors are prisoners of their own preconceived visions of Africa. What is alarming is that many of the students of history, of our own clay, are falling victims to this erroneous conception of Africa, a conception based on a falsified history, an underanalyzed present, and a discounted future. In effect, there has been a greater intermingling of people in the thousand and more years in which Arabs and Africans have lived together in the Sudan than is usually accepted. That intermingling created the nucleus of our unity, and its denial amounts to a denial of our history itself.

There is abundant evidence in the past to prove the existence of cultural interpenetration up and down the Nile—as far north as Egypt. Historians and archaeologists have drawn attention to Egyptian paintings revealing horns of cattle curved in a way comparable to those of Dinka oxen. They also have drawn attention to the resemblance of the burial of the Shilluk Reth to that of ancient kings of Egypt. And there have been allusions to the very close similarity between musical instruments used by the Azande and those used in ancient Egypt.

In modern history there is abundant evidence of such influences. The Annals of Emin Pasha on his days with the Acholi Chiefs are very revealing in this respect. The influences of the Mahdia concept on some of the Nilotic tribes are well known. The Dinka, for example, have assimilated the concept of the Mahdi (the guided one) into their religious thought, making of him a divinity linked with Deng, a deity only next to God in importance. In contemporary history the foremost nationalist movement in the Northern Sudan, the White Flag Movement, which came to be known as Arab-inspired and oriented, was led by a Muslim Dinka, Ali Abdel Latif.

In addition to the cultural factor, geography also played its role in keeping the two regions apart. The North and the South are adjacent regions that both lie within the basin of the Nile and its tributaries. Yet the greater part of the South was isolated from the North until the second quarter of the nineteenth century by papyrus swamps. "The physical insulation has been so effective," according to historians, "that there has been a time interval of about thirty-four centuries between the dates at which the Northern Sudan and the Southern Sudan were opened up."[1]

The Southern Sudan's first experience with the outside world was most unhappy. The region was opened up through raids by foreigners to collect ivory and capture slaves. Europeans, who masterminded the operation using some Arab elements and even Southerners as middlemen, tried relentlessly to wash their hands of this responsibility, to the point of obliterating facts and history.

The experience, however, left memories in the minds of Southern Sudanese. Colonial education was geared toward keeping the tragic memories alive in the minds of Southern children, while omitting from the story all that was convenient to omit.

As if those barriers were not enough, the British administration decided to add its own rule (1898-1956) and initiated administrative procedures aimed at sealing off the South from the North. The use of Arabic as a means of communication was severely suppressed. Southerners were pointedly encouraged to shun Arabic names and clothing, and Northern Muslim merchants were dissuaded from doing business in the South, the preference going to Greeks and Christian Syrians and Lebanese. Also, the governors of the three Southern Provinces were made to hold separate administrative conferences in the South, unlike the governors of the rest of the provinces, who met annually in the national capital, Khartoum. The consequence of this policy was the fostering of tribal manners and customs in the South and the predication of the whole structure of society and organization of government on traditional usages.

This policy even lacked the saving grace of being aimed, for reasons of parsimony and political expediency, at the creation of constructive national identity for the Southern Sudan. Still less was it for the modernization and enlightenment of tribal authority in the manner in which British Colonial Administrator Luggard dealt with the traditional autocracy of Northern Nigeria. The main aim of Governor General, Sir John Maffey, the chief architect of this policy, was to turn the South into "a stronghold of tribalism" that might help to check the rising tide of nationalism in the country. This is, perhaps, a generous explanation of the rationale behind that policy. Others may wish to see in it yet another aspect of the condescending paternalism of the colonial administration. An arrogant expression of this thesis was made by a British administrator during the Juba Conference of 1947. He maintained:

we the British, who, whatever our failings, are better qualified than any other race, by tradition and taste and training, to lead primitives up the path of civil progress, are going to stand guard here till the South can dispense

with a guard, and are not going to see the South dominated
by an Arab civilization in Khartoum, which is more alien
to them than our own."[2]

"Their own" never left an imprint on the Southern Sudan despite
fifty years of continued presence—not to mention that that presence
was only made possible after the bloody suppression of the dogged
resistance to colonial invasion by Southern tribes, like the Nuer and
the Dinka Alyab, to mention a few.

Thus, when the British departed, they left behind them an
entirely Muslim North confronting a South that was still mainly pagan,
led by a small educated Christian intelligentsia. Though some people
may wish to argue that the British did not deliberately set Northern
Sudan and Southern Sudan by the ears, this, in fact, has been the
effect of their policy.

A corollary of the British policy of shielding the South from the
North was that it left the South untouched by the winds of change and
modernization. The South remained not only economically but also
educationally backward. The record of the colonial administration
in this regard is both disgraceful and inauspicious. Education was
only introduced to the Southern Provinces in 1924 as a tool for the
implementation of Maffey's Southern Policy, and possibly as a reaction
to the national awakening in the North, which was admittedly oriented
to and influenced by the Egyptian national liberation movement. That
educational policy was not geared toward the betterment of the social
and intellectual lot of the Southerners inasmuch as it was meant to
perpetuate vernacular languages and local usages in a way that would
eradicate all traces of Arabic or Islamic culture. The proceedings
of the language conference at Rajaf in 1926, which was attended by
the Director of Education and the Commissioner of the Northern
Province in Uganda as well as the representative of the Belgian
Congo administration, are very revealing in this respect. It was
therefore not without reason that Sayed Abel Alier, Sudan Vice President of the then still Provisional High Executive Council of Southern
Sudan, said:

> if there was anyone to blame for this state of backward-
> ness in the Southern Sudan, it was the British. At the
> time of independence only six Southerners had had
> university education.

There was a discernible imbalance between the North and the
South in education and political sophistication on the morrow of
independence, with the result that there was more political consciousness in the North than in the South. The difference was one of degree,

since even in the North education was not much advanced, nor were
the educated anything but marginal in the colonial system. For that
reason, the national struggle for independence was mainly spearheaded
by Northerners, and when self-rule was achieved, the administration
of the country fell upon the shoulders of Northerners, who predominated in the civil service and the entrepreneur class.

In that respect, Southerners were not as well qualified. Out of
800 jobs vacated by the British and Egyptians, only 6 went to Southerners. However, it has been argued with much sense that statesman-
ship on the part of the Northern leaders should have led to deliberate
oversight of requisite qualifications regarding Southern applicants.
What would have been lost in efficiency could have been gained in
confidence between the North and the South, and this possibly, could
have averted the conflict.

Our misfortune was that after independence the country, rather
than being run by statesmen, was by and large run by soap-box
politicians whose main preoccupation was the next election and not
the next generation. Informed opinion generally agrees that the result
of the Sudanization of jobs stirred ill feelings in the South. Rightly
or wrongly, some of the Southerners came to understand independence
to mean a change of masters. It was at this time that the demand for
safeguards was made by Southern politicians. They demanded a
federal status for the South to ensure full participation in decision
making regarding jobs, social services, economic development, and
cultural identity.

One of the first expressions of discontent with the state of
affairs after self-government came in the form of an army mutiny
in 1955 started by the Equatoria Corps. It is a chapter in our history
that none of us, Northerners and Southerners alike, would look back
to with pride. Several innocent lives were lost, and the revolt was
put down only after many casualties.

The mutiny and its aftermath had a traumatic effect on the
whole country. In the North, the hawkish and less forward-looking
elements carried the day. In the South, politicians in Parliament
became more vocal about the demand for a federal status for that
region, to the point that only a promise by the Northern parties that
federation would be given careful consideration after independence
was achieved served to unite the North and South in their joint resolution for full independence in December 1955.

After independence, the rallying point of Southern opinion was
the Liberal Party, which again stepped up its demand for federation.
In 1958, after this demand was rejected in Parliament, the Liberal
representatives withdrew. The Northern parties had not yet recovered
from the trauma of the equatorial mutiny. It was at this point that
General Abboud took over power and delivered the country into one

of its darkest periods. The General's answer to Southerners' demands for federation was military repression. This had the effect of alienating Southerners and producing a significant separatist movement in the South in the early 1960s.

THE FAILURE OF POLITICAL PARTIES

Thus, if the British cannot be exonerated from blame for their failure to integrate North and South Sudan, a no less culpable failure was that of the national political parties. They inherited probably the most difficult ethnic integration problem in Africa. Its solution required much understanding of the requirements of integration, and the parties sadly lacked such understanding. They saw in independence an end and not a beginning, a fulfillment and not a challenge. The lack of understanding of the requirement of integration on the part of the political parties was evident on many levels of their activities and in their very untutored approach to the problem.

In the field of political organization, the political parties did little to indicate that they understood the problem of national integration. Political parties in many parts of Africa did serve as instruments for integrating different ethnic and cultural groups. However, the political parties in the Sudan either centered around religious sects—the UMMA around the ANSAR; National Unionist Party (NUP) and Popular Democratic Party (PDP) around the KHATMIYA—or around ethnic groups, like the Liberal Party in the South. Thus, instead of becoming instruments of integration, the parties became catalysts for fragmentation. None of them emerged as a national party in the sense that it was able to embrace membership from different regions and ethnic groups.

Conceptually, the parties failed to see the Southern problem in its proper perspective. No party had the good sense to realize that ethnicity is not bad per se and that, as a determinant of social behavior, it could be used to rally the populace around good causes. All that was necessary, perhaps, was the taming and controlling of ethnicity's reactionary and negative aspects. With its obtuse look to the problem, the national government could only see in the legitimate aspirations of the Southerners unjustified claims; in their natural ambitious aspirations, treacherous exigencies; and in their political agitation, irrational exuberance.

The Revolution of October 1964, which overthrew the Abboud military regime, created an opportunity for the Sudan to find a new basis for integration. The October government undertook, for the first time since independence, a genuine search for a peaceful settlement and called for a Round Table Conference in which both Northern and Southern politicians, as well as observers from friendly African countries, participated. The conference, though it did not produce any agreement between the North and South on the basic constitutional question, reached limited agreement on a number of reforms. If those reforms had been implemented, that might have rebuilt confidence among the Southerners. But in the intervening period, the elements that had brought about the October Revolution were elbowed out of office by the traditional parties. They sabotaged the results of the conference, thereby bringing the country back to square one.

THE MAY REVOLUTION

By the first half of 1969, the Sudan appeared to have been steeped in a stage of large-scale civil conflict of unknown duration and uncertain outcome. This was the time when the Army intervened and took power in May 1969. With the advent of the May Revolution came a refreshing breath of hope. To some people, particularly those with the memories of the clumsy manner in which the Abboud regime dealt with the Southern question, this might sound like a contradiction in terms. Generally, it has become fashionable to describe armies as forces of repression. That need not always be the case. Armies in the Third World, given a determined and purposeful leadership, acting within a framework of popular consent and acquiescence, and supported by a wide political participation, can be important forces of stabilization and modernization. Without those conditions, armies in government can deteriorate into dictatorships driven by impulses of coercion. Coercion may be necessary to check all the central forces of purposeless dissent, but it is hardly the best equipment to deal with complex political problems like national integration and nation building.

This brings us to the aspect of leadership and the role it played in bringing about peace in the Sudan. In 1969, when President Nimeiry came to power, he promised the nation a leadership that would have the political will and determination to do all that had to be done to achieve progress, and more important still, charge the nation with a sense of national purpose. In a country whose energies had been dissipated in war and the merry-go-round of party politics, there could have been no better rallying point. The importance of such a brand of leadership is that it serves as a focus of national purpose by the very dint of its transcendence of all sectoral allegiances. Leadership in the "ancient regimes" was generally based on sectarian allegiances, ethnic and tribal belonging, or socioeconomic status.

Unfortunately, the problem with many European commentators, both East and West, and many of their loyal disciples in our midst, is that they cannot view our society, except within the perimeters imposed by their preconceived notions. Dicey and Lord Acton may make sense in England. Some of the sociological aspects of Marx, particularly as regards the determinants and vehicles of change, may make sense in the industrialized societies of Europe. And even there, with the experiences of Yugoslavia, Czechoslovakia, and Ireland, I am sure many would wish today to revise some of the old assumptions—though revisionism, in some political lexicons, may be categorized under the rubric of pejorative expressions.

We in the Sudan know that the incapacitated system of government based on what is fashionably known as Britain's cricket democracy, far from being overthrown, has in fact collapsed under its own heavy weight. That system did not stem from the people's heritage, nor did it take into consideration their mores, ethos, and patterns of social communication.

Going back to the role of the Army in helping bring about the peaceful solution of the Southern problem, it is not necessary to mention here that the South was the prime reason for the overthrow of General Abboud in 1964 and of the parties' government in 1969— the former for a brutal and clumsy manner of dealing with the problem, and the latter for a myopic and irresponsible approach. The Southerners, understaffed and underequipped as they were, faced the impossible situation of having to fight an interminable and unnecessary war for no good reason other than that the leaders of Khartoum were either frivolously unconcerned with it and its outcome, or politically inadequate to understand its genesis and control its consequences.

With such a bitter experience, the May leaders placed the problem of the South at the top of their priorities. Shortly after he came to power, President Nimeiry, in what came to be known as the Ninth of June Declaration, said that his government recognized the historical, cultural, and geographic differences between North and South, as well as the right of the Southern people to develop their separate traditions and to enjoy administrative regional autonomy within a united socialist Sudan. He maintained that unity could be achieved despite the historical and cultural differences between the North and the South.

The Southern problem, however, was not readily soluble. The problem had its national and African ramifications as well as its political and psychological aspects.

On the national level, the political aspect involved two questions. The first was the need to recognize the importance of national unity. In a world that is progressively advancing toward larger units, development and progress in a variety of fields will be blocked if national fusion and economic consolidation and integration are not achieved. On that score, the Addis Ababa Agreement has gone a long way to

ensure unity. The Agreement was predicated on the principle of
national unity. The second question was the need to recognize that
the Southern aspirations for autonomy were not necessarily a negation
of nationalism. As President Nimeiry said on several occasions
that unity can be maintained despite divergence of ethnic and cultural
traits.

Those aspirations derive from a rejection of being governed
by remote control. Fortunately, the whole philosophy of the May
Revolution is based on the recognition that the locals are better judges
of their cause. The People's Local Government Act, promulgated
in 1971, has as its main purpose the decentralization of government
and diversification of the decision-making centers. Democracy is
a hollow word if political participation is not assured at all levels,
including the grassroots. Nation building is doomed to failure if the
message of change is not carried to the remotest part, which is
generally the most stagnant and traditional.

It is our belief that the measures provided for in the Addis
Ababa Agreement and the legislation emanating from it were the
best way not only to cater to the legitimate aspirations of the Southern
citizens for autonomy but also to promote constructive political
participations, and possibly political initiation, in some parts of the
South. The instruments of power created by such measures are best
suited to articulate the sentiments and convictions of the people of
the region, to ensure national peace and tranquillity by minimizing
local conflicts, and to provide vehicles for wide mobilization of the
masses in the process of development. National integration does not
necessarily mean the disintegration of all forms of communal life,
nor does it necessarily presuppose the deliberate destruction of all
traditional ethnic patterns.

The psychological aspect of the problem, on the other hand,
involved the need to regain trust where trust had been lost. With the
sparks of old bitterness fanned into a blaze by the colonial administration, and the deep disappointment following independence, a state
of mistrust had clouded the thinking of many Southerners. Such
disappointments reached their peak after the failure of the genuine
search by the October government for a peaceful settlement. The
Round Table Conference that was initiated by that government provided
a platform for meaningful dialogue between Southerners and Northerners and prompted the return, from voluntary exile, of considerable
numbers of refugees and Southern intellectuals.

But although enough common ground was already surveyed, the
ensuing mistrust made communication impossible. There is a lot of
truth in the comments of one author, dealing with a different situation:

Social trust is vital in establishing the credibility of
political messages. Variations in credibility of messages

183

lead to fragmented perceptions of political events particularly acute in moment of crisis.[3]

In its initial conception, the idea of the Round Table Conference was a gesture of faith and confidence in the power of peace and wisdom. But under the traditional politickers—who came to power after the October government—it turned into a parody of itself. In some ways, it could be called the only landmark on the long and laborious climb to the Addis Ababa Agreement of 1972.

IMPACT ON AFRICA

On the African level, the problem of the South had a relevance to the neighboring countries, both politically and economically. The new states of Africa are mainly the geographic products of arbitrary division of the continent between the colonial powers in the late nineteenth and early twentieth centuries. The Sudan has its share of ethnic links with contiguous countries. The Nuers and the Anuaks have their kith and kin in Ethiopia. The Acholi of Sudan have blood relations with those in Uganda. The same could be said of the Azande of Sudan and those in Zaire and the Central African Republic, as well as the Kareish in Western Bahr El Ghazal and those in Central African Republic. Peace in the Southern Sudan could account for stability of border areas and create the nucleus, if a small one, of common interest, communication, and understanding.

ISSUES ARISING FROM THE AGREEMENT

In dealing with the Addis Ababa Agreement, some people may wish to highlight such elements as the apportionment of authority between the region and the center, or the integration of the Anya-Nya in the National Army. I believe that those questions might be of more interest to a newspaper correspondent trading in sensationalism, or to a detached politicologue. However, the ease with which the regional government was installed in the South, and the smoothness with which the integration of the Anya-Nya into the National Army was achieved, baffled the most optimistic of us and proved that those problems were of lesser importance to us. Those who are emotionally involved in the problem have other preoccupations. In my opinion, the most important issue is economic development, including the accelerated development of education within the overall social and economic development plan. Those two factors, development and education, will play the determinant role in achieving unity and progress in the Sudan.

184

Under the Addis Ababa Agreement, responsibility for educational planning and national economic development falls within the purview of the central government. But what is important here is not who will do what, but what the Sudanese, both in the North and in the South, should do together to achieve national integration and social and economic progress. In our part of the world, the tenure of governments shall, and should, be determined by their ability to satisfy the social and economic expectations of the people they govern.

THE ROLE OF EDUCATION

The need for the accelerated development of education in developing countries is perhaps more poignant than any other need, for if there were to be a permanent change, such a change would best be effected through education. Education, more than any other agent of change, has a determinant role to play both in forging national unity and in creating a common sense of purpose and determination.

The development of education has more to it than the proliferation of schools. Education must be attuned to the needs of the society. It must revolutionize habits and ways of life hardened in centuries of custom. Education must be nationally oriented in the sense that it must foster national pride and reject the concept of colonial education aimed at grooming the nationals in the image of the Europeans. It must be scientific and geared to the developmental needs of the country, rather than engaging in a pedantic acquiescence in patterns already abandoned in Europe and elsewhere. It must be revolutionary since the big gap between us and the developed world, in history and culture, can never be filled through conventional ways and methods.

Another feature of education is political education. Formal education does in some measure contribute to this type of education, but the major part of it falls to the political organizations. Political parties, in the past, have miserably failed to educate the masses. The incapacity of leaders to lead was only matched by their penchant for following the tides of irrational public sentiment, often a figment of their own imaginations. Native will and grit were often confused with political judgment and singlemindedness.

The Sudanese Socialist Union, the only political organization in both North and South, will have a herculean task ahead. Its role will not only be one of political mobilization but also of political initiation and education. Party machinery must allow for constant discussion of local problems by the local peoples themselves. It is only through such methods that natural leadership emerges, popular mobilization in the process of development is assured, and national integration is achieved at will.

185

ECONOMIC DEVELOPMENT

For over half a century, the problem in the South also assumed a developmental dimension. The existing gap between the two regions will have to be closed if the peaceful settlement is to have any sense at all.

But more important than this bridging of the gap is the whole question of the acceleration of social and economic development—the only method that would enable us to compress centuries of social experience into a single generation.

Now, with peace and tranquillity restored and freedom of movement ensured, activities in different fields of development—including foreign and domestic investment in agriculture, livestock, industry, and trade—can safely commence. Freedom of movement in particular has an important role to play in the process of integration. This mobility helps in creating an atmosphere of confidence conducive to a healthy pursuit of a national human relationship between the people of the North and the South, and eventually to the social integration of the people of the Sudan.

Modern Sudan has known the phenomenon of immigration by Southern labor into Northern cities—a phenomenon that is independent of, and predates, disturbances in the Southern Provinces. And despite its disadvantages, typical of urbanization, this movement had an important effect in liberating the immigrants from tribal taboos against certain kinds of jobs or hired work in general. For example, the Dinka, who view hired labor as an indecency, engage in it once away from their tribe. I believe there is a lot of truth in the view that

> a man is more likely to think of the ancestors when there
> is economic stagnation or decline and more likely to
> think of his work and his future if there is economic
> growth and prosperity.[4]

The process of integrating the Southern region with the other regions of the Sudan in a centrally planned economy has its organizational, economic, and sociopsychological aspects. The government of the Sudan, on the basis of the guidelines in the Addis Ababa Agreement, has already launched effectively coordinated programs of rural development, local government reform, transport and communication, building and construction, as well as sustained efforts for social development, including projects and schemes in this domain to be carried out partly by "self-reliance" and partly through resort to international and bilateral assistance.

The impetus and acceleration in the process of resettlement and rehabilitation of returnees will determine, among other things, the time dimension needed for the execution of viable projects in the Southern region. However, we all realize that some time is needed before the contribution of the South in the national economy is felt in real terms. If the solution of the Southern Sudan problem now will have one far-reaching affect on Africa, that affect will be economic.

Now that the Addis Ababa Agreement is in operation, there are strong reasons to believe that some viable regional projects and joint ventures with other African countries, especially those bordering the Southern region, could be sought in the short run. The long-run approach may extend to more serious forms of economic integration.

The drive for cooperation among the African nations should be based on the following aims and objectives:

1. To foster mutual cooperation not only as an economic necessity but also as an inevitable political factor for facing a set of challenges.

2. To effectively utilize the complimentarities between the resources and requirements of the African countries, thus contributing to each other's economic and social progress.

3. To intensify and broaden the movement for cooperation and integration by all practical means.

The Sudan did not contribute much to such a trend in the past, being obstructed by its own internal strife and the fact that the Southern problem constituted a physical barrier for exploring possibilities of cooperation on a regional basis.

The development of infrastructure occupies a position of priority in considering the forms of mutual cooperation that could be developed. The execution of joint regional projects in the fields of rail and road communication, irrigation and power will have far-reaching multiple effects on trade, tourism, industry, employment, and the mobility factor. An immediate preoccupation of the African Revolution should be the transformation of prevailing systems of transport, communication, and telecommunication services in Africa—with a view to promoting direct media of mutual cooperation. The lack of an integrated transport system adversely affects national cohesion and the possibility of developing an export trade beyond what was established within the colonial metropolitan nexus.

The Addis Ababa Agreement, to recapitulate, has the following implications for Africa.

First, it is an example of the feasibility of unity in diversity, both at the national and continental levels. Many commentators and self-styled Africanists are preoccupied with the concept of two

187

Africas—north and south of the Sahara. The Sudan is demonstrating how an Afro-Arab synthesis can be made to work.

Second, the Agreement will serve to bring continental harmony as far as the immediate neighbors of the Sudan are concerned. This is a necessary prerequisite for regional and indeed continental peace.

Third, the Agreement marks a halt to the process of fragmentation of Africa. This has been a primary objective of the Organization of African Unity since its inception, and the main preoccupation of all independent African states.

Fourth, it lays the foundation for the integration of the national economy as a prelude to the process of regional economic integration.

Fifth, and finally, the Agreement represents a triumph for Africa. It is a testimony to the fact that Africans can solve their problems peacefully if left alone. It is lucid answer to the detractors of Africa, as well as to those paternalists who have not always displayed an unalloyed sympathy toward us.

NOTES

1. Arnold Toynbee, Forward to Oliver Albino, The Sudan: A Southern Viewpoint (London: Oxford University Press, The Institute of Race Relations, 1970).

2. Letter of 5 January 1947, from Bahr Ghazal Province to Governor of Equatoria Province; Khartoum Conference on the South March 1965 documents.

3. Ruth Schachter-Morgenthau, Africa in the Seventies and Eighties (New York: Praeger Publishers), p. 73.

4. Ibid.

10

THE OAU AND THE ARAB-ISRAELI CONFLICT: A CASE OF MEDIATION THAT FAILED

Yassin El-Ayouty

INTRODUCTION

On 22 June 1971, the eighth Assembly of Heads of State and Government of the OAU adopted in Addis Ababa a resolution on the Middle East conflict that resulted in an unprecedented involvement by the OAU in the Arab-Israeli conflict. As of that date, the OAU went beyond the realm of adopting resolutions condemning Israel's occupation of a part of the territory of a member state—namely, Egypt—as a result of the war of June 1967, and sought to exert direct pressure aiming at the achievement of a durable and just peace in the Middle East.

The transformation of the OAU's role in that regional conflict from pure exhortatory to action-oriented led, especially after the war of October 1973, the fourth Arab-Israeli war, to a dramatic alteration in African-Israeli interaction when all the African states belonging to the OAU, with the exception of Malawi, Lesotho, Botswana, and Swaziland, severed diplomatic relations with Israel. As part of these trends on the African continent, which began in earnest as of 1971 and represented the intertwining of the diplomacies of the League of Arab States and the OAU with regard to both the Middle Eastern and Southern African conflicts, the Palestine Liberation Organization received the OAU's "full support . . . as the only legitimate representative of the Palestine people in their heroic struggle against Zionism and racism."[1] This contrasts sharply with the situation that had obtained in the 1960s, when Israel maintained diplomatic and/ or consular relations with more than 30 African states, and when President Abdel-Nasser of Egypt sought to avoid injecting "the Israel problem" at the founding conference of the OAU in May 1963.[2]

The presentation and analysis that follow deal primarily with the 1971 effort by the African presidents, who sought unsuccessfully to mediate the conflict (primarily between Egypt and Israel), and with the immediate aftermath of that effort, whose failure contributed to the transformation of the system of international relations between Africa and the Middle East.

THE NATURE AND MEANING OF THE
OAU INITIATIVES

Under the impact of pressures for some action in the Arab-Israeli conflict, especially on behalf of an OAU member, Egypt, the eighth Assembly of Heads of State and Government of the OAU adopted in Addis Ababa its resolution AHG/Res. 66 of 22 June 1971 (see Appendix).[3] The resolution's title makes manifest the political intent of that document. Under the title "Resolution on the Continued Aggression Against the United Arab Republic, the OAU proceeded to issue a forceful call for action for "strict implementation" of U.N. Security Council Resolution 242 of 22 November 1967. Its basic thrust was "full support" for the Jarring Mission, especially for Jarring's initiative of 8 February 1971, "as a practical step for establishing a just and lasting peace in the Middle East." The operative principle is "immediate withdrawal of Israeli armed forces from all Arab Territories to the lines of 5 June 1967," and the impasse of the Jarring Mission is blamed on "Israeli defiance" in refusing to withdraw to Egypt's international frontier.

The OAU's resolution, adopted in Egypt's "Year of Decision," was a clear diplomatic victory for Egypt and its OAU supporters.[4] This was the most forceful OAU resolution on the Middle East crisis since the 1967 war, especially since it called for a specific African initiative directed toward implementation of Security Council Resolution 242 and renewal of Egyptian-Israeli indirect talks under Jarring's auspices. That initiative is expressed in the resolution's request to "the current Chairman of the OAU [President Ould Daddah of Mauritania] to consult with the Heads of State and Government so that they use their influence to ensure the full implementation of this resolution." Under such general terms, the African continental organization ventured for the first time out of its traditional politico-diplomatic bailiwick, which has been governed by the OAU's "unwritten principle of dealing solely with 'African' affairs."[5]

The priority given in the OAU resolution to the principle of withdrawal from "all" Egyptian and other territories occupied since 5 June 1967 is not surprising. The OAU Charter has enshrined the principle of "territorial integrity" of states. Although those Charter provisions are primarily aimed at opposing fragmentation through either secession or colonial action on the continent, their relation to "non-acquisition of territory by war," referred to in Security Council resolution 242, is obvious.

It could therefore be said that the only unifying principle for the OAU membership, as far as the Middle East conflict is concerned, is "withdrawal" of Israeli forces from occupied Arab territories. With equal unanimity, the African states summit in Addis Ababa in June 1971 regarded the reactivation of the Jarring Mission as the focal objective of its history-making initiatives in the Arab-Israeli conflict, initiatives that have, at least in their face value, transferred the crisis from an issue of "sympathy" to an issue of "action."

Against such background, the nature of the African initiatives* could be understood in terms of an African adjunct to the Jarring Mission—whose goal was, to quote the Foreign Minister of Senegal in the General Assembly debates of 13 December 1971, "to enable the Jarring negotiations to break out of the deadlock."[6] The African initiatives were based on an OAU resolution stressing the crucial importance of Security Council Resolution 242; those initiatives were not considered by their authors as supplanting that resolution or replacing Ambassador Jarring. Senegal's Foreign Minister, whose head of state led the on-spot discussions in the Middle East, stated before the General Assembly in December 1971 that the African action was "not to replace by new measures any of the provisions of resolution 242."[7]

As already stated, the OAU Chairman was requested "to consult with the Heads of State and Government so that they use their influence to ensure the full implementation of this resolution." While the political intent and orientation of the resolution were sufficiently clear, as indicated above, the resolution offered no clue as to the method of implementation. The decision on the nature of the African action was apparently left for later consultation by the Mauritanian President. Following the African diplomatic tradition developed under the OAU umbrella for peaceful settlement of disputes in Africa, a group of heads of state and government, numbering ten, was organized in an OAU Commission of Implementation (i.e., use of influence). It was composed of Cameroun, Ethiopia, Ivory Coast, Kenya, Liberia, Mauritania, Nigeria, Senegal, Tanzania, and Zaire. With the exception of Mauritania, all these countries, whose heads of state were included in the Commission, maintained diplomatic relations with Israel.†

---

*The author prefers to use "initiatives" to its use in the singular because the African action had several stages each of which varied in character from the others.

†In 1971 U.N. African membership totaled 41 countries of which 31 countries had maintained diplomatic relations with Israel. Those that had no such relations were the seven North African (Arab)

From the Commission's composition, it is obvious that the
African heads of state attempted to include a variety of political views,
ranging from consistent support of the Arab position to aversion toward getting sub-Saharan Africa or the OAU involved in what is regarded as primarily a non-African problem. Thus Mauritania and
Liberia, for example, could be taken as representing the two extreme
shades of the spectrum of opinion on the Commission of Ten. In that
regard, it could be said that African unanimity on the need for Israeli
withdrawal from occupied Arab territories and for reactivation of
the Jarring Mission does not imply unanimity among the African
states on the order of priorities and commitments in implementing
Resolution 242. These divisions of opinion were to be sharply reflected
in both the General Assembly debates and voting on the U.N. resolution on "the Middle East situation" between 1968 and 1971.

Following the establishment of the Commission of Ten, four
members were designated to ascertain Egyptian and Israeli views.
This committee consisted of President Ahidjo of Cameroun, President
Gowon of Nigeria, President Senghor of Senegal (Chairman), and
President Mobutu of Zaire. Once more the African pattern of action
through the summit prevailed. The committee was to travel to both
Cairo and Jerusalem to find what the delegate of the Ivory Coast, in
his statement to the U.N. General Assembly, called "a ground for
understanding which would make it possible to reactivate the Jarring
Mission."[8] Again, the whole range of African views—from support
for the Arab position on Resolution 242 to neutrality—could be observed in the Committee of Four. If Cameroun and Nigeria could be
said to represent the former sector of views, both Senegal and Zaire
might be described as belonging to the latter. It was also to be expected that the leadership of the Commission of Ten by the President
of Mauritania had to be balanced by the designation of the President
of Senegal as leader of the Committee of Four.

It was therefore not surprising that Senghor, upon arrival in
Israel, on the first of two rounds of consultations undertaken by the
Committee of Four, referred to the need for a "dialogue" between
the conflicting parties as a means of reactivating the Jarring Mission.[9]
Whatever the Senegalese President meant by his call for a dialogue,
neither the Egyptians nor the Israelis expected the efforts of the
Committee of "the Four Wise Men" to accomplish much. From Jeru-
salem the press conveyed an air of pessimism, and from Cairo an

---

countries, Guinea, Mauritius, and Somalia. By 1974, this picture had
drastically changed with all states in Africa, with the exception of
South Africa, Botswana, Lesotho, and Swaziland, severing relations
with Israel.

Egyptian editor was quoted as saying, "We have no illusions of a breakthrough resulting from all this."[10] Nevertheless, both Egypt and Israel saw in the Committee of Four possibilities for advancing their diplomatic arguments about the responsibility for the impasse facing the Jarring Mission.

CONFLICTING HOPES REGARDING THE OAU MISSION

If the Egyptians and Israelis were pessimistic about the possibility that the OAU mission would succeed in reactivating the Jarring negotiations, they nevertheless entertained hopes that it would bolster their respective positions. These conflicting hopes were based on the realization by the two opposing parties that the African mission was not one of mediation but of clarification of positions.

The Israelis hoped that the OAU mission would result in modifying "the pro-Egyptian positions previously adopted by the OAU.[11] Although the mission was considered at the periphery of the ongoing peacemaking diplomacy, it was regarded as potentially significant in Israel's efforts to improve relations with Third World governments.

More important, the Israelis hoped that the mission would be used as a new point of departure or a new context of negotiation. The Jarring initiative of 8 February 1971, which forced the Israelis to say no to a commitment to Israel's withdrawal to Egypt's international borders with Mandated Palestine, had become, for Israeli diplomacy, "a focus of deadlock"—to use Abba Eban's words in the General Assembly debates.[12] The way out of the deadlock was, from Israel's point of view, through what its Foreign Minister described as "free negotiation," which meant "no preconditions"[13] or precommitments, as requested by Jarring in his peace initiative of 8 February 1971.

Any support that the African mission might give to these Israeli diplomatic objectives would be gain, especially if such support was in the form of new points of reference implying "free negotiations" between Israel and Egypt. The embarrassment created by Israel's "no-withdrawal" response to Jarring would therefore be mitigated, if not overcome altogether, a new order of priorities might emerge, giving the objective of "a peace treaty" precedence over "withdrawal" under Resolution 242.

For Egyptian diplomacy, the crux of peacemaking efforts was an Israeli positive response to Jarring's memorandum of 8 February 1971 regarding prior commitment on withdrawal. Particular reference was therefore made in paragraph 3 of the Addis Ababa resolution of June 1971 to Jarring's "initiative for peace of 8 February 1971."[14] Any attempt to replace those terms of reference of

193

8 February and 22 June 1971 was obviously objectionable as it would shift world attention away from the primordial issue of prior Israeli commitment on withdrawal. Thus, the press reported from Cairo, in connection with the African mission's arrival on 5 November 1971, that "the Egyptian leadership was pleased by the [OAU] resolution, but seemed wary of any new peace plans presented by the Africans."[15] It was also reported that the Egyptian Minister of State for Cabinet Affairs, Dr. Issmat Abdel-Meguid, had toured African capitals to indicate that any new resolutions or plans would only "complicate the situation." The same point stressing the importance to Egyptian diplomacy of continuity of the U.N. frame of reference was made by Hafez Ismail, principal foreign affairs adviser to President Sadat. He was quoted as having said that the African mission must not be regarded as a mediation group, but rather as a group seeking implementation of Security Council Resolution 242.[16] Moreover, President Sadat told the mission of the "Four Wise Men" in Cairo that they "represented a new and serious attempt by the OAU, in the context of the African Summit Conference of June 1971, to implement resolution 242." He added that "Cairo sees in every attempt to revive the Jarring Mission an attempt to implement resolution 242."[17]

Moreover, Cairo was keen on using Israel's negative position on the Jarring initiative of 8 February as a means of furthering the isolation of Israel on the international diplomatic level. Specifically, Egypt hoped that Israel's economic and political interests in Africa "might be adversely affected"[18] as a result of its rebuff to the principle of "non-acquisition of territory by war."

These, then, were the guiding principles, rules, and hopes motivating Egypt and Israel in two diametrically opposed directions as the mission of four African Presidents, on behalf of the OAU's Commission of Ten, began its discussions in Jerusalem and Cairo in early November.

MISSION PROPOSALS AND THE RESPONSES

The Committee of Four accomplished its discussions in the Middle East through two visits to Jerusalem, two visits to Cairo, and discussions in Dakar with the membership of the Commission of Ten. At the end of this undertaking, the Commission of Ten transmitted "to the two parties . . . proposals for their considerations" as a means of allowing "the resumption of the Jarring negotiations and the establishment in that region of a just peace, which they wish to be lasting as between brothers."[19]

The African proposals or suggestions were considered by the Commission of Ten as helping to "reconcile the essentials in the respective positions of the two parties.[20] This was a hopeful assessment by the African heads of State, and tended to blur the sharp differences between Israeli and Egyptian positions. A study of the proposals and the parties' responses to them reveals three central elements. First, the parties demonstrated what the Commission described as their "yearning for peace." Second, the parties expressed their desire to see the Jarring Mission resumed, although with differing ordering of the Jarring talks. Third, Egypt clung to a reaffirmation of Resolution 242, the Jarring initiative of 8 February, and the OAU resolution of 22 June,[21] while Israel saw in the African proposals the promise of a new start bypassing the aforementioned "documentary obstacles" to "free negotiations." Said Israel's Foreign Minister: "Israel . . . accepts this [the African formulation] as the occasion and starting point for renewing discussions."[22] It is this third element that lies at the root of the present stalemate. The fact that the African proposals were first communicated officially to the U.N. membership not by their authors but by Israel's Ambassador Tekoah (via an annex to his letter of 9 December to the Secretary-General) was a further demonstration of Israel's desire to do away with the Jarring memorandum of 8 February as a basis for resumption of the talks.

Thus, an important question is posed: Did either Egypt or Israel, on the basis of their replies to the Commission of Ten, find in the African proposals sufficient basis for "reconciliation" of the essentials in their respective positions? An analysis of the proposals and the respective replies[23] leads to an answer in the negative. The essential elements are reproduced as follows:

1. On resumption of the Jarring negotiations: The Commission proposed resumption of these "indirect negotiations under . . . Jarring and within the terms of resolution 242 (1967), in order to reach a peace agreement." Israel agreed "to resume negotiations without prior conditions" under Jarring "within the terms of resolution 242 in order to reach a peace agreement." (Emphasis has been added throughout this discussion.) Egypt, by contrast, agreed to hold indirect negotiations under the Special Representative for implementation of resolution 242 in all its parts and for implementation of Jarring's initiative of 8 February. Once more the issue of "no prior conditions" versus the issue of "prior commitment on withdrawal" could not be reconciled.

2. On an interim agreement for Suez: The African heads of state suggested acceptance of an agreement "for the opening of the Suez Canal and the stationing, on the Eastern Bank of the Canal, of United Nations forces between the Egyptian and Israeli lines." Israel agreed "to work out a Suez Canal agreement" through negotiation that would also cover "measures to ensure supervision and observance of a Suez Canal accord." For its part, Egypt stated that it was ready to undertake arrangements for reopening of the Canal—in return for a

first stage of Israeli withdrawal, and on condition that Israel responded positively to Jarring's memorandum of 8 February. It will be noted that Israel implied that a Suez agreement, was an independent although subsidiary issue. Moreover, Israel, in emphasizing the separateness of a Suez accord, raised the questions of the supervision and observance of such an agreement. The Egyptian response, by contrast, stressed the comprehensiveness of Resolution 242 as covering all aspects relative to peaceful settlement of the entire conflict. Moreover, Egypt insisted on the primacy of a prior Israeli commitment to withdrawal from all occupied territories as a phase of implementing Resolution 242.

3. On secure and recognized boundaries: The African memorandum called for acceptance of such boundaries "to be determined in the peace agreement." It thus seemed to put the achievement of such an agreement as a goal that might take precedence over the prior commitment on withdrawal. Israel replied that it agreed such boundaries "should be determined by negotiation between the parties and embodied in the peace agreement." The Egyptian response, while agreeing with the African formulation, went on to stipulate that any agreement would have to conform to the OAU resolution and to the borders specified in the Jarring initiative. Thus, Israel's rejection of the Jarring initiative through the formula of "free negotiations" was countered by Egypt's insistence on the principle of "non-acquisition of territory by war" contained in the OAU and Security Council resolutions.

4: Security guarantees: The African memorandum stated that the solution to security problems could be found "within the guarantee of the United Nations, in the creation of demilitarized zones, in the presence of international forces at some strategic points." Israel agreed that "in addition to the determination of agreed, secure and recognized boundaries, further arrangements for ensuring security could be negotiated." In contrast to such a generalized and non-committal response, Egypt accepted the entire African formulation except where Egypt referred to demilitarized zones "astride borders." Thus Egypt, which made no reference to the modality for establishing such security guarantees (while Israel stressed negotiations), raised the need for reciprocity of territorial demilitarization. This was an additional stress made by Egypt on the idea of "no fruits for conquest."

5. Withdrawal: The African heads of state proposed that "the terms of withdrawal from occupied territories be embodied in the peace agreement." Instead of reference to "withdrawal from occupied territories," Israel, in response, gave its agreement to "withdrawal to the boundaries negotiated and agreed" to "be embodied in the peace treaty." Egypt, apparently finding that its response to this point was subsumed in its earlier points of reply, made no corresponding reference. Once again, irreconcilable responses failed to bridge

196

the gulf separating Egypt and Israel on the issue of "withdrawal" and "boundaries."

6. Sharm El-Sheikh: The African proposal called for "the stationing of international forces at Sharm el Sheikh" in order "to guarantee freedom of navigation to all ships through the Strait of Tiran." Israel's response referred to the inclusion of that question "in the peace negotiations as specified in paragraph (c) above" (which dealt with secure and recognized boundaries). It also referred to Security Council Resolution 242 as providing for "free navigation in all international waterways such as the Suez Canal and the Strait of Tiran, for all ships and cargoes" to be specified "in the peace agreement." Egypt accepted the African formulation in its entirety. Thus Israel made no response to the African reference to international forces and guarantees as far as Sharm El-Sheikh was concerned, and went beyond that to indicate by implication that that part of Egyptian occupied territory was to be the subject of negotiation on "secure and recognized boundaries."

From the above analysis, it becomes apparent that the Jarring type of African memorandum, which was handed by President Senghor of Senegal to Prime Minister Golda Meir of Israel and President El-Sadat of Egypt in late November 1971, did not succeed in eliciting the reconciliation of essentials in the respective positions. Aside from providing the parties with the opportunity for agreeing with the basic African objective—namely, the need for resuming the Jarring talks—the mission accomplished very little.

Judging by the past OAU position regarding the Middle East crisis—namely, noninvolvement beyond the adoption of resolutions supporting U.N. calls and Egyptian stands—the memorandum of the Commission of Ten was a very ambitious (i.e., unrealistic) undertaking. The membership of the two OAU bodies was not of one mind as to the best means to a peaceful solution of the crisis, and the terms of the memorandum reflected compromises among the African heads of state themselves. By the same token, the interpretation of the African memorandum, and the Egyptian and Israeli responses, caused a division of African opinion in the General Assembly, or allowed that division to come to the surface to a greater degree. Such a division in African ranks was caused by conflicting interpretations of the meaning of the African initiatives, the African memorandum, and the responses to it, as well as the following factors:

1. The method of communicating the African memorandum to the General Assembly through a letter from the Israeli Permanent Representative to the Secretary-General. This caused resentment among African delegations, particularly those whose support for Egypt's position was well known, and whose heads of state took part in the OAU initiatives (e.g., Nigeria and Tanzania). This resentment

197

was caused by what appeared to be Israel's attempt to force its own interpretation of the African proposals on the Assembly membership, particularly African members. This feeling was heightened by Israel's written and oral statements to the Assembly, which implied that certain African delegations would be going against the views of their heads of state on the Commission of Ten if they supported the Egyptian position in the Assembly. The Ambassador of Nigeria, referring to a remark by Abba Eban, later stated in Assembly debates that Israel's Foreign Minister was "talking down to representatives of independent, sovereign countries." He added that the African proposals had, in fact, not been received by all African heads of state, and that most of the African delegations "are not in a position to have received instructions."[24]

2. There was no clear system of reporting on the results of the African initiatives. Beyond requesting its Chairman "to consult with the Heads of State and Government so that they use their influence to ensure the full implementation of this resolution," the OAU gave no clarification of this mandate. Thus, vagueness surrounded both the method of reporting (who reports what to whom at what point) and the method of communicating the results of the inquiry to the African delegations. Israel, on 9 December, reported to the United Nations not only its responses but also the African memorandum, and Egypt hastened the following day to provide the United Nations with its formal reply to President Senghor. Nigeria's Permanent Representative therefore responded that the OAU mission "was not reporting" to the General Assembly. He added, "To whom did the Committee . . . submit those proposals?[25]

3. The OAU resolution contained specific political stands. Paramount among those stands was "immediate withdrawal . . . from all Arab territories to the lines of 5 June"; support for Jarring's efforts to implement Security Council Resolution 242; "solidarity with the United Arab Republic"; and appreciation for Egypt's "positive attitude reflected in its reply of 15 February 1971." However, in the tradition of political compromises, the African memorandum had neither a clear political line nor a sharp philosophical position. It only attempted to place the general hopes of the parties (i.e., peace through Jarring) side by side with the points at issue, stated in the least controversial language. The result was a restatement of positions by both Israel and Egypt, despite the polite expression of "appreciation" of the African efforts during the General Assembly debates on the Middle East situation.

RESULTS OF THE U.N. GENERAL ASSEMBLY
DEBATES

The adoption by the General Assembly of Resolution 2799 (XXVI) of 13 December 1971 signified not only reaffirmation of Security Council Resolution 242 but also endorsement of the Jarring initiative of 8 February 1971. The Assembly's support of "the Special Representative's initiative" relating to prior commitment on withdrawal was formulated in the following points of the operative part of the resolution:

● The Assembly's reaffirmation that "the acquisition of territories by force is inadmissible and that, consequently, territories thus occupied must be restored" (paragraph 1).

● A call for reactivation of the Jarring Mission "in order to promote agreement and assist efforts to reach a peace agreement as envisaged in the Special Representative's aide-memoire of 8 February 1971" (paragraph 3).

● Appreciation of "the positive reply given by Egypt" to the Jarring aide-memoire of 8 February, and a call upon Israel "to respond favourably" to that initiative for peace (paragraphs 5 and 6 respectively).

In addition to the Assembly's insistence on the need to reactivate the Jarring Mission (in terms of the Special Representative's initiative of 8 February), which was at the center of the African initiatives, there were other distinctive features of the resolution of 13 December. It emphasized the duality of principles of "withdrawal" in paragraph 2 (a) and the "right to live in peace within secure and recognized boundaries" in paragraph 2 (b). Taking this into account, one finds that the resolution's references, direct or indirect, to "withdrawal" occur in paragraphs 1, 2, 3, 5, and 6. It might also be noted that, in the African memorandum of November 1971, the reference to "withdrawal" came in the fifth of six proposals. This comparison helps to explain Israel's enthusiasm for the OAU proposals as a "starting point," and Egypt's insistent reference to the OAU's call in its June resolution for "immediate withdrawal" from "all" territories occupied since 5 June 1967.

Another distinctive feature of Resolution 2799 (XXVI) of 13 December 1971 involves the requests addressed to both the Secretary-General (paragraph 8) and the Security Council (paragraph 9) regarding implementation. The Secretary-General was requested "to report to the Security Council and to the General Assembly" on the progress of Jarring's implementation of Resolution 242 and the Resolution 2799 (XXVI). As to the Security Council, it was requested "to consider, if necessary, making arrangements, under the relevant Articles of the Charter of the United Nations with regard to the implementation" of Resolution 242.

As for the OAU initiatives, the Assembly's resolution saw the entire effort not in terms of the African memorandum's accomplishments or nonaccomplishments, but only in terms of "efforts . . . in pursuance of the resolution adopted on 23 June 1971 by the Assembly of Heads of State and Governments" (preambular paragraph 4).

These are the main outlines of the subsequent Assembly resolution on the Middle East conflict, assessed not only in terms of the U.N. handling of the issue but also with reference, where appropriate, to the corresponding features of the proposals of November 1971 made by the ten African heads of state. It would be difficult to ascertain the effect of the African initiatives on the adoption of the Assembly resolution. However, it is instructive to note that 22 African delegations, including six whose heads of state were members of the Commission of Ten (Cameroun, Ethiopia, Mauritania, Nigeria, Senegal, and Tanzania) cosponsored the 22-power draft resolution that, after minor amendments by members of the European Common Market and the United Kingdom, became Resolution 2799 (XXVI). Of the six African delegates whose heads of state were members of the Commission of Ten, three (Cameroun, Nigeria, and Senegal, although Senegal later withdrew its cosponsorship) had been represented on the itinerant committee that visited the Middle East.

An examination of the recorded vote on this resolution and the positions taken by various African members that had taken part in the OAU initiatives would reveal, at least in part, the African outlook on the Middle East situation.

The resolution was adopted by a vote to 79 to 7 with 36 abstentions.26 Included in the yes votes, were 23 African states, 6 of which took part at the summit level in the work of the OAU Commission of Ten (Cameroun, Ethiopia, Kenya, Mauritania, Nigeria, and Tanzania). No African state opposed the resolution, which was rejected by Israel as well as Costa Rica, Dominican Republic, El Salvador, Haiti, Nicaragua, and Uruguay. Included in the abstaining votes were 16 African states, 4 of which had taken part in the work of the Commission of Ten (Ivory Coast, Liberia, Senegal, and Zaire).

Thus, the membership of the Committee of "Four Wise Men," which visited the Middle East, split on the vote on Resolution 2799 (XXVI), with Cameroun and Nigeria in favor and Senegal and Zaire abstaining.

During the debates, while all the African representatives stressed the importance of the reactivation of the Jarring Mission, as well as the principle of the "non-acquisition of territory by war," their varied approach to the means of accomplishing those ends manifested their division of opinion in the crisis. Those divisions centered primarily on the following elements:

1. Lack of agreement on the importance of a positive Israeli reply to the Jarring aide-memoire of 8 February. Calling for that reply, Nigeria asked: "Why should Israel not co-operate with that [Jarring] mission or whatever results therefrom, be it a questionnaire, be it an aide-memoire?"[27] On the other hand, the Ivory Coast, in arguing against the 22-power draft resolution, stated that "a diplomatic victory . . . is of no real interest to us."[28]

2. The place and role of the African initiatives in reactivating the Jarring Mission. The Ivory Coast maintained that the OAU Commission "came to encouraging conclusions with respect to the resumption of negotiations," and therefore that the 22-power draft resolution "might in fact create additional difficulties and might undermine the efforts made by the Heads of African States."[29] Both the Ivory Coast and Senegal seemed to regard the Egyptian and Israeli responses to the African memorandum as sufficient to get the Jarring talks resumed. The Ivory Coast Representative stated that both Egypt and Israel had "accepted the recommendations of the Heads of State" by agreeing to resume negotiations, while the Senegalese Representative pointed out that the African mission had found "acceptance by both sides on the resumption of negotiations under the aegis of Mr. Jarring."[30] Other African states that differed with these views, such as Nigeria, called on those who "wish to support the African group or Heads of State . . . to co-sponsor" the 22-power draft resolution. Nigeria attacked the Barbados draft resolution, (which called for "support" for "the OAU proposal"[31]) saying that that draft "quotes out of context some of the principles enunciated by the Heads of State."[32] Eventually, Egypt's African supporters helped force the withdrawal of the Barbados draft resolution.

More significant, the Senegalese amendments—which, inter alia, called for deletion of references in the 22-power draft resolution to the comparison between Egypt's and Israel's positions regarding the Jarring memorandum of 8 February—also were defeated. Despite the fact that President Senghor of Senegal had led the Committee of Four, half of the states represented on the Commission of Ten (Cameroun, Ethiopia, Nigeria, Mauritania, and Tanzania) voted against Senegal's amendments. This is all the more significant because Senegal had proposed in its amendments that the Assembly noted with satisfaction the replies given by Egypt and Israel to the memorandum of African heads of state.[33]

A similar fate met the Costa Rica-El Salvador-Uruguay draft resolution, which, inter alia, seemed to equate in importance the Jarring "efforts" and the "important conciliation efforts of OAU."[34]

3. The admission by those who called for a stronger projection of the African memorandum in the Assembly's resolution that the

African heads of state had encountered serious difficulties. These were expressed by Senegal and the Ivory Coast in terms of two fundamental issues: "withdrawal" and "peace within secure and recognized boundaries."[35] With such an admission, no serious case could have been made in the Assembly to represent the meager findings of the OAU as a breakthrough meriting consideration as a new basis for an Arab-Israeli "dialogue."

Here one should also take into account that both the Ivory Coast and Senegal insisted on the need for Israeli withdrawal from occupied Arab territories.[36] Senegal, intermittently subjected to Portuguese incursions as a result of the Guinea-Bissau war of national liberation, could not take a different stand. Moreover, as indicated above, the principles of territorial integrity and acceptance of the inherited frontiers in Africa have almost been canonized in the OAU Charter. These principles were strongly reflected in the various OAU resolutions adopted on the Middle East crises in 1968, 1969, 1970, and 1971.

There also were outside (i.e., non-African) factors that contributed to the division of African opinion in the United Nations between support for and abstension on the 22-power draft resolution.

First, the Secretary-General's report of 30 November 1971 on the Jarring Mission clearly made a positive Israeli response to the Jarring memorandum of 8 February 1971 the essential element in the resumption of the Jarring talks. In that report, the Secretary-General stated unequivocally, "it is a matter for increasing concern that Ambassador Jarring's attempt to break the deadlock has not so far been successful. I appeal, therefore, to the Government of Israel to give further consideration to this question and to respond favourably."[37]

The Secretary-General's report was cited by several African delegations supporting the 22-power draft resolution. This argument caused the Ivory Coast to withdraw its request for a separate vote on the draft resolution's paragraph relating to the call on Israel "to respond favourably to the Special Representative's peace initiative." In appealing to the Ivory Coast not to insist on a separate vote on that crucial paragraph, the Delegate of Mali stated, "Mr. Jarring and the Secretary-General have laid down this response as an indispensable condition for resumption of the talks."[38] When Barbados wished to force a nose count on the issue of a favorable Israeli response to Jarring, by insisting on a separate vote on the word "favourably" in the pertinent paragraph in the 22-power draft resolution, Zambia, seconded by Tunisia, opposed the Barbados proposal, basing its argument on the Secretary-General's report of November 1971. The Barbados motion was finally rejected by 69-9, with 49 abstentions.[39]

It could therefore be said that the African forces in the General Assembly—which had wished to replace an Israeli positive response to Ambassador Jarring's aide-memoire by the general responses given by Egypt and Israel to the proposals of the ten African heads of state—could not find support in the Secretary-General's report on the situation. Their views of the Middle East crisis, which were generally characterized by "neutrality," caused them to abstain in the vote on Resolution 2799 (XXVI).

A second outside factor in the division of African opinion between "supporters" and "neutrals" on the Middle East situation was the Israeli public stance in the Assembly and in press communiques.

A press release issued on 9 December 1971 by the Israeli Permanent Mission commented on what later became the 22-power draft resolution by stating, inter alia: "Three of the four delegations representing members of the African Mission [meaning Cameroun, Nigeria, and Senegal] have given their names to a resolution different in letter and spirit to what their Presidents and other African Presidents submitted to Israel and Egypt only two weeks ago."[40] A few days later, Abba Eban of Israel, speaking in the General Assembly, characterized the 22-power draft resolution as "a repudiation of the effort by the African Heads of State."[41]

Rejecting such interpretations, the Nigerian Delegate stated, "This is typical of the attitude of trying to divide and rule; trying to embarrass us by saying, 'Will you now go back on the recommendation of your Heads of State?' That is not the issue."[42]

And a third outside factor was the impact of support given by the members of the European Economic Community and the United Kingdom to the 22-power draft resolution. That support, given in the form of amendments that were accepted by the sponsors, [43] strengthened the hand of African supporters of the draft. The main West European amendment involved the introduction of the features of Resolution 242 balancing between "withdrawal" and the "right to live in peace within secure and recognized boundaries"—paragraph 2 of Resolution 2799 (XXVI).

The importance of the West European position to the African stand derives from the cultural and aid influences that the European Common Market, especially France, exerts in Francophone Africa. That position was articulated by France's Ambassador in his statement to the General Assembly on 10 December 1971 stressing the need for a positive Israeli response to the Jarring memorandum. He stated that:

> Egypt, for its part, had responded in the positive as it had indicated its readiness to sign a peace accord with Israel if the legitimate requirement of Israeli evacuation from the occupied Arab territories were satisfied in accordance with Security Council resolution 242. He added that he was also awaiting a similarly positive response from Israel on the question of withdrawal.[44]

It is difficult to assess the precise impact of this West European stand on the African states, which eventually abstained from voting on Resolution 2799 (XXVI) instead of voting against it. However, it should be noted that nearly half of the African abstaining votes were cast by Francophone West African and Malagasy states.[45]

Let us now turn to the main beneficiary of General Assembly Resolution 2799 (XXVI), namely, Egypt. In this context, let us briefly examine the nature and effects of Egyptian diplomacy toward not only the African initiatives but also the general question of peace and war in the Middle East.

The following elements could be discerned: Egypt avoided reminding the delegates of its "Year of Decision," much less what that meant; shunned bellicose statements about possible Arab military endeavors to liberate the occupied territories; concentrated on the need for resuming the Jarring talks through an Israeli prior commitment on withdrawal to Egypt's international borders; reminded the African delegations of the parallels between Israeli practices in the occupied territories and the situation in Southern Africa;[46] and stressed Egypt's organic links with the continent. Moreover, Egypt emphasized the paramount importance of reading the African memorandum of November 1971, not in terms of the Israeli responses but in terms of the mainstream of political and diplomatic efforts represented by Security Council Resolution 242 and the Jarring efforts as endorsed by the OAU resolution of June 1971.

There is no need here to produce a great deal of evidence on all these aspects of Egyptian diplomacy at the United Nations. Suffice it to refer here to several statements made by Egypt's Foreign Minister, Mahmoud Riad, and Egypt's Permanent Representative, M. H. El-Zayyat clarifying these attitudes. Describing the OAU resolution of June in the General Assembly, Riad said: "For Egypt, it was an act of solidarity on the part of our sister African States."[47] Soon afterwards, Riad declared in a CBS television interview on 5 December 1971: "I came to the General Assembly to ask once again for the continuation of Ambassador Jarring's Mission. I hoped that the General Assembly would ask Israel to answer in a favorable way so that Jarring may continue his mission." When one of the interviewers remarked that the African heads of state "did not ask for preconditions," Riad replied, in apparent reference to the OAU resolution: "The African chiefs said that Israel must give a favorable response to Jarring and should withdraw to the lines of 4 June 1967." Riad also stated, "War is already in the Middle East. . . . I hate war." Throughout this interview, he uttered not one bellicose statement.[48]

Ambassador El-Zayyat, commented on the African initiatives, on the day of adoption of Assembly Resolution 2799 (XXVI), by stating: "We have given it . . . every possibility of succeeding, because we

have no doubt that they, the African States, will never accept, even
if we should, the idea of the acquisition of territories as a result of
war being enshrined."[49]

All these statements reflected a pragmatic Egyptian diplomatic
approach that had one single aim in view: the adoption by the General
Assembly of Resolution 2799 (XXVI). The success Egypt attained in
this regard could be interpreted not only in terms of the African votes
cast for the resolution but also in terms of the absence of negative
African votes.

CONCLUSIONS

The African initiatives in the Middle East situation were based
on an OAU resolution of June 1971 that left it to the OAU Chairman
to organize an effort for exerting African influence in the direction
of implementation of Security Council Resolution 242. Although the
OAU resolution was vague on how those initiatives were to be undertaken, and to whom their result would be communicated, its political
thrust was manifestly clear: It supported the Egyptian position in the
conflict, called for total Israeli withdrawal from "all" Arab territories occupied since 5 June 1967, urged the reactivation of the Jarring
Mission, and called on Israel to give a favorable reply to the Jarring
memorandum of 8 February 1971.

The establishment of an OAU Commission of Ten Heads of
African States, under the leadership of the President of Mauritania,
which in turn established a Committee of Four headed by President
Senghor of Senegal, was the first OAU incursion in a political/military
issue that did not traditionally fall within the purview of the OAU.
Aside from the OAU resolution of June 1971, these initiatives were
considered an Egyptian diplomatic success since they involved the
OAU, for the first time and in a concrete way, in the Middle East
problem. However, the scope of the African mission remained limited
to the Egyptian/Israeli aspect of the conflict, as a result of Israel's
military occupation of the territory of Egypt, an OAU member.

Following a Jarring pattern of simultaneous submission of
"principles" to the two parties (Egypt and Israel), the Commission of
Ten developed a memorandum whose import and significance became
controversial among African states. The division of African opinion,
which may be termed identification with divergent approaches to a
peaceful solution, was represented by two groups of states. One
group, which was more numerous (23 states, including 6 represented
on the Commission of Ten), felt the OAU resolution remained the
main African instrument for the reactivation of the Jarring Mission.
The second group (16 states, including 4 represented on the Commission)

205

looked upon the Israeli and Egyptian responses to the Commission
as a sufficient basis for the reactivation of the Jarring Mission.
Members of the second group therefore desired a strong reflection
of the African memorandum in the General Assembly resolution, placing
less importance on the need for an Israeli prior commitment to withdrawal to Egypt's international borders before the Jarring talks could
be resumed.

As a result of these differences in African perceptions of the
Middle East conflict, the African votes on General Assembly Resolution 2799 (XXVII) were divided between yes and abstention. Various
factors could be discerned in the absence of a major cleavage within
the African group, as might have been represented by negative votes
on the Assembly resolution. The most important of these factors, in
the author's view, is that the two wings of the African group were
united on the need for withdrawal from occupied territories, a principle
enshrined in the OAU Charter in provisions relating to territorial integrity, and the importance of implementation of Security Council
Resolution 242 in order to achieve a peaceful settlement in the Middle
East.

One may represent the various shades of African opinion on the
Middle East conflict in 1971 by dividing the 10 states whose chiefs took
part in the African initiatives as follows:

1. Group A: (Primary importance to withdrawal to reach a peace
agreement—Cameroun, Mauritania, Nigeria, and Tanzania.

2. Group B: Primary importance to peace negotiations to reach
a peace agreement—Ivory Coast and Liberia.

3. Group C (the middle group): Parallelism between negotiation
for peace agreement and affirmation of nonacquisition of territory by
force—Ethiopia and Kenya, with tendencies to regroup with Group A;
Senegal and Zaire, with tendencies to regroup with Group B.

Measuring the effectiveness of the African initiatives in terms
of advancing the U.N. efforts toward a political settlement in the Middle
East, one is led to believe that they were of a peripheral value. The
"findings" of the mission were already well advertised by the parties
to the conflict. Both Egypt and Israel had repeatedly stated, before
the launching of the African initiatives, that they were for "peace"
and in favor of the resumption of the Jarring Mission. The Egyptian
and Israeli responses to the African memorandum clearly reflected
the parties previously expressed positions.

In spite of the meager accomplishments of the African mission,
Israel saw in it "a new starting point" for unblocking the Jarring
Mission, because of the low priority given in those proposals to the
question of prior commitment to withdrawal, and the absence of refer-
ence to the Jarring memorandum of 8 February 1971. However,
Egypt insisted on the OAU resolution of June 1971 as the only valid

document representing the consensus of all African heads of state and government.

The vagueness of the modalities of reporting the African mission's "findings" contributed to the polemics between representatives of the two wings of African opinion in the General Assembly. It was unclear whether the Commission of Ten had acted in the spirit of the OAU resolution of June 1971, or whether its findings were properly communicated to all heads of state and government in Africa. In fact, the African memorandum was circulated to the U.N. membership as an annex to a letter to the Secretary-General from Israel's Permanent Representative. It soon became clear that most African delegations had not received instructions from home on the results of the African mission.

Consequently, the only valid approach that remained before most of the African delegates in voting on the Assembly's resolution on the Middle East was to reaffirm Security Council Resolution 242 and Ambassador Jarring's initiatives to implement it, including his initiative of 8 February 1971.[50]

With regard to the right to self-determination, it should be noted that Assembly Resolution 2787 (XXVI) of 17 December 1971 "confirms the legality of the peoples' struggle for self-determination and liberation . . . notably in southern Africa . . . as well as of the Palestinian people, by all available means consistent with the Charter of the United Nations" (paragraph 1). This represented one of the first linkages between African and Palestinian national movements within the same U.N. concern with liberation.

Another impact of the OAU Commission to the Middle East emerged when Jarring made a special trip to Africa in 1972. According to a "Note to Correspondents" issued by the U.N. Office of Public Information,[51] Jarring, with the agreement of the Secretary-General, would "pay a visit to the President of the Republic of Senegal, Leopold Sedar Senghor, upon his invitation." The same note added that Jarring would "also travel to Mauritania for talks with President Moktar Ould Daddah, who is the President of the OAU and the Commission of Ten of the OAU on the Middle East question." Those visits by the Secretary-General's Special Representative were in harmony with the basic premise of the African initiatives, namely, that they were never intended to replace the Jarring Mission. On the contrary, they were designed to achieve the "unblocking" of that Mission, as stated above. (Since 10 January 1972, Ambassador Jarring has been at U.N. headquarters for consultations with the Secretary-General and the representatives of the parties to the Middle East conflict.)

In conclusion, it could therefore be said that the OAU's failure in its attempted mediation of the Egypt/Israeli sector of the Middle Eastern conflict precipitated a series of transformations in the

international relationships between Africa and Israel. These transformations isolated Israel, brought the League of Arab States and
the OAU together in the process of harmonization of policies regarding
both the Middle East conflict and the Southern Africa conflict, and
created more ideological interaction between the Palestine Liberation
Organization and the African liberation movements. Since the October
1973 war, these processes have accelerated, particularly in terms
of Afro-Arab cooperation in the aftermath of the rise in oil prices.

These trends have been reflected in the various resolutions
adopted by the OAU since 1972 with regard to the Middle East conflict.
Thus in 1973, the OAU Concil of Ministers, at its meetings in Addis
Ababa on 5-12 February, condemned Israel "for its obstinate refusal
to withdraw from all occupied Arab Territory and for its expansionist
policy which led to the uprooting of the Palestinian people from their
rightful homes".[52]

Moreover, in the commemorative tenth anniversary session of
the OAU, held in Addis Ababa on 27-28 May 1973, the Assembly of
Heads of State and Government adopted a resolution that inter alia,
recalled "the negative attitude of Israel towards the mission of the
ten African Heads of State mandated by the OAU to work for the implementation of Security Council resolution 242 of 22 November
1967." It also declared that "the attitude of Israel might lead OAU
Member States to take, at the African level, individually or collectively, political and economic measures against it, in conformity with
the principles contained in the OAU and U.N. Charters."[53]

Following the October war of 1973, in which Egypt recaptured
by force of arms part of its occupied territory, the OAU Council of
Ministers, at its eighth extraordinary session in Addis Ababa (19-21
November 1973), recalled the resolution adopted by the OAU summit
in May 1973. Inter alia, the Council noted with satisfaction "the gains
achieved by Egypt during the October war of liberation against Israel."
The Council, in that resolution, also recommended that OAU member
states "maintain the severance of relations with Israel until it with-
draws from all the occupied Arab territories and until the recovery
by the Palestinian people of their legitimate national rights."

In response to a question addressed to him by Jon Woronoff,
the former Administrative Secretary-General of the OAU, Nzo Ekangaki attributed the changes in Africa's outlook on Israel to "the disappointment the group of ten [which sponsored the mediation] felt during
the contacts they had in seeking an amicable settlement."[54]

It seems that those who attribute the change in Africa's attitude
toward Israel to "Arab oil money" either seek simplistic answers
or do not attribute sufficient credibility to Africa's capacity to make
its diplomatic decisions in the light of its own long-range interests
and the principles contained in the OAU Charter.

Letter dated 13 July 1971 from the Executive Secretary of
the Organization of African Unity to the United Nations
addressed to the President of the Security Council trans-
mitting the text of resolutions adopted at the eighth session of the Assembly of Heads of State and Government of
the OAU

[Original: English/French]
[21 July 1971]

In accordance with Article 54 of the United Nations Charter, I
have the honour to transmit to you, for the information of the Security
Council, the resolutions enclosed herewith, which were adopted at the
eighth session of the Assembly of Heads of State and Government of
the Organization of African Unity (OAU).

(Signed) Mamadou Moctar THIAM
Executive Secretary of the Organization of
African Unity to the United Nations

Resolution on the Continued Aggression
Against the United Arab Republic
(AHG/Res.66 (VIII))

The Assembly of the Heads of State and Government of the OAU,
meeting at its eighth ordinary session in Addis Ababa, from 21 to 23
June 1971,

Having heard the declaration of the Minister of State for Foreign
Affairs, Head of the delegation of the United Arab Republic,

Recalling its previous resolutions AHG/Res.53 (V) of September
1968, AHG/Res.57 (VI) of September 1969 and AHG/Res.62 (VII) of
September 1970, concerning the situation prevailing in the Middle
East in general, and in the United Arab Republic in particular, calling
for withdrawal of foreign troops from all Arab territories occupied
since 5 June 1967 in accordance with Security Council resolution 242
(1967) of 22 November 1967 and appealing to all Member States of
the OAU to use their influence to ensure a strict implementation of
that resolution and support the present efforts of the United Nations
Special Representative of the United Nations Secretary-General,

Mindful of the constructive efforts of the United Arab Republic
aiming at the establishment of a just and lasting peace in the Middle

East, especially the positive position recently taken in response to Ambassador Jarring's peace initiative of 8 February 1971,

Seriously concerned that the present grave situation resulting from the continued Israeli occupation of the territories of three Arab States, one of them a Member in this Organization, constitutes a serious threat to the regional peace of Africa and to international peace and security,

Determined that the territory of a State should not be the object of occupation or acquisition by another State resulting from threat or use of force, which is a basic principle enshrined in the United Nations Charter and reiterated in Security Council resolution 242 (1967), as well as the Declaration on the Strengthening of International Security adopted by the General Assembly in its resolution 2734 (XXV) of 16 December 1970),

1. Takes note of the declaration of the Minister of State for Foreign Affairs, Head of the delegation of the United Arab Republic;

2. Reaffirms emphatically the contents of its resolutions AHG/Res.53 (V) of September 1968, AHG/Res.57 (VI) of September 1969 and AHG/Res.62 (VII) of September 1970, and calls for immediate withdrawal of Israel armed forces from all Arab territories to the lines of 5 June 1967 in implementation of Security Council resolution 242 (1967) of 22 November 1967;

3. Expresses its full support to the efforts of the Special Representative of the United Nations Secretary-General to implement Security Council resolution 242 (1967), and to his initiative for peace of 8 February 1971, in particular;

4. Reaffirms its solidarity with the United Arab Republic and appreciates the positive attitude reflected in its reply on 15 February 1971 to the Special Representative's initiative for peace as a practical step for establishing a just and lasting peace in the Middle East;

5. Deplores Israel's defiance to that initiative and calls upon it to make a similar positive reply to the Special Representative's initiative for peace of 8 February 1971;

6. Requests the current Chairman of the OAU to consult with the Heads of State and Government so that they use their influence to ensure the full implementation of this resolution.

NOTES

1. Adopted by the OAU summit of African Heads of State and Government in Mogadiscio, Somalia, in June 1974.

2. Nasser's Speeches, vol. IV (Cairo: The Government's Department of Information, n.d.), p. 361.

3. UN Doc. S/10272, 21 July 1971, pp. 2-3.

4. Al-Ahram (Cairo), 23 August 1971, article by Shawki Mustafa (all quotations in this chapter from Al-Ahram have been translated by the author from the Arabic).

5. Jon Woronoff, "OAU/Middle East," Africa Report, January 1972.

6. UN Doc. A/PV.2016, 13 December 1971.

7. Ibid.

8. UN Doc. A/PV.2016, 13 December 1971.

9. Time, 15 November 1971.

10. Ibid.

11. The New York Times, 3 November 1971.

12. UN Doc. A/PV.2016, 13 December 1971.

13. Ibid.

14. UN Doc. S/10272, 21 July 1971, p. 3.

15. The New York Times, 6 November 1971.

16. Ibid.

17. Al-Ahram (Cairo), 9 November 1971.

18. Al-Ahram (Cairo), 23 August 1971.

19. UN Doc. A/8566 and S/10438, 9 December 1971; annex to letter dated 9 December 1971 from the Permanent Representative of Israel to the United Nations addressed to the Secretary-General.

20. Ibid.

21. See Ambassador El-Zayyat's statements in the General Assembly on 13 December 1971 in UN Doc. A/PV.2016.

22. See Foreign Minister Eban's statements in the General Assembly on 13 December 1971 in ibid.

23. For Israel's responses, see Ambassador Tekoah's letter of 9 December 1971 to the Secretary-General (UN Doc. A/8566 or S/10438). For Egypt's response, see Ambassador El-Zayyat's letter of 10 December 1971 to the Secretary-General (UN Doc. A/8576 or S.10443).

24. UN Doc. A/PV.2016, 13 December 1971.

25. Ibid.

26. Ibid.

27. Ibid.

28. Ibid.

29. Ibid.

30. Ibid.

31. UN Doc. A/L.651.

32. UN Doc. A/PV.2016, 13 December 1971.

33. UN Doc. A/L.656.

34. UN Doc. A/L.652/Rev. 1.

35. UN Doc. A/PV.2016, 13 December 1971.

36. Ibid.

37. UN Doc. A/8541, paragraph 21.

38. UN Doc. A/PV. 2016, 13 December 1971.

39. Ibid., p. 167.

40. Statement by a spokesman for the Permanent Mission of Israel, in press release dated 9 December 1971, New York.

41. UN Doc. A/PV.2016, 13 December 1971.

42. Ibid., p. 141.

43. UN Doc. A/L.657.

44. UN Doc. A/PV.2012, 10 December 1971.

45. The ratio was 7 to 16. The seven votes were cast by Central African Republic, Dahomey, Gabon, Ivory Coast, Madagascar, Senegal, and Upper Volta.

46. On which the Assembly adopted Resolution 2851(XXVI) of 20 December 1971 by a vote of 53 to 20 (including 7 African states) with 46 abstentions. Commenting on this resolution, a press release by the Permanent Mission of Israel dated 20 December described the resolution as "devoid of any moral, political and juridical validity." The Egyptian Mission criticized that press release in a release of its own dated 22 December 1971.

47. UN Doc. A/PV.1999, 3 December 1971.

48. Notes by the author on the interview telecast by CBS, New York City, 5 December 1971.

49. UN Doc. A/PV.2015, 13 December 1971.

50. In an article dated 10 September 1971 in Al-Ahram, Hassarain Haikal stresses the Africans, and other groups, in terms of the importance of their moral support of Egyptian actions in the conflict.

51. UN, Office of Public Information Note No. 3729, 20 January 1972.

52. Egypt's Permanent Representative to the UN, Dr. Ahmed Esmat Abdel-Meguid, requested the circulation of that resolution as an official document of both the UN Security Council and the General Assembly. It was circulated as UN Doc. S/10891.

53. OAU Resolutions, AHG/Res. 70 (X).

54. Africa Report, September-October 1973, p. 22

11

OAU COLLABORATION WITH THE UNITED NATIONS IN ECONOMIC AND SOCIAL DEVELOPMENT

Berhanykun Andemicael

At this point in the history of international organizations, when several governments are concerned about the rapid multiplication of intergovernmental organizations and the concomitant issues of compatibility, control, and complementarity, it seems especially important to deepen our understanding of the relationships between the United Nations and the major regional organizations. It is the purpose of this chapter to throw some light on the complex issues of relationship between the United Nations and the Organization of African Unity in the economic and social field.

While the U.N. Charter provides specifically for relations with regional intergovernmental organizations in the peace and security field (in Articles 33, 52, 53, and 54), and even with international nongovernmental organizations (in Article 71), it includes no provisions for relations with non-U.N. intergovernmental organizations in the economic and social field. However, as the importance of the regional approach for postwar economic reconstruction and development became fully recognized in the early years of the United Nations, the progress that was made both toward geographic decentralization within the United Nations and toward the formation of non-U.N. regional bodies for economic cooperation has resulted in the rapid multiplication of inadequately coordinated regional structures.

Within Africa, the main problem for the United Nations and the OAU has been the existence of competitive regional structures— the creation of the OAU five years after the establishment of the United Nations Economic Commission for Africa (ECA) has entailed

---

This chapter is based on the findings of a larger study on U.N.- OAU relations by the same author prepared under the auspices of the United Nations Institute for Training and Research (UNITAR).

the setting up of a new set of specialized commissions parallel to
ECA. On the other hand, at the level of global U.N. bodies, the main
problem has been how to harmonize the global and regional policies
to bring about collaboration for more effective development action.
The most significant relations of the OAU at this level have been with
ECOSOC (the U.N. Economic and Social Council), with certain subsidiary
bodies of the General Assembly, especially the United Nations Conference for Trade and Development (UNCTAD), the United Nations
Industrial Development Organization (UNIDO) and the Office of the
High Commissioner for Refugees (UNHCR), and with the United Nations
Development Program (UNDP). The essence of the relationship has
been the OAU quest for effective participation in the proceedings of
the United Nations bodies both through a representation of its Secretariat and through a concerted effort of African delegations in those
bodies.

The overall framework for U.N.-OAU relations is provided
on the one hand by General Assembly Resolution 2011(XX) and on
the other by Resolution AHG/Res. 33(II) of the OAU Assembly of
Heads of State and Government. Both resolutions provide for reciprocal representation at the meetings of relevant bodies and encourage
the establishment of close cooperation between the two organizations.
Within this context, the various bodies of both organizations concerned with African development have made specific arrangements
for cooperation, the most significant of which is the 1965 U.N.-OAU
agreement on cooperation between ECA and the OAU.[1]

As the relations between the United Nations and the OAU in the
economic and social field are conducted essentially at the regional
level, the focus of this chapter will be on OAU's relations with ECA.
An attempt will be made to analyze problems arising from basic
structural and functional overlapping as well as deficiencies in co-
ordinative mechanisms or organizational competition, and to explore
feasible remedies and possibilities for strengthening ECA-OAU
cooperation.

ECA AND THE OAU: THE PROBLEM
OF PARALLEL STRUCTURE

In studying the problem of parallel structures, we will concentrate on the relevant policy-making bodies of ECA and the OAU.
The organizational structure of ECA and the OAU are shown in Figures
11.1 and 11.2.

The special policy-making bodies concerned are the Council
of Ministers of ECA and the relevant specialized commissions of
the OAU. These OAU bodies consist of the Economic and Social

FIGURE 11.1

ECA Organization Chart

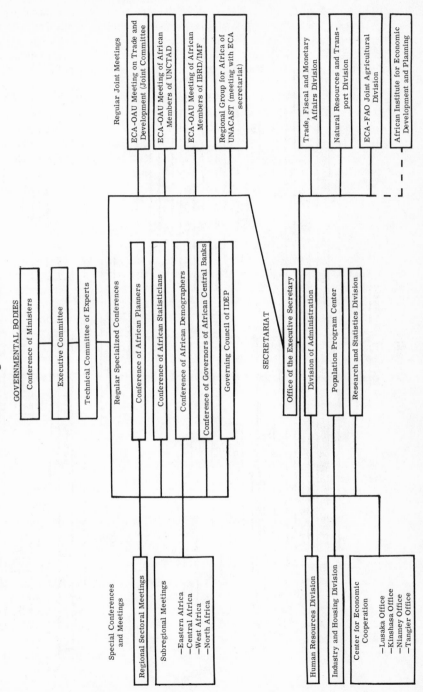

215

FIGURE 11.2

OAU Organization Chart

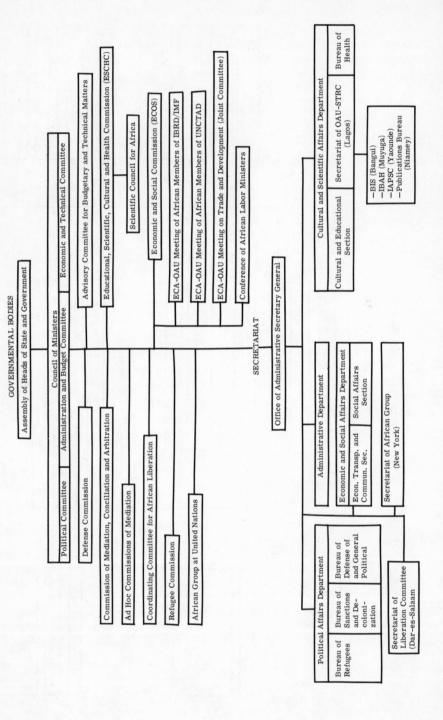

Commission (OAU-ECOS), of which the former Transport and Communications Commission (OAU-TRC) has become a part, and the Educational, Scientific, Cultural and Health Commission (OAU-ESCHC), which now combines the former Educational and Cultural Commission (OAU-EDC), the Scientific, Technical and Research Commission (OAU-STRC) and the Health, Sanitation and Nutrition Commission (OAU-HSNC).

ECA and the OAU Economic and Social Commission

In May 1963, when the OAU was established, ECA had already been operating for five years. It was established by ECOSOC in response to a recommendation of the General Assembly and on the basis of Article 68 of the United Nations Charter in order to:

a) Initiate and participate in measures for facilitating concerted action for the economic and social development of Africa, including its social aspects. . . .
b) Make or sponsor studies of economic and technological problems and developments within . . . Africa . . . and disseminate the results. . . .
c) Undertake or sponsor the collection, evaluation and dissemination of economic, technological and statistical information. . . .
d) Perform . . . . advisory services to the countries and territories of Africa. . . .
e) Assist the [Economic and Social] Council at its request in discharging its functions [in Africa] in connexion with any economic problems, including problems in the field of technical assistance; and
f) Assist in the formulation and development of co-ordinated policies as a basis for practical action in promoting economic and technological development in the region. . . .[2]

These functions were designed to be performed within the framework of the policies of the United Nations and, of course, within the limits of its resources; no action with respect to any country would be taken without the agreement of that country's government.

At its first session, ECA laid down certain principles to guide its work. It decided that it should undertake projects that individual countries by themselves would find difficult to handle, and also those whose scope might extend beyond national frontiers.[3]

217

By the end of its fifth year—that is, by the time the OAU specialized commissions held their first round of sessions (December 1963-
February 1964)—ECA not only had completed building up its institutional structure, including the Secretariat, but also had established
or was completing the establishment of African institutions, notably:
the Annual Conference of African Statisticians, the African Institute
for Economic Development and Planning, and the Conference Development Bank as an independent organization. At the subregional
level, ECA had established branch offices of its Secretariat in sub-
regions. In addition to the building of institutions, its principal
activities during this period comprised information gathering and
research. However, its operational activities—such as training, the
provision of advisory services to governments, and coordination of
national development plans, policies, and actions—have gained emphasis only since the beginning of the second five-year period.[4]

The OAU Economic and Social Commission, the body with the
closest resemblance to ECA, was established to study problems
relating to economic and social development, especially those concerning:

1. The creation of a free trade area among the African countries, and of developing trade among them.

2. The establishment of a common external tariff and a common
fund for raw material price stablization.

3. The restructuring of international trade.

4. The setting up of an African payments and clearing union
and a pan-African monetary zone, following the progressive freeing
of national currencies from all nontechnical external attachments.

5. The harmonization of existing and future national development
plans.

6. The raising of social standards and the strengthening of
inter-African cooperation through the exchange of social and labor
legislation, the organization of vocational training courses for African
workers, the establishment of an African Trade Union, an African
youth organization, an African scouts union, and annual African sports.[5]

In addition, the OAU-ECOS is charged with the coordination of
means of transport and the establishment of inter-African transportation companies. By incorporating the Transport and Communications
Commission, the OAU-ECOS has not only regained exclusive competence within the OAU over these matters but also expanded its
area of responsibility to include the coordination of African telecommunications and postal services.[6]

By comparison with ECA's areas of specific activity, the only
subjects in the OAU-ECOS terms of reference that fall largely outside

the ECA sphere of direct interest are those concerning African labor unions and sports. ECA had already become keenly interested in all the other subjects before the establishment of the OAU.

ECA and the OAU Educational, Scientific, Cultural and Health Commission

The OAU-ESCHC combines all the objectives for which its predecessors—the OAU-STRC, the OAU-EDC, and the OAU-HSNC— had been separately established. Within the educational, scientific, and cultural fields, the OAU-ESCHC is concerned with developing effective means of cooperation among the African states in matters of science and technology relevant to the development of Africa. It has inherited the following responsibilities from the OAU-STRC: to formulate scientific policies; to conduct scientific surveys of Africa's natural resources; to execute joint programs of scientific and techno- logical research and promote effective utilization of the results by the African states; to promote training and exchange of scientific, technical, and research personnel and to provide facilities for the dissemination of scientific information to them; and to channel external aid for relevant OAU-sponsored projects.[7] The tasks derived from the OAU-EDC include the promotion of educational and cultural activi- ties with relevance to both economic development and African unity. A major objective of the Commission in this regard is to help in the implementation of the UNESCO Plan for African Educational Develop- ment—the Addis Ababa Plan of 1961.[8]

All these areas of responsibility of the OAU-ESCHC, except those primarily concerned with cultural development, were of direct interest to ECA long before the establishment of the OAU.

Rationale for the Establishment of the OAU Specialized Commissions

Since the African states were presumably fully aware of the scope of ECA objectives and activities, and since they had full control over the proceedings of the ECA sessions, it should be explained why they felt the need to create the OAU specialized commissions with objectives similar to those of ECA.

The African states appeared in 1963 to be somewhat disillusioned with ECA. They had come to realize that it was not quite the powerful African instrument that they had imagined it to be when they won, over the opposition of the colonial powers and with the help of other developing countries, majority support for a General Assembly resolution directing ECOSOC to establish ECA. ECA had a slow start, partly due to the prolonged debates on political issues at its sessions, especially that concerning the membership of the colonial powers and South Africa.

Being primarily a research organization, it devoted most of its energy to data gathering and analysis while the African states were also expecting from it operational activities that could produce quick returns. In the view of many of them, ECA's ambiguous relationship to the United Nations family of organizations had made it neither an effective channel for aid to Africa nor an instrument serving strictly African demands and priorities.[9]

Thus when the relevant provisions of the OAU Charter were drafted, the logic of creating specialized commissions in the economic, social, and related fields was hardly questioned by the African states. Indeed, all the charters of previous African Summit Conferences,[10] which were presented for consideration by the "founding fathers" of the OAU together with a new draft Charter proposed by Ethiopia,[11] envisaged a comprehensive African organization with the necessary institutions in the political, economic, social, and related fields.

When the various plans for an African organization were considered by the Preparatory Conference of Foreign Ministers, preceding the African Summit Conference of 1963, some delegations seemed to imply that the committees or commissions to be established should strengthen ECA by securing political consensus and support from the higher political organs, but without themselves engaging in operational activities.[12] Some of them even opposed a proposal, which was subsequently adopted, that the Summit Conference should appoint a committee of African experts to study, in consultation with ECA, various African economic and social problems, arguing that ECA with its adequate facilities and its vast experience in these subjects should be invited to accomplish the task.[13] However, the majority, while agreeing that the African states should give greater importance to their responsibilities within ECA than in the past, felt that ECA as a United Nations body could not be a substitute for the envisaged "genuinely African institutions" to guide African affairs. They insisted that new African institutions should be established even though they might "create the impression that they were duplicating in a way the work of international organs."[14]

The consensus reached at the Summit Conference was to establish four specialized commissions in the economic and related fields (OAU Charter Articles 20-22) to coordinate and harmonize the general policies of the African states. It did not appear that the commissions were intended for technical operations. But it became increasingly clear during the first session of the OAU-ECOS that this Commission would embark on substantive studies in areas where ECA had already been engaged, and not merely limit itself to considering the results of ECA's work with a view to making recommendations to its superior organs. The OAU-ECOS general program of work implied that this body would be engaged, simultaneously with ECA, in studies concerning national development plans and intra-African trade, transport, and communications, while for the time being leaving for ECA the tasks concerning natural resources development and the social aspects of economic development.[15]

Some effort was made at the first session of the OAU-ECOS to minimize overlapping of responsibilities with ECA—the ECA representative at the meeting was in fact invited to help in the drafting of the pertinent resolutions, including the ones on the work program of the OAU-ECOS and on relations with ECA. But the division of tasks between the two organizations remained far from clear. Since the resolution did not clarify the respective roles, the extent to which the OAU was to undertake programs of research, institution building, and various operational activities such as those of ECA, depended on whether or not it was able to set up effective subsidiary bodies and corresponding secretariat units.

Consequences of Overlapping Bodies

The creation by ECA and the OAU of organs with parallel or overlapping responsibilities seems to have had adverse affects on some aspects of the work of the two organizations.

There has been a tendency in both organizations to multiply the number of their meetings, which has entailed not only additional financial strain for the Secretariats concerned and for the member states but also an increase in the call upon hard-pressed African ministers and other officials, with the result that the number as well as the quality of participants in meetings has been progressively declining. On the OAU side, many of the technical meetings envisaged by the specialized commissions could not be convened; for lack of quorum, the specialized commissions themselves have had to postpone repeatedly for over five years their scheduled third round of sessions.[16] Similarly, many meetings of ECA that had been provisionally scheduled had to be postponed or canceled, partly due to difficulties in coordinating them with the meetings of other organizations, including the OAU, and partly to doubts concerning the degree of attendance. Even though ECA has begun holding biennial instead of annual sessions, the number of nonattending members recently reached thirteen, in contrast to a maximum of four during the sessions prior to 1967.

The establishment of bodies with overlapping responsibilities also seems to have led ECA and the OAU to compete in inviting African experts, whose numbers are too limited to meet even the needs of the African governments themselves, to serve in the technical bodies and Secretariats of the two organizations. While the OAU has been anxiously trying to build up the core of its Secretariat, ECA has been intensifying its efforts to raise the ratio of its African professional staff from the level of about 50 percent existing at the end of 1966 to a maximum of 75 percent in response to the demands of the African states and in accordance with a principle concerning regional recruitment laid down by the U.N. Secretary General.[17]

Even though the OAU specialized commissions had decided to establish only a few subsidiary bodies with close resemblance to certain technical bodies of ECA, considerations of finance, personnel, and time induced the OAU as well as ECA to seek remedial measures to the problem of wasteful overlapping, both within each organization and between them. The OAU Assembly found it necessary not only to limit the number of all technical meetings but also, and more significantly, to reduce the number of the specialized commissions and their subsidiary bodies. Similarly, ECA, although better off than the OAU in financial and personnel resources, found it necessary to keep the number of its technical meetings at a minimum and to reduce the number of its subsidiary bodies. Both have carried out institutional reforms with some positive results, but as each has underlined its policy-making function in the areas of mutual concern, the issue of respective roles has remained unresolved.

THE PROBLEM OF DELIMITATION OF RESPONSIBILITIES AND DIVISION OF LABOR

The establishment in ECA and the OAU of organs with overlapping responsibilities has raised jurisdictional issues as well as problems of cooperation and coordination in activities of mutual interest. These problems have led to a call for an agreement between the two organizations on principles governing their respective roles. Such principles could represent one or more of the following:

1. Acceptance of hierarchical relationships between the two organizations as regards decision making on important issues.
2. Division of roles between them based on the nature of the functions performed (assuming that a clear separation can be made between technical activities and the formulation of policy).
3. Recognition of each other's spheres of special interest and of exclusive responsibility as regards subjects of economic development within the general areas of common concern.

4. Acceptance as a basis for cooperation of the presumption of equality of competence in all fields of mutual interest and at all stages of the decision-making and implementation process.

The question of respective roles and division of work between ECA and the OAU has been the subject of considerable debate at many meetings of the two organizations, especially during the two years preceding the conclusion in November 1965 of an agreement on co-operation.

The respective approaches of the two organizations can be examined in the light of the principles implied in the above four bases of relationships.

The OAU Approach

The OAU approach seems to imply hierarchical relationships between ECA and the OAU, and as such seems to call for a combination of points (1) and (2) above. The OAU Secretariat has maintained that, even though it did not doubt the ability of ECA to respond to the wishes and aspirations of the African governments (they collectively form its policy-making body), the final policy decisions on economic issues with significant political implications, particularly those crucial to the objectives of African unity, should be taken by the highest political organ of the OAU, the Assembly of Heads of State and Government.[18] Accordingly, the role of the OAU in the economic field was to be defined in the light of the political nature of that organization and its objective of bringing about "close co-operation . . . [and] unity of action and purpose among African Governments, by deliberate and conscious efforts."

In the view of its first Administrative Secretary General, the OAU was an organization with a built-in mechanism for the taking of decisions at the political level, and especially suited to deal with issues that were "half political and half economic which ECA [was] not particularly suited to [handle] because of its nature as a United Nations organ."[19]

These arguments reflect a claim that the OAU should have institutional preeminence over ECA because: (1) the African states are represented in its highest organ by their heads of state or prime ministers, in contrast to the ministerial (or lower) representation in ECA; (2) OAU's capability as a politically oriented organization should entitle it to play a special policy-making role in economic and social development within the present political setting.

The OAU-ECOS adopted a resolution on the respective roles of the two organizations on the basis of these arguments, and also bearing in mind the fact that ECA already had a well-established structure, a body of experience, a wide range of projects in progress, and technical and financial resources far exceeding those of the OAU. This resolution notes that

> the Economic and Social Commission of the Organization of African Unity is basically a policy-making and executive body while the role of the Economic Commission for Africa is generally limited to technical and advisory functions.[20]

Although there was very little difference between the subjects included in the program of work accepted by the OAU-ECOS and the studies and investigations this OAU body requested ECA to continue, subsequent recommendations by the Administrative Secretary General indicated that among the political economic issues the OAU, by its very orientation, was especially qualified to handle were the problem of economic integration in Africa, involving the creation of an African common market and the harmonization of national and regional development plans and policies.[21]

The OAU Secretariat has argued that, irrespective of the number of technical studies undertaken on the establishment of an African common market, one has to recognize in the final analysis that its creation has to be decided at the highest political level. On this basis, the following conclusion was drawn on the division of work between ECA and the OAU: ECA would, in addition to undertaking a study of the technical problems, provide a technical forum; the OAU would provide machinery to consider "the political and other aspects of the problems" of economic and social development, as well as coordinate the policies of the African states. Such an arrangement not only would promote intimate collaboration between the two Secretariats but also would permit the OAU to benefit from the large reservior of expertise at the disposal of ECA. Moreover, by thus combining the efforts of the two organizations, it would ensure considerable saving in time for government officials dealing with this problem.[22]

Implied in this approach to relationships are not only organizational hierarchy between the two organizations in decision making and qualitative division of work in regard to specific fields of activity, but also a heavy reliance on ECA and other bodies of the United Nations for technical assistance. Arguing that the OAU by its very nature cannot be a suitable recipient of bilateral assistance, the OAU Secretary General has indicated that much of the necessary assistance for the OAU economic and social programs would have to be obtained "through the medium of the United Nations and its Specialized

Agencies."[23] The significance of this factor of international assistance has been such that the ninth ordinary session of the OAU Council of Ministers listed the maximization of such benefits as one of the cardinal principles guiding the OAU in its relations with the United Nations system.[24]

The ECA Approach

In contrast to the OAU approach to the problem of respective roles—which is based on the premise that ECA and the OAU differ in the basic nature of their functions, in the nature and extent of their resources, and therefore in their relative suitability to take final policy decisions concerning Africa—ECA's approach tends to stress practical division of tasks and cooperation on the basis of formal equality and organizational independence.

Thus, commenting on the OAU Secretariat's assertion that there was a fundamental difference between the two organizations— namely, while the OAU was not subordinated to any higher authority, ECA's decisions were subject to approval by ECOSOC—the ECA Secretariat stressed that ECA's constitutional position as an integral part of the United Nations could not adversely affect its African character since the orientation of its work was determined by its members, the African states. If, as suggested by the OAU Secretariat, ECA should find it necessary to adapt its working methods to fit the new African context resulting from the creation of the OAU, such changes would have to be in accord with its terms of reference, that is, "within the framework of the policies of the United Nations and subject to the general supervision of the Economic and Social Council." But ECA's claim that it was a genuinely African institution and the fact—pointed out by the OAU Secretariat itself—that there had been no instances of action by ECOSOC making its supervisory functions over ECA distasteful to the African states, tended to reduce the significance of the issue of relative suitability of the two organizations for policy making.[25]

As regards the related issue arising from the claim of basic differences in the functions and orientations of the two organizations, the ECA Secretariat seems to distinguish between the consideration of the political aspects of economic problems and policy making in the economic and social fields. Concerning the political aspects, it did not dispute the claim that it was for the OAU "to weigh their character and indicate how they should be dealt with."[26] But this was not to imply any hierarchical relationship because the OAU would be expected to provide recommendations rather than directives. On any matter of a political nature concerning ECA's work, the final

225

decision would have to be taken by the U.N. General Assembly. This issue was clarified at the ninth session of ECA in connection with the designation of representatives of the peoples of certain non-self-governing territories, which were already associate members of ECA, to participate in the proceedings of the Commission.[27]

On the function of policy making and the implementation of economic and social programs, ECA felt that the OAU notion concerning respective roles would be inconsistent with ECA's terms of reference. Far from limiting its role to that of providing technical and advisory services, the relevant provisions in its terms of reference stipulate that ECA may: (1) "initiate and participate in measures for facilitating concerted action" for African economic and social development; (2) "assist in the formulation . . . of co-ordinated policies as a basis for practical action."[28] These functions have been interpreted by the United Nations Secretary General not merely as involving the provision of technical services for the study and exploration of African economic problems but also as implying a role for ECA as a center for consultations where governments can freely define and elaborate the form of their cooperation. In his view, ECA was conceived as a flexible institution that could "retain its value and usefulness through changes in political and constitutional patterns" in Africa.[29]

On the technical assistance aspect of ECA-OAU relationships envisaged by the OAU, there seem to be no significant differences between the two organizations. Upon the authorization of the U.N. Secretary General, ECA has indicated its readiness to provide the OAU Secretariat with as much technical assistance as its normal resources could permit.

It can be inferred from these considerations that ECA's approach to the problem of relationships was based not on any notion of "fundamental differences" between the two organizations but on the fact that the relevant OAU specialized commissions—which, like ECA itself, were subject to the supervision of higher political organs— were engaged in activities similar to its own. Arguing that it would not be feasible to divide responsibilities between them on the basis of fundamental principles, ECA has maintained that the tasks should be shared on pragmatic grounds; the two organizations could, for example, engage in joint programs or in complementary activities dealing with different aspects or phases of a problem.

Accordingly, rather than basing the relationships on an a priori definition of respective roles, the ECA approach relied on the application of agreed procedures to divide work between the two organizations in concrete cases and to coordinate their activities. This approach did not, of course, exclude the possibility that each organization might concentrate on the fields of activity in which it had a

special interest and for which its orientation, experience, or expertise
was appropriate, so long as it did not claim exclusive jurisdiction.

Agreement on ECA-OAU Cooperation

The problem of guiding principles was not the only issue between
ECA and the OAU during their two-year debate over the question of
their mutual relationships, which culminated in the 1965 Agreement
on Cooperation. There was also disagreement over the degree of
formality of the collaborative arrangements to be concluded. While
the OAU advocated the conclusion of a formal agreement providing
"a legal guarantee to every common action,"[30] the ECA Secretariat
preferred a "simple exchange of letters" between the two Secretariats
to provide a framework "flexible enough to be immediately adapted."[31]

The 1965 Agreement on ECA-OAU Cooperation is indeed a
compromise between the two organizations as regards the above two
issues. As a formal legal instrument signed by the U.N. Secretary
General and the OAU Administrative Secretary General, it meets
the OAU demand for a binding arrangement that precisely defines
framework of cooperation. This concession by the ECA Secretariat
conformed with the recommendation of the seventh session of its
Commission, which endorsed the relevant aspects of the resolutions
of the OAU-ECOS.

On the more fundamental issue of respective roles, however,
the concession was made by the OAU. The preamble of the Agreement
expresses the desire of the two organizations to establish effective
cooperation "within their respective spheres of responsibility" and
in accordance with their respective Charters and the terms of reference
of their relevant Commissions.[32] No provision was included that might
imply functional differentiation or organizational hierarchy between
them. In line with the pragmatic approach of ECA, consultations are
to be held, when circumstances so require, between the administrative
heads of ECA and the OAU to seek agreement on the most effective
manner of undertaking specified activities.[33]

However, the absence of a definition of respective roles from
the Agreement should not imply that the OAU has abandoned its claim
of preeminence in policy making. Even after the conclusion of the
Agreement, representatives of the OAU Secretariat continued to claim
that the "OAU must be the sole forum for the drafting of decisions
on economic policy, for the formulation of the most appropriate programs and for the selection of projects best adapted to African realities." They have not only stressed the shortcomings of the Agreement
but also suggested that it might be desirable to amend the terms of
reference of ECA in order to ensure that this body would "limit its

efforts to seeking the most effective technical and financial means"
to implement the programs formulated by the OAU.[34]

On the other hand, the ECA Secretariat has maintained that,
since it has not proved impractical to apply the existing Agreement,
there would be no immediate need to modify it. It would envisage
no radical changes in the Agreement or the terms of reference as
such changes could be detrimental to the effectiveness of ECA.[35]

Evaluation

Although, in signing the 1965 Agreement, the two organizations
had moved their contrasting positions toward a compromise solution,
the problem of delineation of their respective functions has continued
to be an issue between them. Whether or not the OAU will continue
to press for acceptance by ECA of the OAU approach—that of reserving
for itself the role of policy and program formulation (or the power
to approve ECA's policies and programs) as well as the main responsibility for fields such as trade, economic integration, and the harmonization of national development plans—might depend upon the extent
of development of the OAU activities in the economic and social fields.

At present, the OAU preoccupation with political problems and
its inability to build up a strong machinery for economic and social
programs seem to indicate that the need for a fundamental division
of responsibilities may not be regarded as very urgent. The OAU
position on the distribution of powers and areas of specialization,
if adopted, might not only jeopardize the independence of ECA but
also, in the short run, reduce the latter's flexibility of action in attaining maximum impact from its diverse, interrelated programs,
as well as adversely affect the continuity of some of them. In the
long run, however, if the OAU intensifies its activities in the economic and social fields, it might be necessary, in order to avoid
rivalry and wasteful duplication of effort, to agree upon a more
fundamental distribution of work based on the orientation, experience,
and resources of each organization. In the meantime, if the existing
Agreement—which provides procedures for mutual consultation and
for cooperation in the planning and implementation of various projects—
is strengthened and applied more effectively than in the past, each
organization may gradually develop areas for special concentration.

It seems clear from the statements of the ECA Secretariat
that ECA would not accept a position of subordination vis-a-vis the
OAU as regards the power of decision making on matters that concern
its work. However, Resolution 190(IX) of the ninth session of ECA—
which, as will be shown later, is a landmark in ECA-OAU relations—
seems to have created a problem for the ECA Secretariat. This

resolution reiterates the OAU Assembly's view that this organ remains "the highest body for encouragement and orientation in matters of economic and social policy development on the African continent" and recommends that reports on ECA's activities "be presented regularly" for the consideration of the OAU Assembly. The ECA Secretariat would have preferred the resolution to be phrased in such a way as to attract the support of African heads of state for ECA's programs and their advice on any questions having political implications, but without any implications of "legislative control" over ECA.

POSSIBILITIES FOR STRENGTHENING ECA-OAU COOPERATION

There are essentially five forms of coordination between ECA and the OAU: (1) the procedures of cooperation contained in the 1965 Agreement; (2) a tripartite arrangement made in February 1969 by the administrative heads of ECA, the OAU, and the African Development Bank (ADB); (3) the Executive Committee of ECA; (4) the African delegations to both the ECA Council of Ministers and the OAU-ECOS; and (5) the reporting procedure between ECA and the OAU Assembly of Heads of State and Government. Taken individually, these forms of coordination have certain elements regarded as shortcomings by one organization or the other. But to a large extent the weaknesses of each form of coordination are compensated for by certain elements of the other forms.

The main shortcoming of the 1965 Agreement is that it provides no guidelines for delineation of respective functions between ECA and the OAU, nor does it specifically provide for systematic coordination of policies, programs, and priorities. However, the absence of specific provisions for coordination at the stage of policy and program formulation is now meant to be remedied by the tripartite arrangement for regular biannual meetings of the administrative heads of ECA, the OAU, and the ADB. The shortcoming of this arrangement lies in the fact that, being entirely based on the initiatives of the three administrative heads, it lacks the degree of institutionalization that could withstand the ups and downs of personal relationships.

The Executive Committee of ECA—composed of the Executive Secretary of ECA, the Chairman, two Vice Chairmen, and Rapporteur of the ECA session, as well as two African members of ECOSOC and two of the UNDP Governing Council, plus some additional members to ensure that each subregion is represented by two countries—is an ingenious device for coordinating policies of African states in various intergovernmental organizations and for providing an influential

229

pressure group for implementation of ECA programs. But the OAU Secretariat's participation in the Executive Committee is limited to attending with observer status, in spite of the OAU's active role in coordinating the policies of African groups in international organizations and its efforts to establish close links with subregional groups and organizations in Africa.

It appears that this shortcoming of the ECA Executive Committee was meant to be remedied by the expected role of the African ministers and senior officials representing their countries in the sessions of ECA and the OAU-ECOS. But the OAU-ECOS has been dormant for several years and its raison d'etre has become questionable, especially following the 1969 reorganization in ECA. By transforming ECA's biennial sessions into ministerial conferences, the African states have given ECA's policy-making role a special emphasis. In addition, they have sought to enhance the operational role of ECA by calling for the strengthening of its Secretariat and for more decentralization of the activities of the United Nations system in Africa in favor of ECA. Yet, in spite of the confidence shown by the African states in ECA's future role, it appears that the main tasks of the nonfunctioning OAU-ECOS will most likely continue to be performed by the Economic and Technical Committee of the OAU Council of Ministers. The problem of coordination might thus continue to arise at the level of this Committee. It ought to be mentioned that delegates in that Committee are often foreign ministry officials and are usually not those who represent their countries in the sessions of ECA. Communication between this Committee and the ECA bodies could be made more effective if, as far as possible, the officials who attend ECA sessions were also to attend the meetings of the Committee.

No provision has been made in ECA Resolution 190(IX) for coordination between ECA's Council of Ministers and the Economic and Technical Committee of the OAU Council of Ministers. What the resolution recommends is the submission of reports on ECA's activities to the OAU Assembly of Heads of State and Government. It can be expected that, when such reports are submitted to the OAU, they would be studied first by the Economic and Technical Committee and then submitted through the Council of Ministers to the OAU Assembly. This one-sided procedure of submitting reports might raise fears of undue control by the OAU over ECA, especially in the absence of effective coordination of policies and programs between ECA and the OAU bodies dealing with economic and social matters.

In the light of the foregoing, an attempt will be made to explore possibilities for overcoming the present obstacles to effective cooperation between ECA and the OAU. The author has proposed elsewhere certain measures designed merely to improve existing forms of cooperation.[36] Therefore, we will concentrate here on possible long-range solutions involving basic structural changes.

Possibilities for Fundamental Structural Changes
in ECA-OAU Relationships

In view of the difficulties faced by the OAU in making the OAU-
ECOS fully operational and the wasteful rivalry with ECA, the following new forms of ECA-OAU relationship might deserve serious
consideration as alternatives to the maintenance of parallel commissions: (1) the establishment of joint sessions of ECA and the
OAU-ECOS; (2) the abolition of the OAU-ECOS, accompanied by the
strengthening of ECA's relations with the OAU political organs.

The problems arising from the existence of ECA and the OAU-
ECOS as parallel organs are mainly the following: duplication of
conferences in spite of the limited financial and personnel resources
and the constraints of time faced by the two Secretariats and the
ministries of African governments; the resulting decline in the rate
and level of attendance by African officials at the meetings of the
OAU commissions; the difficulty in coordinating respective programs
and activities; and the clash over issues of preeminence, jurisdiction,
and respective roles.

Joint Sessions of ECA and the OAU-ECOS

If joint sessions could be arranged between the Council of
Ministers of ECA and the OAU-ECOS, all of these problems might
be solved. But to do this on a regular basis might require an amendment of the terms of reference of ECA and of the OAU-ECOS. Since
there is no precedent for such joint sessions between other regional
commissions in the economic and social fields and their counterparts
in non-U.N. intergovernmental organizations, acceptance of the idea
by ECOSOC and by the competent organs of the OAU may not be easy.

The legal, political, financial, and administrative implications
of the measure would first have to undergo a thorough examination.
While there would hardly be any problem concerning recommendations
on any matter within the competence of ECA and the OAU-ECOS
addressed by the joint session directly to the African states, any
resolution involving wider economic and social policies or having
financial implications for either organization would need endorsement
by the competent higher organs. Conceivably, a problem could arise
if differences of policy or opinion emerge between such higher organs,
particularly ECOSOC and the OAU Council of Ministers, when they
consider the resolutions of the joint session.

But since there seem to be no basic differences between the
objectives and policies of the United Nations and the OAU in the economic and social field, the problem referred to is perhaps merely
theoretical. The technique of joint conferences has been successfully

231

carried out by ECA and the OAU with regard to certain specialized subjects—namely, trade, industry, telecommunications, and refugees. The fact that the recommendations of such conferences have been endorsed on the one hand by the sessions of ECA and by ECOSOC, and on the other by the OAU Council of Ministers seems also to indicate that it is not unreasonable to expect similar treatment for the resolutions of joint sessions of ECA and the OAU-ECOS.

The financial and administrative implications of a joint session may be beneficial for both organizations, provided that agreement can be reached on the modalities of sharing conference expenses and distributing conference work between the two Secretariats on an equitable basis. The joint session itself may decide on the extent of the programs and projects to be implemented jointly, as well as on those to be carried out by either the ECA or the OAU Secretariat.

In view of the present legal and procedural obstacles to establishing joint sessions of ECA and the OAU-ECOS on a permanent basis, it might be worthwhile for ECA and the OAU to consider the possibility of convening a joint session on an experimental basis in accordance with parallel resolutions of the competent bodies of the two organizations. The experience gained from such an ad hoc arrangement would show whether it would be desirable to make it permanent through an amendment of the respective terms of reference and the rules of procedure.

Abolition of the OAU-ECOS

An alternative course of action worth considering is the abolition of the OAU-ECOS, simultaneously with the restructuring of the Executive Committee of ECA to permit greater participation by the OAU.

In view of the difficulties that the OAU has been facing in convening sessions of the OAU-ECOS, and considering the useful role that the Council of Ministers' Economic and Technical Committee has been able to play since 1967, the member states of the OAU might come to realize that there is no compelling need to retain the former body. The abolition of the OAU-ECOS would represent not a relinquishment by the OAU of its objectives in the economic and social fields but essentially a transfer of the functions of the Commission to the Economic and Technical Committee. However, as this Committee cannot be a substitute for the OAU-ECOS in all respects—its perspective is basically political rather than economic—abolition of the latter body might, on the one hand, necessitate greater OAU reliance on ECA with regard to the economic and social aspects of the problems concerned and, on the other hand, might call for greater harmonization of any differences in perspective between the two organizations.

Collaboration between ECA and the OAU could take place effectively at the level of the ECA Executive Committee if this body were to be converted into a joint body or were otherwise to establish special links with the Council of Ministers' Economic and Technical Committee. The Chairman of this OAU body, as well as the Administrative Secretary General, might represent the OAU in the Executive Committee. Together with the existing joint ECA-OAU Committee on Trade and Development, a joint Executive Committee would not only ensure inter-Secretariat cooperation in all relevant fields but also facilitate regular coordination of the policies and actions of African states in global, regional, and subregional intergovernmental bodies dealing with economic and social development in Africa. It could lay the foundation for a harmonious relationship between the economic perspective of ECA and other relevant United Nations bodies and the basically political perspective of the OAU with regard to issues of development in Africa.

With the abolition of the OAU-ECOS, ECA's Council of Ministers would provide the sole regional forum for considering the reports and recommendations of the joint committees. On the OAU side, the Council of Ministers, under the authority of the Assembly of Heads of State and Government, would provide a forum for the consideration of ECA's economic policies and plans within a political context. Once the policies and plans for African economic and social development have received the political support of the OAU, they could be submitted to ECOSOC for adoption.

The abolition of the OAU-ECOS would involve drastic action on the part of the OAU, as it would require an amendment of the OAU Charter. However, it may not be unreasonable to expect such a course of action if ECA succeeds in building upon the measure of confidence in its potential role expressed by the African states during its ninth session. There have been some factors favoring a rise of confidence in ECA, namely: (1) the fact that, through the ECA Executive Committee, representatives of African states are now more deeply involved in policy formulation and implementation; (2) the fact that the representation of African states in ECA's superior organ, ECOSOC, has now been increased following that organ's enlargement; and (3) the progress that is being made toward the "Africanization" (raising the ratio of African to non-African members of the staff) of the ECA Secretariat. However, in order to induce the OAU member states to abolish the OAU-ECOS through the time-consuming procedure of Charter amendment, ECA might need to transform its Executive Committee into an organ for more effective collaboration with the OAU.

For the OAU, the main advantage of abolishing the OAU-ECOS would be to enable it to concentrate on the coordination and harmonization of the economic and social policies of African states, for which

233

it is well suited, and thus avoid dissipating its extremely scarce resources in trying to introduce its own projects or take over the direction of existing ones. If the technical competence of the OAU Council of Ministers' Economic and Technical Committee is improved by involving in its work not only foreign ministers and their staff but also senior officials from ministries responsible for economic and related matters—as far as possible those who attend ECA meetings—then this Committee would be able to examine the work being done in Africa by ECA and a multitude of organizations, groupings, and governments and to determine the nature and extent of the obstacles to progress. On the basis of the conclusions and recommendations of this Committee, the OAU Council of Ministers and the Assembly of Heads of State and Government would be able to urge member states to give full support to all projects in high-priority areas and to change any policies that impede cooperation and development.

Furthermore, by abolishing the OAU-ECOS, the OAU would be able to devote greater effort to the work of the OAU-ESCHC and its subsidiary bodies. The OAU-ESCHC constitutes an integrated regional complement of the various United Nations specialized agencies active in Africa in the fields of education, science, culture, and health. As such, it serves a highly useful purpose and deserves to be strengthened.

NOTES

1. Text in General Assembly Official Records, 20th Session, Annexes, Agenda Item 108, document A/6174, Report of the Secretary General, Appendix.
2. General Assembly Resolution 1155(XII), 26 November 1957, and ECOSOC Resolution 671A(XXV), 29 April 1958.
3. UN Doc. E/3864/Rev.1 (E/CN. 14/290/Rev. 1): Statement by the Executive Secretary of ECA Before the Sixth Session of the Commission, p. 175.
4. UN ECA Doc. E/CN. 14/294, Statement by the Executive Secretary on ECA Activities Since the Sixth Session of the Commission, 27 January 1965, p. 1.
5. OAU-ECOS Resolution ECOS/16/Res. 2(I), 13 December 1963.
6. For the terms of reference of the Transport and Communications Commission, see OAU Assembly Resolution AHG/Res. 20(I), 21 July 1964.
7. OAU-STRC Resolution STR/35/Res. 1(I), 7 February 1964.
8. OAU-EDC Resolution EDC/28/Res. 1(I), 8 January 1964.
9. J. S. Magee, "ECA and the Paradox of African Co-operation," International Conciliation, no. 580 (November 1970): 7.

10. These were: The African Charter of the Casablanca Conference as elaborated in the Protocol of 1961; the Charter of the Inter-African and Malagasy Organization, adopted at the Lagos Conference of 1962. For texts, see Colin Legum, Pan Africanism: A Short Political Guide, rev. ed. (New York: Praeger Publishers, 1965), pp. 211-15.

11. For text of the Ethiopian draft, see Summit Conference of Independent African States, Proceedings of the Summit Conference of Independent African States, vol. I, section I (Addis Ababa, May 1963; publication of the Ethiopian government), Doc. COMM.I/EMPC/1, 17 May 1963.

12. Proceedings of the Summit Conference of Independent African States, Verbatim Records, Preparatory Conference of Foreign Ministers, 15-25 May 1963, Committee I, second meeting, C-I-II, pp. 2, 5, 6, 9, 11, 12.

13. Ibid., Committee I, third meeting, C-I-III, pp. 34-38.

14. Ibid., pp. 35-36.

15. OAU-ECOS Resolutions: ECOS/16/D/Res. 2(I) and ECOS/17/1/Res. 3(I), 13 December 1963.

16. OAU Doc. CM/71, Report of the Administrative Secretary General, October 1965, pp. 30-31; OAU Council of Ministers Resolution CM/Res. 126(IX), 10 September 1967.

17. See summary of statement by the Executive Secretary before the eighth session of ECA in UN ECA Doc. E/CN. 14/SR. 128-139(VIII), Summary Records of the Eighth Session of ECA, 13-23 February 1967, p. 35.

18. OAU Doc. CM/71, op. cit., p. 44.

19. Ibid., pp. 43-44.

20. OAU-ECOS Resolution ECOS/17/Res. 3(I), 13 December 1963.

21. OAU Doc. CM/71, op. cit., pp. 19, 44.

22. Ibid., pp. 44-46.

23. Ibid., p. 45.

24. OAU Resolution CM/Res. 122(IX), 10 September 1967.

25. ECA Doc. E/CN.14/L.298, Statement on Relations Between ECA and OAU, 20 February 1965, pp. 3-5.

26. Ibid., p. 4.

27. UN ECA Resolution 194(IX), 12 February 1969.

28. UN ECA Terms of Reference, paragraph 1.

29. Quoted in the statement of the ECA Secretariat before the seventh session of ECA, UN ECA Doc. E/CM.14/L.298, pp. 4-5.

30. OAU Doc. ECOS/13(II), January 1965, p. 6.

31. UN ECA Doc. E/CN.14/L.298, p. 6.

32. Text of the Agreement is included as annex to UN Doc. A/6174, December 1965.

33. Article I, paragraph 2 of the Agreement.

34. UN ECA Doc. E/CN.14/SR.128-139(VIII), <u>Summary Records of the Eighth Session of ECA</u>, pp. 131-32.

35. Ibid., pp. 132-33.

36. See chapter 11 of a forthcoming UNITAR publication entitled <u>Relations Between the United Nations and the Organization of African Unity</u>, by B. Andemicael.

12

THE ROLE OF OAU IN
PUBLIC ADMINISTRATION
AND MANAGEMENT
Galobawi M. Salih

THE OAU CHARTER

What can be the role of the Organization of African Unity in the field of public administration and management? This is a question raised by some African scholars who are concerned with the promotion and strengthening of the OAU on the occasion of its tenth anniversary. This exploration is inspired by that event.

There is no doubt about the concern of OAU with the problems of public administration in the young African continent, especially at this early stage of its intensive efforts for nation building, and its constitutional and administrative construction. Many provisions of the OAU Charter point to this interest; the following could be cited as examples:

1. "Conscious of our responsibility to harness the natural and human resources of our continent for the total advancement of our peoples in spheres of human endeavour" (Preamble).

2. "The organization shall have the following purposes . . . to co-ordinate and intensify co-operation and efforts to achieve a better life for the people of Africa . . . to promote international co-operation, having due regard to the Charter of the United Nations and the Universal Declaration of Human Rights" (Article 2: Purposes).

3. "The Assembly [of OAU] shall establish such specialized commissions as it may deem necessary, including the following: (a) Economic and Social Commission, (b) Education and Cultural Commission . . . (e) Scientific, Technical and Research Commission" (Article 20).

The views expressed in this paper are those of the author and do not necessarily represent those of the United Nations.

Reading Article 2 on the purposes and objectives of the OAU,
it is obvious that immediate and urgent priorities naturally are mainly
directed to the factors that promote pan-Africanism and unity in the
first place. That is why "promotion of unity and solidarity of the
African states" comes to the fore as a significant target, followed by
such means as "coordination and cooperation"; "defence of sovereignty, territorial integrity and independence"; and "eradication of
all forms of colonialism from Africa." For these ends, the member
states are urged in Article 2:

> to coordinate and harmonize their general policies,
> specially in the following fields: (a) political and diploma-
> tic co-operation; (b) economic co-operation, including
> transport and communications; (c) educational and cultural
> co-operation; (d) health sanitation and nutritional coopera-
> tion; (e) scientific and technical co-operation; and (f) co-
> operation for defence and security.

It should be noted that only factors favoring unity and solidarity
are employed and given prominence and priority. Most of these are
the concern of "external" political affairs—e.g., political and diplomatic cooperation, eradication of colonialism, defense and security, and
independent sovereignty and territorial integrity. Even the "internal"
issues tackled afterward are given attention because of their influence
and impact on the bigger goal of African unity—e.g., economic, educational, and cultural cooperation; health, sanitation, and nutritional
cooperation; and cooperation in science and technology. This priority
policy has influenced the shape and institutional setting of the two
most active organs of OAU, the Council of Ministers and the OAU
General Administrative Organization of the Secretariat.
The Council of Ministers is the second most important organ
of OAU, coming directly after the Assembly of Heads of State and
Government, "the supreme organ of the Organization" (Article 8).
In the Council of Ministers, ministers of foreign affairs are given
preferential status in relation to other national ministers, as indicated
in the following article: "The Council of Ministers shall consist of
Foreign Ministers or such other Ministers as are designated by the
Governments of Member States" (Article 12). In the general organization chart, the preference given organs dealing with unity and solidarity
questions is most obvious (see Figure 12.1). Besides the Council of
Ministers (which is dominated by ministers of foreign affairs, as
noted) there are also such organs as the Commission of Mediation,
Conciliation and Arbitration; the Liberation Committee; and the Defense Commission. There is no doubt that this policy of favoring
political solidarity, unity, and integrity has produced obvious results

FIGURE 12.1

Structure of the OAU

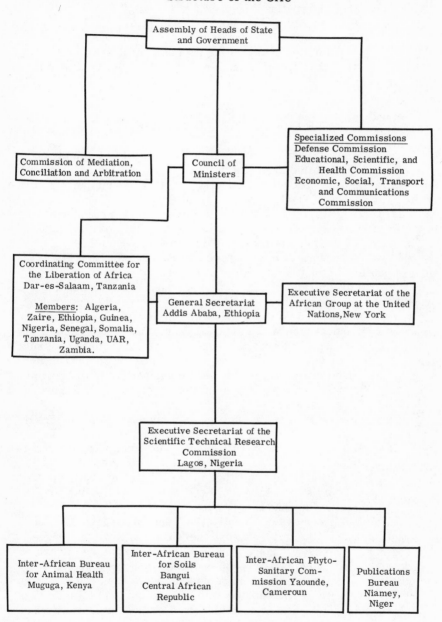

and substantial progress; e.g., 32 independent African countries originally signed the OAU Charter but membership has now increased to 41 independent member states, a very influential bloc in the United Nations and other international arenas.

Thus, OAU has so far done very little, or almost nothing, in the field of administrative improvement in Africa. It was too busy with the higher priorities of liberating its member states and consolidating their efforts to defend and maintain their newly attained political freedom.

THE CHALLENGING NEW TASK

It has become a well-known fact that OAU could so quickly and confidently amplify the continent's voice in world affairs. If this success in the field of foreign affairs was so marvelously accomplished in the first decade of OAU existence, great expectations have been expressed that OAU would address itself more, in its second decade, to the internal construction, consolidation, and modernization of the governments of its member states. This objective could best be served by an ambitious crash program and concerted action in the field of public administration and management.

Several arguments can be brought forward in support of this proposition. More than three-quarters of the present 42 independent African states achieved their independence in or after 1960. The first years of their independence are naturally spent in gradual transformation, political change, and organizational adjustment from the colonial pattern to the freedom one. There is a great need for radical change in administrative and organizational set-up during this initial period. The whole orientation and philosophy of the government machinery, and also its functional structure, is in need of change.

During colonial times, the government machinery was oriented to maintaining peace and order; no serious effort was made in the fields of economic and social development. The administrative structure was modeled along the one in the colonial power. Most, if not all, leadership and senior posts are filled by expatriates drawn from the colonial power; only some of the middle ranks and all lower officials are drawn from the indigenous nationals.

Ambitious programs of "localization" and "Africanization" of personnel in the public services were therefore the first challenges that confronted the newly independent countries. Hence, on the eve of independence, for political expedience, attention was directed to the quantity of nationals who could replace colonial expatriates, rather than to their quality. Confronted by an acute shortage of local personnel, the newly independent countries used their limited qualified

240

national personnel in the sensitive areas of national security and pride—e.g., the army, the police, administration, and diplomacy; the other posts were filled by newly contracted expatriates.

As rightly expressed by a recent conference report of the Economic Commission for Africa:

> Most African governments during the past decade have been engaged in the preparation and implementation of development plans, as a means of accelerating their economic and social development. Often, however, the inadequacies and defects inherent in their administrative structures and management procedures, at various levels of government, have persistently constituted major obstacles to the full realization of their plan objectives or targets. Recognizing that a very important step towards the eventual removal of these constraints on development is to assist African Governments to identify and bridge the gaps between their administrative structures and procedures is to establish sound modern and efficient administrative and management services.[1]

This is the prevailing situation of African countries today in the field of public administration: a struggle against underdevelopment in the fields of administrative organization and reform, financial management, local government reform, personnel management and training. The gravest problem of all is that these shortcomings and constraints are prevailing in an environment of underdevelopment. The recent survey conducted by the United Nations Development Program showed that 16 of the 25 hard-core least-developed of the developing countries are located in Africa. As a matter of fact, it is generally agreed that a very large proportion of African countries fall within this category. Africa as a whole can thus be considered the least developed among developing countries.[2] The result is that the African economies and governments are still run by a great number of expatriates; hence, the African countries are suffering great losses and wastes from mismanagement and maladministration. Determined effort and concerted action to cope with these problems and handicaps —which should involve a special program using special measures to improve the administrative and managerial capability of African countries, is most urgently needed.

A SUGGESTED APPROACH

What is the most advisable approach for OAU in this area of concern? First, before initiating any specific action program, it is appropriate to see what other national, regional (pan-African), and international organizations are doing in this field. A second question is: What order of priorities is most suited to African development needs in this area? In the light of the answers to these two important questions, OAU can draw its strategy in public administration.

The OAU policy should preferably emphasize coordination and cooperation with programs of other interested organizations, and it should not compete and overlap with them. It should address itself to areas where gaps are prevailing and felt needs are urgent.

The remaining portion of this chapter will be devoted to exploring answers to the two questions cited. We will examine existing programs of national, regional, and international institutions that are serving Africa in this area; from this survey, OAU can see the facts about the prevailing programs, and also, the gaps and needs that need to be filled.

National Centers of Public Administration

At the national level, all the newly independent African countries have shown their will and concern to meet the challenges of administration and management by establishing their own national centers for public administration. In almost all cases, these were created after independence was attained, in many cases with U.N. assistance. Most of these centers are designated Institutes of Public Administration (IPAs) in the English-speaking African countries, or Ecoles Nationales d'Administration" (ENAs) in the French-speaking countries. A few —especially those cosponsored by the International Labour Organization—are designated Productivity Centers or Management Training Centers. The majority of the IPAs and ENAs work under their own autonomous boards of directors; others are controlled by central governments. In a few cases, they act under the umbrella of a national university.

As indicated by Table 12.1, there are now about 65 such centers, in 39 African countries. They generally provide administrative training for national public servants, conduct research on administrative problems, and provide management consultancy services for governmental and quasi-governmental agencies. Although these schools are undertaking invaluable services for African public services, they operate under many constraints of human and material shortages and shortcomings. Hence, they are in the greatest need of moral, political, substantive, and material support from all national, regional, and international organizations. This is one of the best strategic areas for OAU intervention and action.

TABLE 12.1

African IPAs and ENAs

Country	Number of IPAs and ENAs	Language*
Algeria	2	A & F
Egypt	6	A & F
Botswana	1	E
Burundi	1	F
Cameroun	1	F & E
Central African Republic	1	F
Chad	1	F
Congo	1	F
Dahomey	1	F
Ethiopia	1	E
Gabon	1	F
Gambia	1	E
Ghana	2	E
Guinea	1	F
Ivory Coast	2	F
Kenya	3	E
Lesotho	2	E
Liberia	1	E
Libya	1	A & E
Madagascar	2	F
Mali	1	F
Malawi	1	E
Mauritius	1	E & F
Mauritania	1	F
Morocco	2	A, E & F
Niger	1	F
Nigeria	5	E
Rwanda	1	F
Senegal	2	F
Sierra Leone	1	E
Somalia	1	E
Sudan	3	A & E
Tanzania	3	E
Togo	1	F
Tunisia	2	A & F
Uganda	2	E
Upper Volta	1	F
Zaire	1	F
Zambia	3	E
Total	65	

*E = English; F = French; A = Arabic.

Source: Mainly International Institute for Administrative Sciences, Brussels (April 1972).

REGIONAL ORGANIZATIONS

ECA

At the African regional level, substantial interest in public administration has been shown by a host of pan-African United Nations intergovernmental and nongovernmental organizations. The United Nations Economic Commission for Africa comes at the top of these organizations. Since its inception in 1958, ECA has established a Public Administration Unit in its Secretariat at Addis Ababa, to sponsor and implement a program in public administration. ECA also has passed several historical resolutions and statements in support of this program, the most eminent of which are Resolutions 70(V), 172 (VIII), and 202 (IX). Also in its renowned Resolution 218 (X) on Africa's Strategy for Development in the 1970s, ECA stressed the high priority that should be given to integration of national economies, which has physical, organizational aspects because "it requires an effectively coordinated programme concentrating on regional physical planning, integrated rural development, reform of local government."[3] The same resolution emphasized the inclusion of the public administration component among the various vital elements that should comprise such ECA strategy in the following provision: "improvement of the institutional structure with respect to public administration, planning, project evaluation, etc., with special attention to measures designed to ensure increasing national participation."[4]

Consequently, and in line with this, ECA has announced a program in Administration and Management in Africa, focusing mainly on "localization of professional qualifications in the fields of Administration and Management as a measure for attaining administrative, managerial and executive effectiveness."[5] The objective of this program is to

> develop well-designed educational and training programmes that will produce a continuing supply of professionally qualified, experienced and competent Africans capable of holding effectively positions in managerial, administrative, executive and supervisory capacities. The ECA considers these categories of manpower to be of strategic importance (i) to the completion of the cycle of localization of personnel initiated by African Governments on attainment of independence, and (ii) in providing for the efficient management of change, development and modernization of the economy.[6]

244

However, it should also be noted that the ECA human resources devoted to public administration are very limited; the Public Administration Unit was manned by only about five professional staff members and regional advisers in the early 1960s, diminishing to only three in the early 1970s. OAU had maintained close cooperation and working relations with ECA; this was the fruit of an agreement signed between the United Nations and OAU on 15 November 1965, under which the two organizations can easily draw up a collaborative program in public administration.[7] This agreement emphasized two-way consultation between ECA and OAU, exchange of information, mutual participation in meetings, and reciprocal assistance with regard to experts.[8]

CAFRAD

At the initiative of Morocco, and with the support of nine African countries (Algeria, Cameroun, Gabon, Guinea, Mali, Senegal, Sudan, Tunisia, and the United Arab Republic), a resolution was unanimously adopted by the twelfth session of the UNESCO General Conference (1963), authorizing UNESCO to cooperate with African countries in the establishment of an African Training and Research Centre in Administration for Development (CAFRAD) in Tangier, Morocco. This project was started by an agreement between the Moroccan Government and UNESCO signed on 13 May 1964, and later revised, consolidated, and replaced by a permanent multilateral agreement signed on 18 December 1967 by eleven African countries and left open for ratification by other African member states willing to join in the future. The membership at present totals twenty: Algeria, Cameroun, Central African Republic, Egypt, Ghana, Ivory Coast, Kenya, Liberia, Libya, Mauritania, Morocco, Niger, Nigeria, Senegal, Sierra Leone, Somalia, Sudan, Togo, Tunisia, and Zambia. The CAFRAD functions are defined by its establishing agreement as follows:

1. To undertake, promote, and coordinate comparative studies and research administrative problems connected with social and economic development in Africa.
2. To organize scientific meetings, seminars, and in-service training courses for high-ranking officials from the public and private sectors in African countries.
3. To compile, analyze, and disseminate documentation on the structure, organization, and administrative methods of different African countries.
4. To publish appropriate material.

5. To act as a host and a scientific liaison body for the particular benefit of institutions and schools of administration, universities, and any agencies whose activities come within the scope of the competence of CAFRAD.

CAFRAD has been supported by a UNDP Special Fund project since June 1971. The United Nations Public Administration Division is substantively supporting this project (as the executing agency) in collaboration with UNESCO.

AAPAM

The African Association for Public Administration and Management (AAPAM) was formally inaugurated on 4 November 1971 in Freetown, Sierra Leone, as a purely professional association founded by eminent African administrators and managers. Its main purpose is the development of competent administrators and managers for rapid economic and social development in Africa. Other objectives are:

1. To maintain the tradition of providing senior administrators and managers with the opportunity of exchanging ideas and experiences in public administration and management.
2. To foster the professionalization of public administration and management in Africa, and particularly to develop an increasing appreciation of the value and importance of public administration and management.
3. To advance the study of the techniques in public administration and management.
4. To undertake comparative studies in the field of public administration and management.
5. To promote research in African administrative problems.
6. To promote the adoption of more effective and adequate administrative and management systems and practices.
7. To foster affiliation and maintain liaison with international bodies and organizations interested in the progress of public administration and management.

In his inaugural address to AAPAM, Dr. Stevens, the President of Sierra Leone, said: "The formation of such an Association could not have come at a more opportune moment, for if there is anything that we in Sierra Leone, and every African country for that matter, are short of, it is administrative and management capability for present-day tasks." AAPAM is perhaps too new to appraise its impact and contributions, but certainly cooperation of OAU with AAPAM in this program will be most fruitful and forward-looking.

246

AOAS

The Arab Organization for Administrative Sciences (AOAS) is one of the specialized agencies affiliated with the League of Arab States, whose seat is in Cairo. The AOAS was established by the Arab League in January 1969 to serve its 20 member states in the field of public administration and management. Eight of the 20 member states are African countries: Algeria, Egypt, Libya, Mauritania, Morocco, Somalia, Sudan, and Tunisia. The objectives of AOAS are set out in its establishing agreement as "to promote administrative sciences, improve administrative machinery and develop the financial and administrative capabilities" (Article 3). The following methodology of cooperation is adopted in the AOAS agreement:

1. "Facilitating cooperation between Universities and Institutes of public administration" (Article 3).
2. "Cooperation with institutions and organizations concerned with administrative studies and exchange of relevant data and information with them" (Article 4).

AOAS has established contacts with ECA, CAFRAD, and OAU. Therefore AOAS might prove a useful channel of effective collaboration with OAU in that part of the continent, because it possesses the required linguistic and technical capabilities in the administrative field.

Other Pan-African Regional Organizations

There are many other regional organizations with similar objectives that would be happy to collaborate with OAU in this field. Reference could be made in this respect—for example only—to (1) the United Nations-supported African Institute for Economic Development Planning (IDEP), Dakar, which has a significant public administration component; (2) the African Political Science Association (APSA), Dar-es-Salaam, established in December 1973; and (3) the African Purchasing and Supply Association, Addis Ababa.

INTERNATIONAL ORGANIZATIONS

There are several international programs of technical assistance in public administration and management, dedicated to Africa. Some of them are from multinational and others from bilateral sources. Some of these are briefly reviewed below:

United Nations Public Administration Division

The Public Administration Division (PAD) of the United Nations Department of Economic and Social Affairs, New York, is substantively backstopping and supporting a significant program of public administration in Africa. As of March 1974, PAD was supporting 19 public administration projects in 17 African countries, including 11 major-scale projects costing more than $100,000 each. These projects are manned by about 132 U.N. experts and supported by a large number of fellowships. The major projects include providing support to CAFRAD, $1,535,000; the East Africa (Community) Railways and Harbours Training and Development Project, $1,501,720; the Bureau of Organization and Methods, Senegal, $1,434,900; the Strengthening Institute of Administration, Ife University, Nigeria, $522,100; and Administrative Reform in Mali, $993,152. The research and development component of PAD's work also includes several comparative study projects on African management problems. PAD also is continuously making special efforts to support, coordinate activities, and collaborate with other regional organizations dealing with Africa, such as ECA and AAPAM.

United Nations International Labour Organization

The International Labour Organization, Geneva, has a significant program in the area of management training and manpower planning. There are a number of such ILO projects in Africa. Management training normally is supported by the newly created Productivity Centers or Management Development Institutes, which contribute to management research, training, and consultation, usually by providing supervisory personnel (industrial and commercial) for public and private enterprises. An agreement between OAU and ILO, similar to that concluded with the U.N. in 1966, was negotiated, defining the scope of cooperation between the two organizations. Under this umbrella, collaboration in the area of management could be secured. [9]

Other Global Programs

Many other global programs have special interest or work projects focusing on public administration in Africa. These include some United Nations specialized agencies, such as UNESCO whose interest and input in CAFRAD has been noted. Other programs are affiliated with some of the international nongovernmental organizations, such as (1) the International Institute for Administrative Sciences (IIAS),

248

Brussels, which played a key role in working with and supporting the African group of IPAs and ENAs; (2) the International Union of Local Authorities (IULA), The Hague, which cooperated in many African programs in collaboration with either ECA or other African ministries and agencies dealing with local government administration.

Other types of programs that might fall under this category are the bilateral programs offered to the African region or to individual African countries in the field of public administration and management by USAID: British Ministry of Overseas Development (MOD); Swedish International Development Agency (SIDA); the German Foundation for International Development (Public Administration Promotion Centre, Berlin); Canadian CIDA; French government; Japan, Ford, and Rockefeller Foundations; and the governments of the People's Democratic Republic of China, the USSR, and the Eastern European countries.

SUMMARY AND CONCLUSIONS

1. It is obvious from the findings and analysis in this chapter that the problems of public administration and management in Africa constitute a major and formidable constraint to progress and economic and social development, especially during the current development decade of the 1970s.

2. Therefore, OAU is urged to take a new positive interest, assume leadership roles, and foster new concerted action in this area, which should contribute to the public administration and managerial revolution in Africa. In this connection, attention is drawn to the role played in this field by the Organization of American States (OAS), i.e., providing member states with experts and fellowships in public administration and management.

3. To be able to assume that leading role, it is suggested that OAU authorize one of its commissions—e.g., most appropriately, the Economic and Social Commission—to adopt a specific program of action in this field.

4. In drawing up the proposed program of action, OAU should supplement and complement existing programs and simultaneously use its good offices to cooperate and collaborate with other interested national, regional, and global organizations; to coordinate programs; and to encourage contributions to fill the gaps.

5. OAU itself is urged, where appropriate, to pursue its own program, which might aim to (a) decrease dependence of African countries on the services of foreign expatriates, and hence assist African countries to train their nationals with a view to Africanizing posts currently held by foreigners; and (b) to conduct management research and training programs for the benefit of the staff of pan-

African regional organizations and for national officers dealing with the management of African solidarity affairs.

NOTES

1. ECA, Administration for Development (UN Doc. E/CN.14/UAP/14-Sales No. E. 71. II. K. 13), p. vii.

2. ECA Resolution 218 (X) of 13 February 1971, paragraph 40.

3. ECA Resolution 218 (X) of 13 February 1971, paragraph 2.

4. Ibid., paragraph 41 (iv).

5. See ECA brochure, "Administration and Management in Africa" (August, 1973).

6. Ibid., p. 2.

7. For the text of this agreement, see UN Doc. E/CN.14/INF/32, dated 16 February 1967.

8. See OAU, Report of the Assistant Secretary General, 1965-66, paragraph 7.

9. Ibid., paragraph 8.

253

East Africa (Community) Railways and Harbours Training and Development Project, 248
East African Community (Common Market), 70, 72, 75, 109
East African Standard, 163-64
Eban, Abba, 193, 195, 198, 203
ECA. See Economic Commission for Africa
Economic Commission for Africa (ECA), 57, 58, 69, 70, 71, 72, 213-14, 217-34, 241, 244-45, 247, 248, 249; Administration and Management in Africa, program in, 244; Africa's Strategy for Development in the 1970s, Resolution on, 244; Council of Ministers, 214, 229, 230, 233; ECA-OAU Committee on Trade and Development, 233; ECA-OAU Cooperation, 1965 Agreement on, 227-29; Executive Committee, 229-30, 232, 233; institutions established by, 218; Public Administration Unit, 244, 245
Economic Community of Eastern Africa, 70
Economic Community of West Africa, 70
ECOSOC. See United Nations: Economic and Social Council
Effiong, Col. Phillip, 167
Egypt, 52, 53, 81, 85, 86, 103, 121-23, 124, 125, 127, 128, 129, 130, 176, 178, 189, 190, 192, 193, 194, 195-98, 199, 201, 203, 204, 205-06, 207, 208, 245, 247; Year of Decision, 190, 204 (see also United Arab Republic)
Ekangaki, Nzo, 76, 208
El Salvador, 200, 201
El-Zayyat, M. H., 204-05

Emin Pasha, Annals of, 176
Enahoro, Chief Anthony, 158
Entente, 70, 75; Council of, 70
equality, sovereign, of states, 89-94
Equatorial Guinea, 91
Eritrea, 115
Eritrean Liberation Front, 122
Ethiopia, 5, 18, 31, 32, 35, 36, 42, 43-44, 52, 64, 81, 83, 85, 86, 92, 115, 122, 123, 124, 138, 145, 156, 159, 164, 169, 184, 191, 200, 201, 206, 220
ethnic problems, 63, 94-96
European Common Market. See European Economic Community
European Economic Community, 89, 200, 203
Ewe (tribe), 169

FNLA. See Frente Nacional de Libertacao del Angola
Ford Foundation, 249
France, 64, 88, 93, 106, 127, 130, 141, 168, 203, 249
Francophone states, 64-65, 66, 67, 70, 72, 75, 203, 204
Freetown, 246
FRELIMO. See Frente de Libertacao de Mocambique
French Equatorial Africa, 64-65, 94
French Revolution, 98
French Somaliland, 91, 135
French West Africa, 64-65
Frente de Libertacao de Mocambique (FRELIMO), 137, 139, 140, 149
Frente Nacional de Libertacao del Angola (FNLA), 137, 138, 139, 140, 149
Frente para a Libertacao e Independencia de Guine Portuguesa (FLING), 137

Front for the Liberation of
Zimbabwe (FROLIZ), 137,
150
Fwatua, 28

Gabon, 155, 165, 168, 245
Gaddafy, Muammer, 105
Gambia, 91
Gaya, 28
Gbenye, 122
Geneva, 59, 165, 248
Germany, 49; Foundation for International Development, 249
Ghana, 4, 5, 7-9, 10-11, 12,
13, 14-15, 15-16, 21, 22,
23-24, 24-29, 30, 31, 44-45,
46, 48, 75, 103, 110, 111,
120, 140, 152, 154, 156, 157,
159, 164, 169, 245
Ghana-Guinea-Mali Union, 66,
67
Gowon, Yakubu, 153, 154, 157,
160, 162, 167, 169, 192
Great Britain, 49, 88, 104, 105-
06, 110, 111, 127, 136, 141,
145, 148, 155, 162, 177, 182,
200, 203; Ministry of Overseas Development (MOD), 249
Greater Maghreb, 66
Greece, 97
Guinea, 12, 21, 41-42, 44, 64,
107, 108, 109, 122, 124-25,
127, 129, 143, 169, 245
Guinea-Bissau, 91, 125, 135,
136, 137, 138, 139, 140, 145,
146, 148-49, 150, 202; National Assembly, 149
Gumei, 28

Hague, The, 249
Haile Selassie, 5, 18, 66, 115,
125, 156, 159, 161, 162, 164,
166
Haiti, 200
Harlley, I. K. W., 164

Horin, 28
Houphouet-Boigny, Felix, 26, 27,
64, 65, 66, 69, 72, 73, 112,
114, 152, 162
Human Rights, Universal Declaration of, 86, 98, 237

Ibo (tribe), 153, 154, 156, 158,
159, 160, 163, 166, 169
Ife University, Nigeria, Strength-
ening Institute of Administra-
tion, 248
independence, national, 4, 7-24
Indian Union, 19
Inter-African and Malagasy
States Organization. See
Monrovia Group
Inter-American Treaty of Recip-
rocal Assistance, 119
International Court of Justice
(ICJ), 83, 92, 107, 147
International Institute for Admin-
istrative Sciences (IIAS), 248
International Labour Organiza-
tion (ILO), 242, 248
international law and the OAU,
79-101
International Union of Local
Authorities (IULA), 249
Iraq, 52
Ireland, 182
Irie, 26
Ironsi, Major-General Aguiyi,
153
Ismail, Hafez, 194
Israel, 49, 60, 94, 110, 111,
121, 122, 123, 127, 128, 130,
152, 189, 190, 191, 192, 193,
194, 195-98, 199, 200, 201,
202, 203, 204, 205-06, 207-
08, 210
Italy, 83, 106
Ivory Coast, 26, 31, 65, 112,
125, 140, 141, 152, 155, 160,
165, 167, 168, 191, 192, 200,
201, 202, 206, 245

255

Morocco, 52, 93, 120, 152, 245, 247
Morrallane, Eduardo, 140
Movemento Popular de Liber-
tacao de Angola (MPLA), 137, 138, 139, 140, 149
Mozambique, 107, 135, 136, 137, 139, 148, 149, 150
MPLA. See Movemento Popu-
lar de Libertacao de Angola

Nadawansa, 26
Namibia, 96, 99, 107, 135, 137, 138, 139, 147
Nasser, Gamal Abdel, 20-23, 48, 66, 73, 189
National Unionist Party (NUP), 180
NATO, 114, 148
neocolonialism, 48-49, 60
New Delhi, 59
Ng(o)uabi, Marien, 98
Ngwana, 91
Niamey, 57, 159, 160, 161
Niassa, 149
Nicaragua, 200
Niger, 24, 25-28, 29, 31, 156, 159, 161, 245
Nigeria, 6, 17, 24-25, 26, 29, 31, 34, 64, 67, 75, 88, 93, 103, 110, 111, 115, 123, 125, 129, 130, 145, 152, 153-70, 177, 191, 192, 197, 198, 200, 201, 203, 206, 245
Nigumu, 26
Nile River, 176
Nimeiry, Gaafar al-, 181, 182, 183
Nixon, Richard M., 106, 119
Nkrumah, Kwame, 4, 5, 7, 15-16, 17, 18, 20, 22, 23-24, 25, 26, 27, 28, 29, 48, 63, 66, 67, 73, 75, 104, 105, 109, 120, 152

nonaligned conferences, 6-7, 36, 37, 39, 40, 41, 43, 44, 45, 141
Non-Aligned States, Conference of, 141
nonalignment, 6-7, 36-46
nonintervention, 5, 24-31, 103-115, 153, 156
North Africa, 20
Northern Frontier District (NFD), 33-34
Northern Nigerian Railways, 156
Nouakchott, 25
Nuer (tribe), 178, 184
Nyasaland, 35, 44
Nye, Joseph, 104
Nyerere, Julius K., 4, 66, 67, 105, 106, 108, 114, 145, 162
Nzeogwu, Maj. Chukwuma K., 153

OAMCE, 65
OAS. See Organization of Ameri-
can States
OAU. See Organization of Afri-
can Unity
OAU-ECOS. See Organization
of African Unity: Economic
and Social (Cultural) Commis-
sion
OAU-ESCHC. See Organization
of African Unity: Education,
Scientific, Cultural and
Health Commission
Obote, Milton, 66, 103, 104-05, 106, 107, 108, 110, 112, 158
OCAM. See Organisation Com-
mune Africaine et Malgache
Ogoja, 154
Ojukwu, Col. Odumegwu, 154, 156, 157, 159, 160, 163, 165, 166, 167, 168, 169
Okigbo, Pius, 166
Olympio, Sylvanus, 109, 112

Tiran, Strait of, 197
Togo, 14, 26, 75, 103, 109,
   112-13, 120, 169, 245
Toure, Sekou, 66, 67, 75, 105,
   107, 108, 112, 125
Tshombe, Moise K., 72, 93,
   110, 123
Tsiranana, Philibert, 17-18,
   67, 73
Tubman, William V. S., 66,
   156, 164
Tunisia, 9-10, 15, 19-20, 36-
   37, 38, 39-40, 41, 42, 53,
   146, 202, 245, 247
Tunkin, G., 99

U Thant, 88, 91, 92, 163
UAM. See Union Africaine et
   Malgache
UAMCE. See Union Africaine
   et Malgache de Cooperation
   Economique
UAMPT, 70
UAR. See United Arab Republic
UDEAC. See Union Douaniere
   et Economique de l'Afrique
   Centrale
UEAC, 75
Uganda, 21, 34-35, 65, 70, 93,
   103, 104-07, 108-12, 114,
   115, 138, 145, 158, 178, 184;
   People's Congress (UPC), 105
Uli, 167
UMMA, 180
underdevelopment, 54, 57-60,
   241-42
UNDP. See United Nations:
   Development Program
UNESCO. See United Nations:
   Educational, Scientific, and
   Cultural Organization
Unicio Nacional para a Indepen-
   dencia Total de Angola
   (UNITA), 137, 149

Unilateral Declaration of Indepen-
   dence (UDI; Southern Rhodesia),
   152
Union Africaine et Malgache
   (UAM), 65, 66, 68-69, 75
Union Africaine et Malgache de
   Cooperation Economique
   (UAMCE), 69, 70, 72
Union Africaine et Malgache de
   Defense (UAMD), 65, 69
Union Douaniere et Economique
   de l'Afrique Centrale (UDEAC),
   65, 75
United Arab Republic, 7, 20-23,
   24, 31, 36, 44, 52, 155, 169,
   209-10, 245 (see also Egypt)
United Kingdom. See Great
   Britain
United Nations, 32, 43, 46, 48,
   50, 52, 53, 54, 58, 59, 60,
   62, 75, 81, 82, 83, 85-91, 92,
   93, 96, 97, 99, 100, 119, 121,
   122, 124, 125, 127, 128, 129,
   136, 141, 146, 147, 163, 169,
   195, 196, 198, 202, 206, 213-
   34, 237, 240, 242, 245, 247;
   Development Program (UNDP),
   214, 229, 241, 246; Economic
   and Social Affairs, Department of, 248; Economic and
   Social Council (ECOSOC), 87,
   214, 217, 220, 225, 229, 231,
   232, 233; Economic Commission for Africa (ECA), 57, 58,
   69, 70, 71, 72, 213-14, 217-
   34, 241, 244-45, 247, 248,
   249; Educational, Scientific,
   and Cultural Organization
   (UNESCO), 114, 245, 246,
   248; General Assembly, 54,
   87, 88, 89-90, 97, 99, 127,
   147, 191, 192, 197-98, 199,
   200, 202, 203, 204, 205, 206,
   207, 214, 217, 219-20, 226;

YASSIN EL-AYOUTY is Adjunct Professor of African and Middle Eastern studies at the State University of New York at Stony Brook. He is also Senior Political Affairs Officer, U.N. Department of Political Affairs, Trusteeship and Decolonization.

Born in Egypt in 1928, Professor El-Ayouty holds the following degrees: Diploma, Teachers' Institute, Zeiton, Cairo, Egypt; B.S. (education), State Teachers College, Trenton, N.J.; M.A. (history), Rutgers University; Ph.D. (political science), New York University. He is the author of The United Nations and Decolonization—The Role of Afro-Asia, and coauthor and coeditor of Refugees South of the Sahara: An African Dilemma and Africa and International Organization.

Professor El-Ayouty contributes regularly to scholarly journals in the United States, the Arab world, and Europe, dealing primarily with war and revolution in Africa and the Middle East and the roles of international organizations in the Third World.

AFRICAN MANAGEMENT PRACTICES:
Comparative Studies of Management Attitudes
and Worker Perception
                    Ukandi G. Damachi

CHINA'S AFRICAN POLICY: A Study of
Tanzania
                    George T. Yu

THE PROSPECTS FOR AN ECONOMIC
COMMUNITY IN NORTH AFRICA: Managing
Economic Integration in the Maghreb States
                    Abderrahman Robana

THE UNITED NATIONS AND RHODESIA:
A Study in International Law
                    C. Lloyd Brown-John